THE
GREAT POWERS
AND THE
BALKANS
1875-1878

THE
GREAT POWERS
AND THE
BALKANS
1875–1878

BY

MIHAILO D. STOJANOVIĆ, Ph.D.

CAMBRIDGE
AT THE UNIVERSITY PRESS
1939
REPRINTED
1968

Published by the Syndics of the Cambridge University Press
Bentley House, 200 Euston Road, London, N.W. 1
American Branch: 32 East 57th Street, New York, N.Y. 10022

PUBLISHER'S NOTE

Cambridge University Press Library Editions are re-issues of out-of-print standard works from the Cambridge catalogue. The texts are unrevised and, apart from minor corrections, reproduce the latest published edition.

Standard Book Number: 521 07398 7
Library of Congress Catalogue Card Number: 39-17334

First published 1939
Reprinted 1968

First printed in Great Britain at the University Press, Cambridge
Reprinted in Great Britain by John Dickens & Co. Ltd, Northampton

CONTENTS

PREFACE

THE CRISIS of 1875–1878 may be considered as a prelude to the World War of 1914, so far at least as Europe was concerned. It opened in the Balkans with a question which seemed to be a local one, but which in fact cut deeply into the question of predominance in the Balkans, and therefore had great repercussion upon the position of the Powers in general. The main factors which determined the grouping of the Powers in 1914 were already in existence at that time. The Franco-Prussian War of 1870–1 had created an unbridgeable gulf between them; the Crisis of 1875–8 had revealed the irreconcilability of Austrian and Russian aspirations in the Balkans. Like Germany and France after 1871, Austria and Russia were now driven to seek for support from outside in order to be able to maintain their position and realise their aims. The question of predominance on the Rhine was thus connected with the question of predominance in the Balkans and they formed an axis which divided Europe into two hostile camps. It is therefore important to make a more detailed research into this period and see how far those responsible for the conduct of affairs were conscious of the consequences of their actions, and how far they contributed to render the war of 1914 inevitable.

Although both Russia and Austria were prepared to make concessions and to come to an agreement as to the solution of the Eastern Question, the development of the Crisis demonstrated clearly the impossibility of a lasting agreement between them. Russia and Austria could have agreed upon the partition of territories, as they did at Reichstadt in 1876 and at Budapest in 1877, but these agreements could not reconcile their conflicting interests. For both of them aimed at completely dominating the Balkans, which neither could achieve except by expelling the other party. Their agreements had therefore more the character of diplomatic moves, intended to pave the way towards their final goals, than that of a plan which might be realised to the satisfaction of both of them. This comes out clearly from the fact that both Austria and Russia intended after the war to play off their treaty obligations: Russia, to deprive Austria of Bosnia and Herzegovina, which she had already ceded to her, and Austria, to force Russia to submit the terms of peace to the approval of the Powers, though she had engaged to defend them, and to obtain a European mandate for the occupation of the provinces, which had been ceded to her as a reward for her neutrality and her diplomatic support. Andrassy had no illusion as to the possibility of co-operation with Russia, and therefore endeavoured to restrict it to "avoiding collision". Russia only came to this conviction after the Congress of Berlin.

Behind the struggle between Russia and Austria for supremacy in the Balkans was a conflict between Serbia and Austria over the liberation and union of the Southern Slavs. It came to the fore during this Crisis for the first time, and was left to be decided only by the World War. The insurrection in Bosnia and Herzegovina compelled Serbia to intervene in the struggle and solve this question to her advantage. The union with these provinces was considered in Serbia as her vital interest, as the question upon which even her own existence depended. But in Austria it was considered of equal importance to prevent this union. The liberation of Serbia's kinsmen in Turkey and the creation of a great Slav state was looked upon by Austria as a death blow to her own existence. There was therefore no possibility of an arrangement between them. Having subordinated her Slav element, though predominant in the Monarchy, to the domination of the Austrians and the Hungarians, the Vienna Government sought to neutralise their dissatisfaction, especially that of the Southern Slavs, by preventing the creation of a great Slav state on her borders and by annexing Bosnia and Herzegovina to herself. The Congress of Berlin sanctioned Austria's claims, but though Serbia remained small, Austria failed to content her Slavs and suppressed their aspirations for an independent state. Following the path she had taken then, she was logically driven in 1914 to annex Serbia herself, the attempt which brought her into conflict with Russia and provoked the European War.

But the Austro-Russian conflict had not yet become insoluble in 1875. Russia was ready to sacrifice Serbia's aspirations to an agreement with Austria, and Germany was endeavouring to remove their divergences and help on to a definite solution of the

Eastern Question. Nevertheless, the interests which divided the
Powers already at that time could be clearly traced. Although
Germany desired to avoid a conflict between her two allies, the
existence of Austria as a Great Power was considered by her as a
vital interest of her own, and she was prepared to defend it arms
in hand. The promotion of Austria's interests in the East was
therefore a natural task of Germany's policy. Bismarck did it
only with more tact and skill than his successors. France
realised that so long as Germany kept Alsace-Lorraine her
security could be protected by Russia and England only, who
showed in May 1875 that they would not allow her further
weakening. She endeavoured to support Russia's policy and to
mediate with England in her favour. But the antagonism between
Russia and England rendered her action nugatory, and at the
end of the Crisis she found herself on the side of England. Italy,
like France, was not in a position to take a more pronounced
attitude, but her interests were opposed to Austria's spreading
in the Balkans, and her aspirations to the Trentino found
expression in her press. These interests would bring her in 1915,
though a member of the Triple Alliance, to the side of the Triple
Entente. England was equally determined to preserve her interests
in the East and to prevent Germany's predominance in Europe.
Her conduct in the war scare of 1875 and her resistance to
Russia's designs during the Crisis leave no doubt of her intentions. Yet if she had to choose between the two, her interests in
the West would be nearer to her and more vital. For this reason
Disraeli endeavoured to deter Russia from war when in 1877 he
feared Germany's attack upon France. Subsequent events had
demonstrated this more clearly and had thrown her entirely on
the side of France and Russia.

It is therefore safe to affirm that the grouping of the Powers in
1914 was virtually determined by the interests which existed
already in 1875–8. In the course of the next decade Bismarck
succeeded in keeping his opponents divided and turning their
rivalries to his profit. But his successors were not capable of
playing this game, and after his retirement things returned slowly
to their natural position.

The present work was originally written as a thesis for the
Ph.D. degree, and was approved by the University of London

in 1930 under the title: "Serbia in International Politics, 1875–1878." It has been revised and completed since, so that in its present form it differs considerably from the earlier manuscript, comprising both new material, hitherto unpublished, and new views on some questions. These alterations imposed also the change in the title.

The dissertation had been worked out on the basis of the then unpublished documents from the British, Austrian and Serbian archives—the papers of Sir Henry Layard and the archives of the Russian Embassy in London. Much of this material has been made public since in the works of Prof. R. W. Seton-Watson, *Disraeli, Gladstone and the Eastern Question*, David Harris, *A Diplomatic History of the Balkan Crisis of 1875–1878*, and Humphrey Sumner, *Russia and the Balkans, 1870–1880*. Except David Harris, who has hitherto discussed only the first year of the Crisis, the other two writers deal essentially with the policy of a single Power: Britain and Russia respectively. I have discussed the question from a European standpoint and have endeavoured to disentangle and analyse all the factors that determined the character and the development of the Crisis.

The publication of this work has been made possible by grants from the School of Slavonic Studies and the Serbian Minister's Fund in London. To both of them I gratefully acknowledge my indebtedness. I owe a special debt of gratitude to the Serbian Minister's Fund in London for a fellowship which has rendered my studies possible, and particularly to Prof. Dr Dragutin Subotić for his constant support and encouragement. I wish to express my warm thanks to Prof. R. W. Seton-Watson for his invaluable advice and interest in the publication of this work, and to Prof. G. P. Gooch and Baron Alexander Meyendorff, of the University of London, and to Prof. Slobodan Jovanović, of the University of Belgrade, for their important suggestions. Finally, I am greatly indebted to my former colleague, Dr Winifred Taffs, who has been kind enough to read the manuscript, for which I wish to express my special thanks.

M. D. STOJANOVIĆ

BELGRADE
November 1938

LIST OF ABBREVIATIONS

A.A. Austrian Archives (Haus-Hof und Staatsarchiv). Wien, 1875–8.

A.C. *Actenstücke aus den Correspondenzen des Kais. und Kön. gemein-samen Ministeriums des äusern über orientalische Angelegenheiten.* Mai 1873—Mai 1877. Wien, 1878.

A.O. *Documents diplomatiques: Affaires d'Orient,* 1875–7. Paris, 1877.

Andrassy. *Graf Julius Andrassy,* vols. I–III. By E. von Wertheimer. Stuttgart, 1910.

B.A. British Archives (Public Record Office). London, 1875–8.

Disraeli. *The Life of Benjamin Disraeli, Earl of Beaconsfield,* vol. VI. By G. E. Buckle. London, 1920.

D.F. *Documents diplomatiques Français* (1871–1914), I^e série, tome II. Paris, 1930.

G.P. *Die Grosse Politik des Europäischen Kabinette,* 1871–1914. 2 Band, *Der Berliner Kongress und seine Vorgeschichte.* Berlin, 1922.

Layard. Papers of Sir Henry Layard (British Museum). Memoirs, vols. V, VI and VII.

P.P. Parliamentary Proceedings. Accounts and Papers.

Queen Victoria. *The Letters of Queen Victoria.* 2nd series, vol. II. London, 1926.

R.D. Russian Documents. Published by R. W. Seton-Watson in the *Slavonic Review,* 7th series, Nos. 8–12, 14 and 17. The year 1878 is not published.

Salisbury. *Life of Robert Marquis of Salisbury,* vol. II. By Lady G. G. Cecil. London, 1920.

S.A. Serbian Archives (Ministarstvo inostranih dela). Beograd, 1875–8.

Schweinitz. *Denkwürdigkeiten des Botschafters General von Schweinitz,* vols. I–II. Berlin, 1927.

CHAPTER I

*

THE GREAT POWERS & THE BALKANS
BEFORE 1875

THE TURKS reached the height of their power by the
end of the seventeenth century, when the Sultan's army
besieged Vienna for the second time, but this moment
marked also the beginning of their decline. Austria, who stood
as the defender of Christianity, thus uniting both Hungary and
Bohemia with the House of Habsburg, now took the lead in the
struggle against the Crescent, and brought her army through
Serbia down to Kossovo. Russia, emerging from her long
struggle against the Tartars and the Poles, joined the Holy
League under Peter the Great, and for the time being these two
states seemed to be disposed to co-operate in defence of European
civilisation against Islam. In the successive wars with Russia
and Austria during the eighteenth century Turkey lost all her
provinces beyond the Danube and the Save and was pushed from
the Crimea and the Caucasus in Asia. Her rapid decline created
the belief in Europe that she would sooner or later break up, and
in 1782 Catherine the Great proposed to Joseph II a plan of
partition and of creating a Greek Empire—known as the "Greek
Project". In 1807 a similar idea was to occupy the minds of
Napoleon I and Alexander I, and in 1833 it was agreed between
the Emperors of Russia and Austria at the meeting in München-
grätz that in the event of the dissolution of Turkey an understanding should be reached between them for the protection of
their own interests.

To save his Empire from further disruption,the Sultan Selim III
began to introduce some military and financial reforms, but they
were met with strong opposition on the part of the Mussulmans,
who deprecated every novelty and feared losing their privileged
position. In 1807 the Janissaries revolted and deposed the Sultan,
replacing him by Moustafa IV. But a counter-revolution brought

Mahmud II to the throne, who continued to work for reform and in 1826 succeeded in abolishing the order of the Janissaries. This weakening of the Central Power encouraged the already strong separatist tendencies of provincial Pashas, and the Porte had to cope with a series of Moslem revolts, the more important of which were those of Pazvan-Oglou in Vidin, Ali Pasha of Janina, Kapetan Husein Gradaščević in Bosnia and Mehmed Ali in Egypt. The Christians, Serbs and Greeks, who had preserved their national consciousness despite the four centuries of Turkish domination, rose too to shake off the yoke of their oppressor. In 1804 the Serbs revolted and after a long and interrupted struggle succeeded in obtaining an internal autonomy with a Serbian as hereditary Prince. In 1820 the Greeks revolted and enlisted the sympathies of Russia, France and England, who intervened in their favour and helped them to create their independent state. Tottering under the blows of internal revolution Turkey seemed to be on the verge of collapse at the beginning of the 'thirties. She had lost Serbia, Greece and Egypt and had been compelled to ask for protection from Russia.

The emancipation of Serbia and Greece marked the first stage in the struggle of the Balkan Christians for liberty. Their success moved their kinsmen and the other Christians still under the Turkish rule to begin preparing for their own liberation, and the next decades were filled with a series of Christian revolts. The centres of this revolutionary activity which soon inflamed the whole of the Balkan peninsula were Greece and Serbia. In Greece a "National Party" was formed with the aim of liberating all the Greek provinces and uniting them with the mother-country.[1] Their agitation incited the subjugated population in Epirus and Thessaly, where in 1854 a revolution broke out, which nearly involved Greece in a war with Turkey.[2] During the Franco-Austrian War of 1859 King Otto was preparing common action with Serbia and Montenegro against Turkey. This national movement assumed greater dimensions with the accession of Prince George to the throne and the entering into political life of a new generation, born in liberty and educated under the influence of the nationalist gospel of their time. This generation was swayed by the idea of the creation of a great

[1] W. Miller, *The Ottoman Empire*, pp. 176–7.   [2] *Ibid.* p. 266.

Hellenic Kingdom, which should embrace Constantinople and
the southern part of the Balkan peninsula. In 1866 an insurrection
broke out in Crete, whose inhabitants had already participated
in the war of liberation and had revolted in 1841 and 1852. The
Greek Government helped the insurgents and tried to induce
the other Christians to join them. In 1867 she concluded an
alliance with Serbia for that purpose, and for a moment it seemed
that the whole Balkans would be set aflame. But the Great
Powers intervened to prevent it, obtaining only from the Porte
an internal autonomy for Crete.

The national awakening of the Bulgarians began somewhat
later than among the other Balkan Christians. Under the direct
domination of Constantinople, and without much communication with the West, they were little influenced by the revolutionary,
national and liberal ideas which animated European peoples at
that time. A period of revival of national literature and of
educational activity preceded the awakening of their national
consciousness. Its first reaction was, however, turned against
the Greeks, whose economic and ecclesiastical domination was
against the interests of the well-to-do Bulgarian peasants and
tradesmen. Emancipation from the Greek spiritual supremacy
was considered by the Bulgarians as their main task, and all
their efforts were directed towards the establishment of an
independent national church. The centre of their activity was
Constantinople, where a Bulgarian literary society, founded by
Dragan Cankov, carried on a lively propaganda for a free church.
In this campaign they counted upon the support of the Turks and
were ready to co-operate with them.[1] The Central Bulgarian
Committee at Bucarest sent a petition to the Sultan in 1867
begging him to assume the title of Tsar of the Bulgarians and
create a Turko-Bulgarian dual monarchy after the example of
the Austro-Hungarian Monarchy.[2] The idea of dualism was
much propagated in Bulgarian papers, but it found no response
at the Porte.

Turkey favoured Bulgarian aspirations for a free church,
seeing in it a strong weapon to create discord among the
Christians, but Russia opposed it for the same reason. Mean-

---

[1] A. Hajek, *Bulgarien unter Türkenherrschaft*, pp. 166–7.
[2] *Ibid.* pp. 231–2; W. Miller, *op. cit.* p. 344.

while 3000 Bulgarians asked for the Pope's protection and formed a new community of Uniats with their own bishop. The fear of the spread of Catholicism, Greek pretensions upon Constantinople and the failure to preserve Serbia under her influence after the death of Prince Michael—all this induced Russia to move the centre of her interest farther to the East and seek in Bulgaria the main footing of her future policy. In 1870 she supported their claims at the Porte and induced her to grant them an autonomous church.

Parallel with this struggle for a free church, there developed among the younger generation a purely nationalist movement aspiring to the complete liberation of Bulgaria. They formed another Revolutionary Committee at Bucarest and came into contact with the Serbian Government, who helped them with money and arms.[1] A Bulgarian legion was formed in Serbia and many of its members were trained in the military school in Belgrade.[2] The Committee concluded an alliance with Serbia for common action against Turkey, foreseeing the union of the two states into a "Serbo-Bulgarian Kingdom", with Prince Michael as its king.[3] In Bulgaria they inflamed patriotic feelings and organised local committees preparing the people for the rising which broke out in 1876.

The position of Roumania was in many ways different from that of the other Turkish provinces. By the Treaty of Adrianople in 1829 the two provinces, Valachia and Moldavia, obtained administrative autonomy and were put under Russia's protection. The Treaty of Paris put them under European guarantee, but in 1858 Valachia and Moldavia elected the same prince, and the two provinces were henceforth united as Roumania. Though her interests were not identical with those of the other Balkan peoples, her geographical position directed her to co-operation with them. In 1868 she concluded a treaty of friendship with Serbia.

Montenegro enjoyed a certain internal autonomy, though nominally she was still under Turkish rule. The attempt of the Sultan to exercise his sovereign rights over her led to a conflict

[1] S.A., Opis radnje po predmetu opšteg sporazumljenja za ustanak i sjedinjenje. Beograd, 20 April 1876.
[2] Ibid.
[3] V. Popović, Istočno pitanje, p. 129.

in 1852. In 1857 Montenegro raised the neighbouring population of Herzegovina and supported the rising, which, with interruption, lasted till 1864, twice during that period being at open war with Turkey. Cordial relations had always existed between Serbia and Montenegro since the time of Bishop Peter II, and her co-operation in the national cause was secured. The Belgrade Government gave a yearly subsidy to the Prince of Montenegro and helped him both with war material and military instructors. A treaty of alliance was concluded between them in 1866, Prince Nicholas promising to abdicate in favour of Prince Michael of Serbia, who was to rule the future Yougoslav state.[1]

Serbia was the first among the Balkan peoples to rise against the Turks, and by her geographical position and her ethnographical character was called upon to take the leading rôle in their struggle for independence. A strong national movement developed among the younger generation, which conceived the liberation of its kinsmen as its historical mission and endeavoured to prepare for the realisation of that task. Serbia realised that the Balkan peoples could achieve their liberty by a common effort only, and concentrated her efforts upon uniting their separate national movements and organising a general war against Turkey. The programme of her policy was set out as early as 1844 in a memorandum of Ilija Garašanin.[2] Starting with the idea that the Ottoman Empire was doomed to dissolution, he proposed that Serbia should undertake a planned action for the awakening of national feeling among the Balkan Christians and their preparation for an insurrection. This programme was carried out "consequently for a longer period of time", and Garašanin was personally responsible for it. He established secret national committees in the more important places and disseminated his agents all over the Balkans. By the end of the 'sixties Serbia was in alliance with Greece, Montenegro, Roumania and the Bulgarian Revolutionary Committee, and possessed a national militia which at that time was the best organised and the strongest army in the Balkans. The Balkan Alliance became a factor which began to be seriously reckoned with both at

---

[1] S.A., Opis radnje po predmetu opšteg sporazumljenja za ustanak i sjedinjenje. Beograd, 20 April 1876.
[2] Published in *Delo*, XXXVIII, pp. 321–36, 1905.

Constantinople and in Europe. The position of Prince Michael was as strong and influential among the Balkan peoples as that of Napoleon III in Europe.[1] Italy, Hungary and Prussia took Serbia into their calculations and asked for her collaboration in their struggle for freedom. In Vienna Serbia was considered the most important element in the development of the Eastern Question. Russia regarded her as her outpost in the Balkans, threatening both Turkey and Austria.

But in their struggle for independence the Balkan peoples had to reckon not only with Turkey, but also with the Great Powers, who had an interest in preserving the Ottoman Empire or aspired to its partition. Projects of partition had occupied the minds of European statesmen ever since the Turkish invasion, but they continually failed to materialise, and the enemies of Turkey soon turned into her defenders when they were no longer able to participate in her partition. Like the other Powers Russia adopted by turns both the policy of partition and of preservation of Turkey. Her constant aim was to secure a free access to her fleet in the Mediterranean. Having failed to agree with Austria in 1782 and with France in 1807 upon a plan of partition, she endeavoured to consolidate and enlarge the privileges which, since the Treaty of Kuchuk Kainardji (1774), had already given her a preponderant position in the East. In the Treaty of Unkiar Iskelesi in 1833 she engaged Turkey to keep the Straits open to her fleet and closed to the other Powers and promised in return to defend her against "internal and external enemies".

Russia's supremacy in the East provoked resistance on the part of England and France and in 1841 she was compelled to consent to the Straits being closed to all the Powers. Meanwhile the policy of the maintenance of Turkey did not prevent Russia from working for her partition. In 1853 she tried to win over England to it, though without success. The maintenance of the Ottoman Empire was England's traditional policy. Its existence secured her domination in the Mediterranean and her possessions in Asia, and she opposed therefore all plans for partition. Together with France she waged war on Russia in 1854 and pushed her out of the Balkans and the Black Sea. At the Congress of Paris

[1] S. Jovanović, *Druga vlada Miloša i Mihaila*, pp. 214–15.

in 1856 Turkey was recognised as a great Power and her independence and integrity were guaranteed by a special treaty
between England, France and Austria. Russia was deprived of her
protectorate over the Christians, who were now put under the
protection of the Great Powers. Their aspirations for liberty
were met with a programme of reform, which was intended to
remove their grievances and consolidate the Ottoman Empire.
Protected from outside by the three Great Powers, Turkey was
able now to cope with the nationalist movement of her Christian
subjects.

But the hope that Turkey was capable of regeneration was
soon shattered. Imposed from above, the reforms were supported
by a small number of enlightened men only, while the bulk of
the people resisted them as an encroachment upon their privileged
position and a threat to their religion. Even the more sincere
efforts of Fuad Pasha and Ali Pasha brought about no result.
Some administrative changes were introduced which promoted
economic development and helped the formation among the
Christians of a class of rich peasants and tradesmen, who became
the chief agents of revolution. But the moral position of the
Christians remained unchanged. The Sultan himself shrank
from too radical reforms from fear of alienating the Moslem
masses who were the only support of his power. Twenty years
after the Congress of Paris Turkey stood where she had been
twenty years before. But it was now clear to European public
opinion that Turkey was incapable of reform, and that this
could no longer be used as a pretext for resisting the aspirations
of the Balkan Christians.

Russia had advocated the creation of provincial autonomies,
which, in her opinion, were more adapted to the racial and
religious diversity of the Ottoman Empire. The massacres in
Syria in 1860 had compelled the Powers to wrench it from
Turkish hands and grant it autonomy. The same example was
applied in Crete after its rising of 1866. Russia proposed that
this principle should be extended to the other provinces of
Turkey, as it alone could give sufficient protection to the
Christians and prevent their revolts. But this idea found no
response with the other Powers, who feared lest it should only
accelerate the break-up of Turkey.

After the Crimean War it was clear that Russia was not strong enough to fight against a European coalition guarding the Ottoman Empire. But what she had failed to accomplish alone, she intended to do now with the aid of the Balkan peoples, whose struggle for independence offered her an opportunity to realise her aim without coming into conflict with Europe. Russia had always protected them and supported their aspirations. In the first Serbian rising she had sent to their aid a detachment of her army. By the Treaty of Bucarest she had forced Turkey to grant internal autonomy to Serbia, and later on had compelled her to honour the obligation. When the Greeks rose against the Turks, she had actively supported their claims and forced the Porte, arms in hand, to yield to the demands of the Great Powers. Montenegro had always enjoyed special favour with the Tsars, who protected her and materially helped her on many occasions. After the Crimean War Russia saw in the Balkan peoples her natural allies and took an active part in their preparation for war, believing, like them, that Europe could not oppose by force their struggle for emancipation. She had extolled Serbia as the leader of the Balkan peoples and had induced them to collaborate with her. She had helped her both with money and arms to organise an army and carry out revolutionary propaganda.[1] Having failed to win over the Great Powers for partition, she aimed at dividing the Ottoman Empire now with the Balkan Christians, who, with her aid, were to blow it up from inside.

While the Ottoman Empire was being undermined from within, the wall of protection which the three Powers had set up around it began also to break up. Two of her protectors, France and Austria, came soon into conflict about Italy. To weaken the nationally heterogeneous Austria Napoleon III assumed the role of protector of the subjugated nations and began to nourish their aspirations. He had no illusion about Turkey, and preferred her supersession by the free Christian states to her division between Russia and Austria. His idea was to gather all the Balkan Slavs around Serbia, to make her the centre of his policy and a defence against Russia and Austria alike.[2] This policy

---

[1] S.A., Opis radnje po predmetu opšteg sporozumljenja za ustanak i sjedinjenje. Beograd, 20 April 1876.

[2] V. Popović, *Politika Francuske i Austrije na Balkanu*, pp. 11-12, 169.

was, however, soon abandoned, for the question of the domination of the Rhine opened as soon as that of Italy was settled, and
Napoleon now wanted Austria's support against Prussia.

Austria had firmly adhered to the policy of the preservation
of Turkey, though the idea of annexing Bosnia and Herzegovina
occupied her statesmen as early as 1853 and was henceforth
strongly advocated in military circles. Consisting of a great
number of diverse nationalities, Austria, like Turkey, was exposed
to many disturbances during the nineteenth century, which
shook the very foundation of her Empire. The success of the
national principle in the Balkans would have encouraged her
nationalities to revolts and brought, after the Turkish, her own
dissolution to the order of the day. She strove therefore to
prevent the break-up of Turkey, and in 1856 joined France and
England in guaranteeing her integrity. She realised, however,
that this guarantee could not check the growth of the nationalist
movement, and that the Eastern Question might be raised while
she was engaged in defending her possessions in the West.
Inspired with the idea of revenge after 1866, she endeavoured
to reconcile Russia by some concessions and secure the maintenance of peace in the Balkans. In 1867 she proposed that a
conference of the Guaranteeing Powers should be held to inquire
into the condition of the Christians in Turkey and propose
measures necessary for their improvement. This conference was
also to revise the Treaty of Paris in favour of Russia.[1] Together
with France she pressed reforms upon the Porte, induced it to
evacuate the fortresses in Serbia and to grant a special organisation to Crete; but they also protested in Serbia against her
armament and prevented Greece from joining the Cretans.

Peace was preserved in the Balkans, but Austria and France
could not escape their fate. France was defeated in the war with
Prussia in 1870-1, and Austria, already expelled from Italy and
Germany, lost all hope of restoring her position in the West.
The Crimean bloc was destroyed. Among the friends of Turkey
England alone was still capable of giving her effective protection,
but she was isolated, and her public opinion was no longer
disposed to repeat the Crimean adventure. European politics
were now dominated by the Franco-German antagonism, which

[1] F. Beust, *Aus Drei Vierteljahrhunderten*, II, p. 56.

determined the grouping of the other Powers and their policies in the Balkans. For the alliance of the three Emperors, which superseded the Crimean bloc, the existence of Turkey was not a European necessity; on the contrary, her dissolution was considered inevitable and her partition as a European interest.

The formation of a powerful military empire in the centre of Europe had not only deprived Turkey of her protectors, but had had a decisive influence upon the reconciliation of her chief enemies, Austria and Russia, whose rivalry constituted hitherto the best guarantee of her security. After 1871 both Russia and Austria endeavoured to win Germany over to their side. Russia was already closely tied up with Germany by a sincere friendship which existed between Alexander II and William I, a friendship which had been only strengthened by the many services she rendered Germany during her struggle for unity. She hoped that Germany would keep Europe in check and leave her a free hand in the East. To secure her support she offered her in 1873 a military convention guaranteeing the territorial *status quo* of both states.[1] Austria too desired to establish cordial relations with the new German Empire in order to avoid isolation and the pressure of Russia in the East. In 1872 a meeting between Francis Joseph and William I, to which subsequently the Tsar was also invited, took place at Berlin, and the reconciliation was soon effected. Bismarck accepted the military convention under the condition only that it should be accepted also by Austria. He did not wish to serve as an instrument of Russian policy and remain completely dependent upon her. By bringing Austria into his alliance with Russia, he hoped both to prevent a European coalition against Germany and to preserve her freedom of action.[2] It was by his mediation that Gortchakov and Andrassy came into contact at the meeting of Berlin and exchanged their views, assuring each other of their pacific tendencies in the Balkans. In June 1873, a month after the military convention was signed in St Petersburg, Austria and Russia signed another convention at Schönbrunn, to which Germany acceded, "finding its contents conformed to the idea which underlay the agreement signed at St Petersburg".[3] This convention provided no military

---

[1] Krasnyi Archiv, I, *Relations entre la Russie et l'Allemagne*, 1873–1914, p. 28.
[2] Bismarck, *Gedanken und Erinnerungen*, pp. 510–14.
[3] Krasnyi Archiv, I, *Relations entre la Russie et l'Allemagne*, 1873–1914, p. 34.

assistance in case of war, but left that question to be regulated by a special agreement "if in the course of this entente military action became necessary". The two Emperors mutually promised to agree among themselves, even in case of their interests being divergent on special questions, in order to maintain their entente. In case of European peace being compromised by a third Power, they would come to an understanding, without seeking for or concluding new alliances, "as to the line of conduct to be followed in common".[1] The hopes of both Russia and Austria that Germany would lend her assistance to the realisation of their aims in the Balkans were shattered. Germany was ready to support them in so far only as they were able to co-operate. In entering the Imperial Alliance they were compelled to abandon the aspiration of solving the Eastern Question to their exclusive advantage. An agreement upon a common settlement of this question they could not reach, but they set up the maintenance of their entente as the principal aim of their policy, to which their divergences in the Balkans were to be subordinated. Whatever course events took in the future they were engaged to agree among themselves.

On the eve of the rising in Herzegovina which reopened the Eastern Question in 1875, Turkey stood undermined from within and isolated from without. The Balkan peoples represented no great danger to her, since they were unprepared and divided. But for her destiny it was much more important that her protectors were no longer able to assist her, while the other Powers, whatever their divergences, were ready to accept her partition, rather than go to war for her.

[1] Krasnyi Archiv, I, *Relations entre la Russie et l'Allemagne*, 1873–1914, p. 30.

CHAPTER II

✻

THE INSURRECTION IN BOSNIA AND HERZEGOVINA

THE CHRISTIAN population in Bosnia and Herzegovina had occupied a special position in the Ottoman Empire from the outset. The Turkish conquest had not freed them from their feudal masters, as was the case with their co-religionists in the other provinces, for the great majority of the Christian landlords had accepted Islam and saved their lands and their privileges. In the course of time the nobles increased their privileges by various services rendered to the Sultans, and took into their hands almost the whole administration of the two provinces. When the central power in Constantinople began to dissolve separatist tendencies sprang up in Bosnia and Herzegovina stronger than elsewhere. The masters of the land, the nobles, resented every encroachment on their power and their privileges. In 1831 they revolted against Mahmud II and defeated his army at the field of Kossovo, and Kapetan Husein Gradaščević, the leader of the dissatisfied Moslems, became virtually an independent ruler of the two provinces. Order was restored the following year, but opposition to the reforms was not overcome till 1851.

The Christians, themselves divided into Orthodox and Catholics, remained in complete political and economic subjection to their old masters, succeeding only in preserving their religion and their nationality. But the Serbian revolution stirred their minds and raised their hopes, and, when Serbia started propaganda for a general rising of the Balkan peoples, she found a most fertile soil in Bosnia and Herzegovina. Through men devoted to the Slav cause—particularly priests and merchants— the Serbian Government spread among the people of the two provinces the idea of national revolution and their union with Serbia. The centres of this activity were two theological colleges established and supported by Serbia in Mostar and Banja-Luka, and local committees of the Omladina which gathered all the best patriots. A Central Revolutionary Committee was established in Sarajevo which undertook necessary preparations for insurrection. Many emigrants from these provinces were supported in Belgrade and trained as future leaders of the rising. Thus in 1866 all seemed ready for action; men capable of bearing arms were conscripted, detachments were formed and officers were appointed.[1]

Meanwhile the hopes of a general rising and of Serbia's help began to vanish after the death of Prince Michael. With a young prince on the throne and a Regency at the head of affairs, and with a strong agitation for liberal reforms, Serbia was both too weak and too much occupied with her internal problems for an active foreign policy. Military preparations were abandoned, and propaganda slackened until it died away altogether. The military school for training the emigrants was disbanded; the connections with local agents, which the Regency still endeavoured to maintain, were dropped as soon as Prince Milan took the reins into his own hands. The Regency had tried to obtain from the Porte the administration of Bosnia, Herzegovina and Old Serbia in consideration of paying a yearly tribute. For that purpose Nicholas Hristić was appointed as diplomatic agent in Constantinople in 1870.[2] The Hungarians had for some time favoured the idea of Serbia getting a part of Bosnia and Herzegovina, hoping thereby to separate her from Russia and neutralise her influence with the Austrian Slavs.[3] It seems that in the autumn of 1870 an overture was made to the Belgrade Government to that effect if she engaged to maintain neutrality in the event of a conflict between Austria and some other Power.[4] But Serbia did not wish to divide the two provinces with Austria. Her efforts at Constantinople remained without result.

Unable any longer to lead the Balkan peoples, Serbia was soon abandoned by them, and the idea of common action was superseded by mutual rivalry. Russia had strongly opposed Milan's

[1] S.A., Opis radnje po predmetu opšteg sporazumljenja za ustanak i sjedinjenje. Beograd, 20 April 1876.
[2] J. Ristić, *Spoljašnji odnošaji Srbije*, III, pp. 307–17.
[3] Andrassy, I, pp. 461–2.
[4] J. Ristić, *op. cit.* pp. 140–2.

candidature for the Serbian throne, where she desired to place Prince Nicholas of Montenegro, as a man capable of continuing the policy pursued by Prince Michael. When despite her wishes Milan was proclaimed Prince of Serbia, Russia transferred all her sympathies and assistance to Nicholas and extolled him as the leader of the Balkan peoples. Nicholas, who was earlier prepared to abdicate in favour of Serbia, now separated from her and began to work for his own hand.

Relations with the Bulgarians were no better. Their national leaders were already estranged from Serbia by the conduct of the Regency towards them. Those who fought for the national church now used it as a means for proselytising the Serbian and the Greek elements in Macedonia, which brought them into conflict with Greece and Serbia.

The Greeks had expected assistance from Serbia and Russia in the Cretan rising and were much disappointed at their attitude. The ecclesiastical separation of Bulgaria was a great blow to their supremacy, which they could not forget, and the Slavophil propaganda inspired them with fear of Slav preponderance in the Balkans. They believed that Serbia and Bulgaria were merely agents of Russian policy, which was directed as much against Greece as against Turkey.

In such circumstances the Christians in Bosnia and Herze-govina began to prepare for independent action. In 1872 the Herzegovinian emigrants met in Belgrade and resolved to act alone. In 1873 they sent a memorandum to the Tsar, who was staying in Vienna, telling him that they were compelled to rise against the Turks and asking not to be abandoned. In autumn 1874 some national leaders from the district of Nevesinje met in Biograd and decided to take up arms the next spring. This decision was communicated to Serbia and Montenegro, who were asked for help in arms and ammunition. But the Turks discovered the plot and began to arrest the leaders, who fled to Montenegro for refuge. Almost at the same time great persecutions started among the Christians in Bosnia. In 1872 thirty citizens from Banja-Luka signed a memorandum to the Austrian consul complaining of Turkish misrule and asking for Austrian protection. Next year twenty-four merchants from Gradiška took refuge in Austria from fear of being killed by the Turks.

They addressed a memorandum to the Guaranteeing Powers pointing out the unbearable conditions in Bosnia and demanding the fulfilment of earlier promises and guarantees against future misrule.

Prince Nicholas did not wish for new troubles in Herzegovina at the time when he hoped to settle his differences with the Porte and obtain some concessions for himself. By the aid of the Austrian Government he succeeded in securing an amnesty for the refugees and sent them home. At the intervention of Austria the Porte gave amnesty to the Bosnian refugees also and freed those who were arrested in Sarajevo. But the Christian preparations and the Turkish persecution had already created an atmosphere of irritation and hatred which was bound to explode at the first spark. And this spark was thrown in the summer of 1875 when the Turkish authorities began to exact by force the excessive taxes which the Christians refused to pay. At the beginning of July they revolted in Herzegovina, and a few weeks later Bosnia was also set aflame.

The insurrection in Bosnia and Herzegovina was the continuation of that process of emancipation of the Balkan Christians, which started at the beginning of the nineteenth century with the Serbian revolution and was followed later on by the Greek revolution. More directly, it was the result of the propaganda and preparations which Serbia carried out with the view of organising a general rising of the Christians. In spite of mutual jealousy and friction which divided them at the moment the rising broke out, it made a strong impression upon them, and especially upon the Slavs. The Balkans were, in fact, spiritually prepared for a struggle with Turkey. Volunteers from Serbia, Bulgaria, Montenegro, as well as from Russia and the Slav provinces of Austria hastened to their help. In Belgrade a committee was formed to raise funds for the relief of the refugees and to mobilise and arm the volunteers. Similar committees were established in Vojvodina and Croatia, where Svetozar Miletić, the leader of the Omladina, and Bishop Strossmayer, a Croat champion of the Southern Slav cause, fought energetically in favour of the insurgents. The Slavophils in Russia hailed the rising as a struggle for the Slav Idea and started a great propaganda for "our Slav brethren", sending them both

money and war material.[1] Assisted from all sides and inter-
woven with various interests, the rising raised a much larger
question than it represented by itself. Though it failed to inflame
the whole Balkans, it inflamed almost the whole Slav world, and
there lay its power and its weakness.

The effect of the rising was particularly great upon Serbia.
For decades the Serbian people had been imbued with the idea
of its historical mission to liberate and unite all its subjugated
brethren, and for the realisation of this task great preparations
and sacrifices had been made. The Bosnian rising provoked
therefore enormous enthusiasm in Serbia. Among all the provinces Bosnia was nearest to the Serbian heart. "Bosnia is the
sensitive point for all Serbian politicians," wrote the Austrian
consul in 1868, "it is the centre round which all their desires
and hopes have long turned."[2] Meetings and demonstrations
against the Turks were held throughout the country. Volunteers
came in masses, and a committee was formed to arm and despatch
them across the frontier. Belgrade was soon flooded with groups
of young men, who walked armed through the streets. "War
on the Turks! Give us war!" cried a detachment of volunteers
accompanying Prince Milan, who was coming from Vienna.

The warlike agitation was stimulated by the electoral campaign
which took place at this moment. The Liberals, though in a
majority, had been in opposition ever since the coming of age of
Prince Milan, and were fighting in vain against his autocracy.
Nationalists by conviction, they supported the agitation in the
country, seeing in it both the means of gaining power and of
realising their national programme. Their papers declared that if
Serbia left the insurgents to be crushed by the Turks, she would
compromise for ever her rôle of Piedmont.

The attitude of the Government contributed largely to stimulate
the excitement in the country. They took no measures to prevent
inflammatory speeches and demonstrations. On the contrary,
they distributed arms to the volontéers from the military
magazines and sent two detachments across the frontier.[3] To

---

[1] S.A., Correspondence between Prince Nicholas and A. Yonin, the
Russian Consul at Ragusa, 1875–6.

[2] R. W. Seton-Watson, "Les Relations de l'Autriche-Hongrie et de la
Serbie entre 1868–1874", Le Monde Slave, No. 5, p. 9, 1926.

[3] S. Jovanović, Vlada Milana Obrenovića, I, p. 244.

the Prince who was in Vienna they telegraphed that people believed his journey to be in connection with the insurrection and that they were ready to assist it. The telegram closed with the words: "Very difficult, perhaps impossible to resist it."[1] But although the Government yielded to the national excitement in the hope of preserving their position, they were turned out at the elections, which gave an overwhelming majority to the Liberals.

This warlike excitement and the results of the elections created a very difficult position for Prince Milan. Educated in France till the age of fourteen, Milan was not imbued with the feelings of his milieu. He did not believe Serbia was strong enough to measure herself against the Ottoman Empire. She was unprepared and isolated, and a war in such circumstances would inevitably bring her to catastrophe, which might cost him his throne. But though the policy of war seemed to lead to disaster, Milan could nowhere find support to resist the popular current. He had failed to win the sympathy of his people and his army; his autocratic inclinations and his unbalanced character had estranged from him both the Liberals and the Conservatives. Besides, Prince Nicholas, the Russian candidate for the Serbian throne, had already secretly sided with the insurgents, while his second rival, Prince Peter Karadjordjević, was commanding a detachment of volunteers in Bosnia and standing out as a national hero. Milan realised that open action on the part of Montenegro would force him to follow her at once, and that his rival in Bosnia rendered his position still more difficult. The question was whether an opposition to national aspirations would not provoke an internal revolution and bring his own life into jeopardy. Compelled to choose between these two courses, both of which seemed to be catastrophic for the state and his throne, Milan felt himself unable to find a way out and began to think of abdication. "Whatever course events take", wrote the Austrian Consul, "it is very probable that the result will be fatal to the house of Obrenovitch."[2]

Unable to take any decision in such circumstances, Milan endeavoured to gain time and study the situation more closely.

[1] S.A., Bogićević to Cukić, 19 July 1875. Tel.
[2] A.A., Wrede to Andrassy, Belgrade, 24 Aug. 1875, No. 62.

His hatred of the Liberals and their constitutionalism was now increased by their warlike agitation. He feared lest a Liberal Cabinet should plunge the country into a war, and desired therefore to create a coalition Government between the Liberals and the Conservatives. But all his efforts in this direction remained unsuccessful and, after a fortnight of futile deliberations, he was compelled to form a Liberal Government with Stevča Mihailović as Premier and Jovan Ristić as Minister for Foreign Affairs.

He also avoided giving any-definite promise to the Great Powers, who advised him to maintain peace, pointing out the difficulties of his position. He told Andrassy frankly that he could not abstain from action if Montenegro entered the war.[1] The attitude of Montenegro was of vital importance for him, as he could not allow Nicholas to take the lead of the Southern Slavs. Already by the end of July he asked Nicholas what attitude he was going to take towards the events in Herzegovina and whether an understanding as to common action was desirable.[2] Like Milan, Nicholas was also in a difficult position. His people hailed the insurgents and went in masses to their help. Nicholas was afraid of coming into conflict with Turkey, and gave reassuring declarations to the Powers who asked him to preserve neutrality. But he felt it impossible to oppose his people and, after some hesitation, he began secretly to assist the insurrection. The Belgrade Government tried also to approach Greece with the view of a joint action in the event of Montenegro's entering the war, but their proposal to send a secret envoy for that purpose found no response in Athens.[3]

Another question of importance for Prince Milan was the rising in Bosnia. He was informed in advance that it was being prepared. Before it actually broke out he asked the Russian Consul whether Russia would prevent an Austrian occupation of Serbia if he declared war on Turkey.[4] Prince Wrede wrote to Andrassy that Milan was prepared now to favour war, seeing in

---

[1] A.A., Extrait d'un compte rendu d'une conférence à Vienne le 5 août 1875.
[2] S.A., Tel. to the Government of Montenegro, Belgrade, 13 July 1875.
[3] M. Lhéritier, *Histoire diplomatique de la Grèce*, III, p. 382.
[4] A.A., Langenau to Andrassy, 16 Aug. 1875, Tel. no. 26.

it the only means of keeping himself on the throne.[1] In fact he was only reconnoitring the ground before taking his decision.

In his opening address to the Skupština, which met on 1c September at Kragujevac, Milan preserved his non-committal attitude. He spoke of the sufferings of the insurgents and the Turkish abuses, of the efforts of the Great Powers to restore peace and his readiness to assist them. "I shall endeavour", he added, "in the limits of our small power to reach the result which would satisfy the insurgent provinces."[2] But the conduct of the new Government rendered further temporisation impossible. Hailed by the public as the "Ministry of Action", the Government endeavoured to follow the popular stream. Before the Skupština opened they decided to continue assisting the insurgents and to aid Bulgarian revolutionaries with money and arms to prepare a rising in Bulgaria. General Ranko Alimpić was sent to the Drina in order to organise the volunteers and transport them to Bosnia. Ristić came into contact with some Bulgarian leaders and gave them instructions as to their work.[3]

In the Skupština opinion differed as to the attitude to be adopted towards the insurgents, but there was a general feeling that Serbia could not, and must not, remain indifferent to thei destiny. The majority of the Committee on the Address to the Throne considered that Serbia could not leave the insurgents to be crushed by force "without thereby giving a death-blow to her most sacred interests, renouncing for ever her holy mission, turning away for ever the sympathies of her brethren...". "The question of Bosnia has been raised without us. We are bound by circumstances to participate in its solution, otherwise Bosnia will be lost to us for ever, and not having enough forces within these narrow frontiers for our national life, we shall at last become the prey of some mightier neighbour." A resolution was moved "to assist the insurrection of our brethren in Turkey with all the consequences which the assistance would involve, even war".[4] In a secret addition to the Address to the Throne the Government was authorised to raise a loan to the amount of three million ducats, two-thirds of which were to be used for

[1] A.A., Wrede to Andrassy, 26 Aug. 1875, Tel. no. 64.
[2] Živan Živanović, *Politička istorija Srbije*, I, p. 323.
[3] *Zapisi Jevrema Grujića*, III, p. 109.
[4] *Ibid.* pp. 112–26.

military preparations and assistance to the insurgents, and one-third to be kept in reserve in case of war.

The Porte did not attach great importance to the rising and did not hasten to suppress it. It feared lest energetic measures should be disapproved by the Great Powers, and endeavoured to exhaust peaceful means before resorting to arms. When by the end of July it dispatched an army against the rebels, it sustained great losses in the first encounters with them. This defeat brought about the fall of the Governor of Bosnia, Dervish Pasha, and led to important changes in the Government. Mahmud Pasha, known as the friend of Russia, which won him the nickname of Mahmudov, became Grand Vizier, and Avni Pasha took the War Office. Avni Pasha considered that the real danger of the rising came from Serbia and Montenegro, who supported it. He began to mass troops on their frontier, resolved to attack them if they continued to assist the insurrection or joined it.[1]

Serbia replied to this measure by sending a detachment of her troops to the frontier and starting military preparations. The presence of the two armies on the frontier resulted in frequent invasions on both sides, which gave rise to many complaints. Serbia asked the Porte to cease concentrating its troops; the Porte on its part asked from Serbia guarantees that she would keep her neutrality. These mutual accusations and the continuation of preventive measures on both sides strained the relations between the two countries to such a pitch that a conflict seemed to be inevitable.

The danger of a war compelled Milan to take a more pronounced attitude against the war party and to prevent the measures which might provoke it. He believed that the Government desired to force his hands by the Skupština resolutions of a war loan and the assistance of the insurgents. He resolved to get rid of Jovan Ristić, whom he believed capable of anything in order to maintain himself in power. Ristić says in his *Diplomatic History of Serbia* that the Government, though resolved to support the rising at all costs, realised that Serbia was unprepared for immediate action, and that they intended to keep the movement alive during the winter and use that time to complete the armaments and eventually to revive the Balkan alliance. Before

[1] B.A., Elliot to Derby, 5 Oct. 1875, No. 633.

taking recourse to arms Ristić wished to exhaust diplomatic means. He hoped that the difficult position of Turkey would induce her to accept the mediation of Serbia and Montenegro in favour of the insurgents.[1] It is evident, however, that the measures the Government took to maintain the rising and to impose their intervention in the solution of the Bosnian question were of a nature to provoke a conflict against their will. Milan was conscious of this. He refused to sign the Skupština's resolutions and publicly disavowed the work of the Government. On 4 October he entered the Skupština, determined to make a personal explanation to the deputies and force the Cabinet's resignation. "He made a long speech in which he did not declare himself against war, but only explained that the country must not be hurried, for we were unprepared both militarily, diplomatically and financially."[2] The Cabinet resigned at once and Milan again took the situation in hand. The new Cabinet, composed of the younger Liberals and Conservatives, with Ljubomir Kaljević as President, was not substantially different in character from the late, but it contained no one of commanding personality, who might have influenced events, no one whom Milan had any reason to fear.

Two days after the fall of Stevča Mihailović's Cabinet the agents of the Great Powers made a collective representation to the Belgrade Government, asking them to refrain from any measure which might serve the Porte as a pretext for considering itself attacked and declaring, that in the event of direct hostilities on the part of Serbia, it would be impossible for the Powers to protect her from a Turkish occupation.[3] Before this step was taken at Belgrade, the Powers obtained from the Porte a solemn declaration that it would not attack Serbia unless it were attacked by her.

It was the concentration of the Turkish and the Serbian troops on the frontier and the danger of an imminent conflict between them that induced the Great Powers to intervene. They had from the outset advised Serbia to keep quiet. The Tsar wrote a personal letter to Prince Milan asking him to abstain from any

[1] J. Ristić, *Diplomatska istorija Srbije*, I, p. 58.
[2] S. Jovanović, *Vlada Milana Obrenovića*, I, p. 259.
[3] *Ibid.* p. 258.

action. Milan's question as to the attitude of Russia in the event of Serbia's entering the war was communicated to Vienna, and Novikov, the Russian Ambassador, proposed that the three allied Powers should make a joint representation in Belgrade against war.[1] Andrassy was prepared to prevent Serbia by force from occupying Bosnia, but he did not wish to threaten her in advance and leave the impression that he was opposed to her aspirations, fearing lest this would throw her and the insurgents into the hands of Russia. He desired to preserve the sympathies of the Christians and his influence over them.[2] He refused Novikov's proposal, but promised to support any step which Russia would make at Belgrade.[3] Meanwhile the Russian Government showed little consideration for the feelings of the Serbs. They were much discontented with the conduct of the Belgrade Government and looked upon them as members of the Omladina, as the revolutionaries, against whose activity they had already waged an internal war. Novikov reproached Cukić, the Serbian agent in Vienna, with the revolutionary character of the Belgrade Government and their double policy, declaring that Russia would leave them to bear all the consequences alone.[4] Baron Jomini told the British Chargé d'affaires that the Powers ought to prevent Serbia from entering the war, either by intervention on their part, or by permission to the Porte to occupy the country. "A punishment deserved by Serbia", he said. "During the Turkish occupation the country might be relieved of its republican socialist element."[5] Yet when the danger of a Turkish occupation became imminent Jomini was the first to ask for an intervention of the Powers at Constantinople to prevent it.

Apart from their endeavour to restrain Serbia from action, the Powers intervened also with the insurgents with the view of dissuading them from further fighting and inducing them to enter into negotiations with the Porte. The initiative for this intervention came from Russia. Already by the end of July she drew the attention of Austria to the danger of the revolt's spreading further and bringing European peace into jeopardy, and proposed

---

[1] A.A., Hofmann to Andrassy, 17 Aug. 1875.
[2] A.A., Andrassy to Rodić, 12 Aug. 1875.
[3] A.A., Andrassy to Langenau, 19 Aug. 1875, Tel.
[4] S.A., Cukić to Pavlović, 15 and 22 Sept. 1875.
[5] B.A., Doria to Derby, 29 Sept. 1875.

that the Consuls of the three Northern Powers should be instructed to act in common for a peaceful settlement.[1] This proposal was not welcomed in Vienna. Andrassy did not wish Russia to intervene in the provinces in which Austria was primarily interested and in which she intended to play the chief rôle. He saw in it the proof that Russia had not abandoned her rôle of protector of the Christians in Turkey and that she meant to pursue it regardless of Austrian interests. He suspected her of desiring to create a protectorate of the three Powers over Turkey and to bind Austria's hands for the future.[2] Yet he could not simply refuse her proposal, and therefore endeavoured to counteract its effect by giving the intervention a different meaning. He proposed on his part that the Consuls should advise the insurgents to lay their grievances before the Turkish authorities and tell them that the Powers would ask the Porte to remove those of them which should be deemed justified.[3] Russia accepted this proposal as a basis for discussion, and Vienna was chosen as a centre of action for the three Powers. In a conference between Andrassy, the Russian and the German Ambassadors, it was agreed that the Consuls on the spot should advise the insurgents to cease hostilities and state their grievances to the Turks, and warn them not to expect any support from the Powers if they refused to comply with their advice.

This first attempt at a common action of the three Powers in the Balkans revealed the divergence of interests and tendencies between Russia and Austria. Russia desired to mediate between the insurgents and the Porte in order to bring about a peaceful settlement of the rising. Austria treated the rising as an internal question for Turkey and was in principle opposed to any intervention of the Powers.[4] She consented to this step only after entirely changing its purpose. The Powers were not to mediate, but to discourage the insurgents from further fighting and thus help the Porte to overcome them. Their action was not an interference with Turkish affairs, but good offices offered to the Porte for pacification of the rising. In adopting this measure Russia was in fact advancing Austria's aims.

[1] A.A., Orczy to Andrassy, 25 July 1875, Tel.
[2] A.A., Andrassy to Francis Joseph, 28 July 1875; Andrassy, II, p. 263.
[3] A.A., Andrassy to Langenau, 29 July 1875, Tel.
[4] A.C., No. 109.

The original intention of Russia was to conduct the pacificatory action within the frame of the Dreikaiserbund, without appealing to the other Powers. This was also Andrassy's wish. The German Ambassador was invited to participate in the deliberations which resulted in the common instructions to the Consuls. He restricted his rôle to supporting an agreement between Russia and Austria, as Germany, having no interests of her own in the Balkans, did not wish to take any separate position in this question. But the news of an intervention of the three Powers in Turkey produced some misgivings among the other Powers, who already looked with dissatisfaction at the preponderant rôle the Dreikaiserbund assumed in European affairs. France was particularly afraid lest the three Powers should take advantage of her present eclipse and solve the Eastern Question without her. To prevent such an eventuality she desired to co-operate with them in the work of pacification. Her Ambassador in St Petersburg, General le Flô, protested against the separation of the Dreikaiserbund from the European concert and asked that France should be invited to participate in its work.[1] To appease the French the Tsar sent an invitation to them for a joint intervention at Constantinople, and having done so he extended the invitation to Italy and England too. The Tsar did so without previously consulting his allies; he only informed Austria of what he had done, asking her to send a formal invitation to the other Powers. Such a step was strongly resented by Andrassy, who desired to keep Russia separate from the other Powers and arrange the whole matter with her. He had already difficulties in bringing her to fall in with his plans; they would only increase if every step was to be discussed by all the six Powers.

Italy and France gave their consent at once, but England did so with reluctance and only at the express invitation of the Porte.[2] England was opposed to the intervention of the Powers. She considered the insurrection as an internal affair of Turkey and wished that the latter should be left to suppress it.[3] Her Ambassador had from the outset advised the Porte to show more vigilance in quelling the rising and in preventing its spreading.[4]

[1] D.F., No. 4.   [2] B.A., Derby to Elliot, 24 Aug. 1875, No. 275.
[3] B.A., Derby to Elliot, 12 Aug. 1875, No. 235.
[4] Ibid. 19 Aug. No. 254.

Derby did not believe in the success of the Consular mission and feared that it might open the way to further interference by the Powers. But since the Porte had already accepted it and asked for his participation he could not very well refuse it.

The Porte tried at first to avoid the intervention of the Powers, but Ignatyev was able to convince the Sultan that it was in his own interest, and secured his consent. Server Pasha was sent to Mostar as a special commissioner with large authorisations for pacification. The Consuls of the Great Powers met the insurgents, but failed to induce them to accept their advice. The insurgents refused to believe any longer in mere promises, and asked for serious reforms and European guarantees that they would be executed.[1] Prince Nicholas had informed them in advance of the Consular mission and had sent them instructions as to the demands they should put to the Consuls.[2]

That the mission of the Consuls remained fruitless surprised nobody. It was easy to foresee that the insurgents, after having abandoned their homes and risked their lives, would not stop fighting before they were vanquished or obtained guarantees for the improvement of their position. The real result of that mission was to encourage the insurgents to pursue the struggle, as it gave them proof that the Powers were not indifferent to their cause. The assistance they received from Serbia and Montenegro, as well as from Russia and Austria, enabled them to repulse the Turkish attacks and maintain themselves during the winter.

Despite the pressure of the Great Powers Serbia and Montenegro continued to support the insurrection. Serbia no longer sent volunteer detachments across the frontier, but she helped the insurgents with money, arms and other necessaries. For this purpose and for the completion of armaments the Government was empowered by the Skupština to raise a loan to the amount of two million ducats, and to use the state reserves until the loan was effected. All this action was henceforth conducted by the War Ministry, so that the movement in Bosnia soon came under the control of the Belgrade Government.[3] In Herzegovina Montenegro kept all the threads of the movement in her own

---

[1] A. Beer, *Die Orientalische Politik Oesterreichs*, p. 620.
[2] *Spomenica o herzegovačkom ustanku*, 1875, pp. 8–9, 27.
[3] *Zapisi Jevrema Grujića*, III, pp. 150–1.

hands. Nicholas not only assisted it, but actually directed it through his agent, Peko Pavlović, who was appointed a chief of the rebel's headquarters and who acted according to instructions from Cetinje. Montenegro served in fact as the basis of operation for the revolted province. In Grahovo, a frontier town, magazines of food and arms were established, and detachments were organised, which were sent to Herzegovina when needed.[1]

Apart from Serbia and Montenegro, the insurgents received considerable assistance from Russia and Austria. The Slav Committees began from the outset to advocate the cause of the Christians and to collect money and materials for their help. Through the Russian Consul in Ragusa, Alexander Yonin, himself a fervent Slavophil, they regularly supplied the insurgents with money and war materials.[2] Yonin distributed this help partly directly and partly through Prince Nicholas. He communicated also to him all intelligence relating to the movements of Turkish troops and gave him instructions as to his conduct. Elliot says in his Memoirs that Yonin "did not even think it necessary to conceal his active co-operation with the insurgents".[3]

The neighbouring Slav provinces of Austria took a lively interest in the insurrection. Committees were formed in Vojvodina, Croatia and Dalmatia for the support of the insurgents and volunteers went to the revolted provinces. In Vojvodina Svetozar Miletić fought for the Slav cause in his paper *Zastava* and organised the whole relief of the insurgents. In Croatia Bishop Strossmayer, who already stood in close connection with the Serbian Government, endeavoured to win over Bosnian Catholics for co-operation with the Serbs.[4] General von Mollinary, the Governor of Zagreb, and Baron Rodić, the Governor of Dalmatia, who saw in the rising the wished-for opportunity to annex these provinces, endeavoured to prepare the ground for it by helping the insurgents. They left the Austrian frontier practically open, and the insurgents were able not only to smuggle all their war materials but to cross it whenever they were pursued by the Turks. Mollinary found the means to

---

[1] *Spomenica o herzegovačkom ustanku*, 1875, pp. 34–5.
[2] S.A., Correspondence between Prince Nicholas and A. Yonin, 1875–6.
[3] Sir Henry Elliot, *Some Revolutions and other Diplomatic Experiences*, p. 207.
[4] F. Šišić, *Korespondencija Rački-Strossmayer*, I, p. 372.

relieve the refugees whose number was daily increasing.[1] Baron Rodić proposed in Vienna that Austria should come to an understanding with Serbia and Montenegro and march immediately into the two provinces.[2] Andrassy endeavoured to prevent this fraternisation between his own Slavs and the insurgents and ordered the frontier to be closed, and everyone crossing it with arms to be arrested.[3] But he desired also to retain the sympathies of the Christians "and make it clear to them that they can expect a final settlement of their fate only from us".[4] He therefore maintained neutrality towards Turkey according to the Treaty, but did what he could otherwise to help the insurgents. He sent grain to Montenegro to feed her refugees, but did so with the intention of showing her that she could only protect the insurgents as long as she was protected by Austria.[5] The port of Klek was often closed when the Turkish troops had to disembark, and they were obliged to undergo a quarantine before proceeding to Herzegovina. Andrassy wrote to Zichy that this was being done in order not to compromise the influence of Austria in favour of Russia.[6] Holmes, the British Consul at Ragusa, believed that Austria was behaving more as an open enemy to Turkey than as a friend.[7] The Turks considered her conduct to be "highly equivocal and open to suspicion", and complained to the British Ambassador that "all the arms and ammunition for the insurgents came from Austrian territory".[8]

Supported from all sides, the Christians continued their struggle resolved to "achieve their liberty or to perish to the last man". By the end of October they defeated the Turks, inflicting heavy losses upon them. Hostilities were tacitly suspended during the winter, and the insurgents retreated to the mountains and began to prepare for the next campaign in the spring, when they hoped Serbia and Montenegro would join them.

[1] Anton von Mollinary, 46 *Jahre im oesterreich-ungarischen Heere*, II, p. 291.
[2] Andrassy, II, pp. 266–7.
[3] A.C., No. 106.
[4] A.A., Andrassy to Rodić, 12 Aug. 1875.
[5] Andrassy, II, p. 266.
[6] A.A., Andrassy to Zichy, 1 Sept. 1875.
[7] B.A., Elliot to Derby, 15 Dec. 1875, No. 813.
[8] B.A., Elliot to Derby, 20 Aug. 1875, No. 461, conf.

CHAPTER III

*

THE ANDRASSY NOTE

THE disagreement between Russia and Austria on the question of the Consular mission, its purpose and the manner of its execution, revealed from the outset deep divergences in their aims, which had always divided them in the Balkans. Traditional protector of the Turkish Christians, Russia took every opportunity to enlarge their privileges and bring about their gradual emancipation from the Turkish domination. Unlike the Western Powers, who believed that administrative reforms could remove the causes of conflict between the Christians and the Moslems, Russia held the view that national and religious differences between them were too great to make an equalisation possible, and that Turkey should develop herself in the direction of provincial autonomies suited to local needs and conditions.[1] She was of the same opinion now, though her proposal for intervention referred only to some "equitable reforms". The conviction that an autonomous organisation alone could secure a tolerable life to the revolted Christians and prevent future revolts soon found expression in her press and the unofficial utterances of Prince Gortchakov and Baron Jomini. Gortchakov stated in a private conversation "that it could not be avoided giving Herzegovina and Bosnia a situation analogous to that of Roumania".[2] Baron Jomini, who was in charge of the Foreign Office during Gortchakov's absence, told the British Ambassador that the revolted provinces ought to be granted autonomy, and that an action like that in Syria in 1861 could alone lead to positive results.[3] To the French chargé d'affaires he dwelt upon the weakness of Turkey and the imminence of her dissolution if the rising spread; he insisted upon the necessity of the

[1] É. Driault, *La Question d'Orient*, p. 190.
[2] A.A., Andrassy to Francis Joseph, 30 Aug. 1875.
[3] B.A., Loftus to Derby, 10 Nov. No. 338, 1875.

Powers' occupying themselves in advance with "those who were naturally called upon to take up her succession". He foresaw the possibility of the creation of a Balkan federation with Constantinople as a free city.[1] Both he and Gortchakov believed that Austria was opposed only to a great Slav state, but that her interests would not be offended by autonomy.[2] The Russian press wrote openly in favour of this plan. *Golos* called upon the Powers not to satisfy themselves with "palliatives and vain promises", but to give the Christians autonomy and put them under their protection.[3]

Austria's aspirations in the Balkans were directly opposed to those of Russia. Like Russia Austria considered herself a natural heiress of European Turkey, and did not wish to see Russia preponderating in the East. So long as Austria was occupied in defending her possessions in the West, she endeavoured to preserve the Ottoman Empire. Expelled from Italy and Germany, she turned again to the East, where she hoped to find compensation for her losses. Already in 1853 she tried to obtain France's consent for occupation of Bosnia and Herzegovina.[4] For years military circles made preparations and waited only a favourable moment to carry their plan into execution. Austria's Consuls in Bosnia and Herzegovina developed a great propaganda among the Catholics for union with Austria. General Wagner, the Governor of Dalmatia, made efforts to win over the co-operation of some Croatian circles, who wished to see these provinces united with Croatia and Dalmatia under the Austrian rule.[5] From time to time staff officers were sent there to make military investigations[6] and in 1869 Major von Toemel was ordered to trace out the frontiers of future acquisitions. The occupation was already contemplated in 1867, but the idea was strongly resisted by the civilians and had to be postponed.[7]

There were reasons of internal, as well as of imperialistic, policy which drove Austria towards occupation. Conservative in

---

[1] G. Hanotaux, *Histoire de la France Contemporaine*, IV, pp. 69–70.
[2] B.A., Loftus to Derby, 8 Dec. No. 367, and 21 Dec. No. 396, conf. 1875.
[3] Reprinted in *Journal de St Pétersbourg*, 12 Dec. 1875.
[4] V. Popović, *Politika Francuske i Austrije na Balkanu*, p. 54.
[5] J. Ristić, *Spoljašnji odnošaji*...III, pp. 122–6.
[6] Andrassy, II, p. 257.
[7] A. Fournier, *Wie wir zu Bosnien kamen*, p. 4.

spirit and nationally heterogeneous, Austria was seriously shaken in the first half of the nineteenth century by the corrosive activity of the nationalist and democratic movements. She had survived the revolution of 1848 owing chiefly to Russia's help. After her defeat at Sadowa she was compelled to make concessions to the Hungarians. But their agreement, made to the detriment of other nationalities, provoked resistance among them and a demand for an equal share in the Government. The movement was particularly strong among the South Slavs, who were divided between Austria and Hungary, and whose kinsmen were still under the Turkish rule and in Serbia. Dissatisfied with their position in the Dual Monarchy, they began more and more to look to Serbia, who stood as a champion of an independent South Slav state. The aspirations of Serbia had therefore a special importance for Austria. It was clear that if Serbia succeeded in liberating and uniting her brethren in Turkey, she would become a powerful centre of attraction for Austria's Slavs, and would seriously threaten not only her Dalmatian coast, but her very existence. Unwilling to make any concession to her own Slavs, Austria intended to preclude this danger by preventing the creation of a great Slav state on her boundary. The military circles hoped to achieve this by the annexation of Bosnia and Herzegovina, and found in it one more reason for their plan. But the Hungarians were opposed to annexation, fearing lest a mere increase of the Slav element in the Monarchy should spoil the equilibrium which secured them a preponderant position. "I emphatically declare that all rumours that have been circulated as to our ambitions in Bosnia and Herzegovina are without a shadow of foundation", said Andrassy to Gortchakov in 1872. "Accessions of territory would benefit neither Austria nor Hungary. Hungary, as I have already said, can undertake no additional burden. Austria, on the other hand, has no use for more nationalities within her borders, and if an increase of territory, such as that referred to, were to augment her strength, we Hungarians should object to her receiving it, for it would disturb that balance between her and us which we desire to maintain...."[1] The danger of a great Slav state Andrassy hoped to avert by preserving the Ottoman Empire. "Turkey is almost

[1] *Slavonic Review*, Jan. 1930, p. 400.

of a providential utility to Austria", he declared in a conference in 1875; "her existence is essential to our well-understood interests. She keeps the *status quo* of the small states and hinders their aspirations to our advantage. Were there no Turkey, then all these heavy duties would fall on us."[1]

In this desire to maintain the integrity of Turkey the Hungarians found their chief opponent in Russia, who worked for her dissolution, and from whom the Balkan peoples expected support for their own aims. To counteract her plans they endeavoured to increase Austria's prestige among the Balkan Christians and separate them from Russia. In this struggle against Russia Andrassy laid the utmost stress on winning over Serbia, the pivot of Russia's Eastern policy. As a leader of the Balkan alliance and through her connections with the Slavs in Austria, Serbia had become the decisive factor in the Eastern Question. Andrassy endeavoured to establish cordial relations with her by a series of small services, and to persuade her of the great advantage she might derive from his friendship. The weakening of Serbia after the death of Prince Michael and the consequent discord among the Balkan peoples assisted his aims greatly, and he profited by this to keep them separated and dependent upon the Dual Monarchy. To bind Serbia completely to it, he planned even to give her a part of Bosnia.[2] On the other hand, he established cordial relations with Germany and thus prevented her from putting her weight entirely on the side of Russia. By the Schönbrunn convention he engaged Russia to the maintenance of the *status quo* in the Balkans. In this manner he hoped to avoid the opening of the Eastern Question until Austria was consolidated, believing that by his policy of "peaceful penetration" he would succeed in driving Russia completely from the Balkans and in solving that Question to Austria's sole advantage.

But the preservation of Turkey depended upon her own forces in the first place. Andrassy did not overlook the possibility of her losing Bosnia and Herzegovina. In that event he was prepared to annex them in order to prevent their being united

---

[1] A.A., Protokol über die am 29 Jänner 1875 unter dem Allerhöchsten Vorsitze Seiner Majestät des Kaisers abgehaltene Konferenz. Mil. Kanz. S.M. 69–2/2 v. 1875.

[2] Andrassy, I, pp. 461–2.

with Serbia and Montenegro, but even then he intended to take only what was absolutely necessary for the protection of Dalmatia.

On 29 January 1875 a conference of leading military men and Ministers was held under Francis Joseph's presidency to decide what measures and what objects should be pursued in the event of a conflict between the Turks and the Christians in Bosnia and Herzegovina. The occasion of this conference was the recent conflict in Podgorica, which was already being settled, but which might easily be renewed owing to the difficult conditions of the Christians. The purpose of this preparation was "the rectification of our south-western frontier, and in connection with it the occupation of Bosnia and Herzegovina and the winning of a hinterland to our Dalmatian coast". Andrassy considered this purpose as the right one, and stressed the importance of Austria's being prepared to take advantage of a favourable opportunity, and not letting it pass as she did in 1856 and 1862. In his opinion this purpose could be achieved only if internal disorders in Turkey created conditions which could both internally and externally justify the annexation of these provinces. Direct action against Turkey was dangerous and impossible, for it would be resisted within the Monarchy, and would bring on war with Russia, Turkey and the vassal Christian states. The idea of Austria's taking the lead of the Balkan Christians and starting a movement against Turkey with them must also be rejected. Turkey represented no danger to Dalmatia and so long as she was able to hold her power in these provinces it was not in Austria's interest to break her up. But if a rising broke out in Bosnia and Herzegovina and threatened to extinguish Turkish authority, Austria must be prepared to occupy them in order to prevent their being occupied by Serbia and Montenegro. For if they took possession of these provinces and a new state ensued thereby "which we would not or could not hinder, then we should give ourselves up and take over the rôle of the Sick Man". Andrassy believed that in the present situation in Europe an Austrian occupation could not be opposed by the Great Powers, and he regretted that the conflict in Podgorica did not lead to war, which would enable Austria to solve that question under favourable conditions. The relations between Russia and Austria were based upon the conviction that their co-operation

was in the interest of European peace and he did not think
Russia would have opposed such an action. He was sure of the
consent of Bismarck, and as to Italy the possibility of her
interference was very remote.

Passing on to the concrete case of war between Montenegro
and Turkey, Andrassy laid it down as a principle that Austria
must intervene both in the event of Montenegro being defeated
and of its being victorious. In the first instance she would check
the further advance of Turkey and save her little neighbour from
ruin, which would bring her an invaluable moral profit. It was
necessary therefore that she should intervene alone, for if the
question was to be solved by an international conference, the
rôle of Austria and therefore the advantages she could draw out
of it would be insignificant. If Montenegro defeated Turkey
and started an insurrection in the neighbouring provinces,
Austria would take it as an occasion for occupying the two
provinces. She would thereby prevent a too great weakening or
even a break-up of Turkey, secure her interests by procuring a
hinterland to Dalmatia and oblige Serbia and Montenegro by
giving them some territorial compensations.

Prince Albrecht considered that Austria must preserve a direct
route to Turkey and demanded that the occupation should embrace also the Sandjak of Novipazar up to the heights of the
Balkans. Andrassy did not wish to set up the frontier of future
acquisitions in advance. In his opinion it was necessary to take
into account certain compensations for Serbia and Montenegro,
for they would otherwise become volcanoes as burdensome for
Austria as they were then for Turkey. Austria would at any rate
"eat the meat and leave the bones to the others". The Emperor
agreed with the necessity for compensations, but asked that what
was absolutely necessary for the protection of Dalmatia should
be then settled. He also desired to clear up the question whether
the partition of the Sandjak between Serbia and Montenegro
was in the interest of Austria. Count Andrassy answered that it
was best to annex the whole of Bosnia and Herzegovina, but that
this was impossible because of the projected compensations.
Besides, it was also important to avoid a too great increase of
preponderance of the Slav element in the Monarchy. The
territory westwards from the rivers Bosnia and Neretva and the

ports of Klek and Sutorina was sufficient for the protection of Dalmatia. As to the Sandjak, he considered that its division between Serbia and Montenegro would represent no danger for Austria.

The question was further discussed from the military point of view. Andrassy demanded that the troops intended for occupation should be strong enough to be able to hold Serbia and Montenegro in check, if necessary. The proposed number of 150,000 men seemed to be too large if Austria kept to the basic idea, namely to advance actively only when it became evident that Turkey was no longer capable of holding these provinces with her own power, and to offer compensation to Serbia and Montenegro simultaneously with the entry of the troops. If it was intended to annex the whole of Bosnia and Herzegovina then this number was too small, for sooner or later it would lead to co-operation between Turkey, Serbia and Montenegro.

The conference decided to make all necessary preparations for the event of an insurrection, which was to be used as a pretext for annexation. Preparations were to be made both for the protection of the frontiers and for occupation. The consulates in Bosnia and Herzegovina were to be allotted two to three staff-officers as permanent officials, whose duty was to tour the country and collect necessary information for military operations.[1]

A few months after this conference the military circles induced the Emperor to pay a visit to Dalmatia. This visit took place after the war scare of May 1875, which estranged Germany from Russia, and immediately preceded the outbreak of the rising in Herzegovina. Francis Joseph spent a month in Dalmatia, and on his journey received many deputations of the Christians from Bosnia and Herzegovina, who complained of Turkish oppression and asked him for protection. He returned from this journey convinced that the occupation could not be long delayed; and soon informed Anton von Mollinary, the Governor of Zagreb, that he would appoint him as commander of the troops designed for occupation.[2] The War Office immediately ordered Baron Rodić to undertake the enquiries necessary

[1] A.A., Protokol über die am 29 Jänner 1875 unter dem Allerhöchsten Vorsitze Seiner Majestät des Kaisers abgehaltene Konferenz. Mil. Kanz. S.M. 69–2/2 v. 1875.

[2] A. von Mollinary, op. cit. II, p. 228.

for an entry of troops from Dalmatia.[1] The military circles proposed that Austria should secretly support the rising by all means
at hand and prepare the ground for a military intervention.[2]

This course of action was strongly opposed by Andrassy. He
realised that the Great Powers, and especially Russia, would
not allow an armed intervention of Austria, and that even if she
occupied the two provinces she would be obliged to evacuate
them.[3] He succeeded in inducing his Emperor to reject the
plans of the soldiers and keep strictly to the programme he had
expounded at the conference of 29 January. To Baron Rodić,
who proposed an understanding with Montenegro and an
immediate march into Bosnia and Herzegovina, he wrote that
the Government did not think of an occupation before the
insurgents became masters of the two provinces and their victory
forced the neighbouring states to intervene.[4]

Andrassy succeeded in preventing a precipitate action of the
military party, but the chief problem for him was Russia. Her
intention to mediate between the insurgents and the Porte went
counter to his plan to leave events to develop themselves and
establish Austria's influence as the most interested Power in the
East. What Russia exactly aimed at was not clear, but the ideas
of autonomy privately ventilated from St Petersburg showed that
she not only desired to counteract Austria's designs, but to bar
the way to her expansion in the East even in the future. Andrassy
was resolved to resist this policy with all his power. He wrote to
Francis Joseph that he had foreseen such a situation and had
prepared himself for it. All his policy towards Germany and
Italy was permeated with the conviction that Austria would
need Germany against Russia, and not Russia against Germany.[5]

Ousted by Austria in the first encounter with her, Russia
desired to make the failure of the Consular mission a pretext
for further action of the Powers in favour of the Christians.
Indeed she had no confidence in the success of this mission, and
endeavoured to enlist the support of the Great Powers for her
programme even before it was ended. Gortchakov told the Duke
Decazes, who visited him in Switzerland at the beginning of

---

[1] Andrassy, II, p. 266.   [2] Ibid. p. 259.
[3] Ibid. pp. 267–8.   [4] A.A., Andrassy to Rodić, 12 Aug. 1875.
[5] Andrassy, II, 255–6.

September, that the time had come to make the *entente* of the Powers more precise and to determine its purpose. It was necessary to make this *entente* more intimate in order to bring Turkey to a more equitable appreciation of the wishes and needs of her populations. He proposed that the Powers should ask for serious guarantees against the recurrence of such disorders.[1] Gortchakov spoke in the same vein to Count Shouvalov, the Russian Ambassador in London, who visited him at Vevey on his return to England. Shouvalov was instructed to explain to the British Government that by restraining Serbia and Montenegro from action Russia "had already departed from its neutral attitude in favour of the Turks and thus had assumed a moral responsibility to prevent sanguinary Turkish reprisals and to obtain immediate alleviation for the Christians". Russia attached great importance to "a complete *entente* with England for regulation of the present difficulties in the East". It was urgent that the Powers should act in complete accord in order to induce the Porte to grant the necessary reforms to the Christians. A divergence between England and the other Powers would be injurious to European peace.[2] Shouvalov assured Lord Derby that Russia did not ask for autonomy for Bosnia and Herzegovina, but only for some administrative and fiscal reforms, and that she had no wish to weaken Turkey or raise the Eastern Question.[3]

Russia's efforts to secure the support of the Western Powers and her aspirations for autonomies produced great apprehensions in Vienna. Andrassy desired that the three Powers should alone decide upon the measures of pacification, and merely invite the other Powers to support their action. He was confident that within the Dreikaiserbund he could, with the passive support of Germany, remove all untoward proposals of Russia and lead his allies in the path conducive to Austria's interests. Were all the six Powers brought into the deliberations, Austria would cease to play the leading part in Near Eastern affairs as she wished. She might not be able even to prevent undesirable reforms, nor to present the desirable ones to the Christians as her own service. Taken in connection with the idea of autonomy, Russia's

---

[1] D.F., No. 7.
[2] R.D., Shouvalov to Jomini, 14 Oct. 1875.   [3] *Ibid.*

endeavour to act in common with all the Powers showed that
she intended to circumvent Austria by the aid of the other
Powers and take the lead in their pacifying action. Andrassy
was particularly afraid lest the idea of autonomy should find a
willing ear with the other Governments, and hastened to discredit
it through his press. At his inspiration the *Neue Freie Presse*
started a campaign against autonomy as being impossible in the
provinces with mixed population and likely to stimulate other
provinces to revolt. On 16 October Andrassy sent a circular
note to his representatives abroad explaining his views on the
question of autonomy.[1] Avoiding his chief argument for opposing
such an organisation of the two provinces, namely that it would
close the door upon Austria's expansion in the East, he concentrated his criticism upon internal difficulties. The Porte,
he wrote, would refuse autonomy, and even if it consented to
it, it would prove to be impossible in the provinces whose
population was divided into two closely balanced sections of
Moslems and Christians. No chosen chief would be able to
govern them to the satisfaction of both sections: the Prince of
Montenegro or of Serbia would sacrifice the interests of the
Moslems to those of the Christians; a hereditary Turkish Pasha,
like the Khedive of Egypt, would not ameliorate the lot of the
Christians. The autonomy would encourage the other Christians,
especially the Bulgarians, to rise and ask for the same privileges.
Roumania would declare independence, and Serbia, Montenegro
and Greece could not resist the pressure of their peoples
for territorial aggrandisement. Thus the remedy would be
worse than the disease, for instead of pacifying the rising it
would stimulate other revolts and re-open the whole Eastern
Question.

The plan of autonomy was a distant danger only; it was
unlikely that it would be approved by the other Powers. But in
his efforts to deter Russia from co-operation with the Western
Powers and preserve the leading rôle in the Dreikaiserbund,
Andrassy encountered unexpected difficulties. His greatest
opponent in Russia was General Ignatyev, who suspected
Austria's secret designs upon Bosnia and Herzegovina and considered co-operation with her detrimental to Russian interests.

[1] A.C., No. 183.

During the fourteen years he spent in Constantinople, Ignatyev's chief purpose was to restore Russian influence in the Balkans and prepare a situation which would enable Russia to solve the Eastern Question in her sole interest. He played the chief part in the efforts Russia made during the 'sixties with the view of organising a general insurrection of the Balkan peoples. He endeavoured to maintain good relations with Turkey and to undermine her from within in order to make her completely dependent upon Russia. He was opposed to separate risings as they would only retard the realisation of his plan. "All our art", he says in his Memoirs, "must consist in keeping in our hands the threads of every possible movement in the Balkans, without exciting the Christian population prematurely...without leading them to an open conflict with the Porte. If these movements are sufficiently simultaneous, then we might direct them towards a goal in keeping with their respective just and vital interests and with the interests of Russia."[1] He therefore "constantly deplored" the rising in Herzegovina, and "foresaw the unhappy results of it". He "suspected our supposed allies of trying to bring us into conflict with the Porte, to incite prematurely a Slavonic insurrection, to make use of Slavonic sympathies buried in the heart of every true Russian, in order to involve us in war".[2] Suspicious of Austria's designs, Ignatyev considered it his chief object "to avoid every pretext for Austria to seize Bosnia and Herzegovina". He set himself at once to wrest the leadership from Andrassy's hand and make Constantinople the centre of action. Before the Consular mission was ended he proposed that they should report upon the grievances of the Christians and recommend practical measures which might be accepted by all the Powers, that the Ambassadors of the Powers should be instructed to press reforms upon the Porte, and that Austria should threaten the Porte with military reprisals if she committed excesses in dealing with the insurgents.[3] The Tsar accepted this proposal and tried to win over Germany and Austria for it. Andrassy refused to make any military threat; he consented to the Consuls sending their

[1] A. Onou, "Memoirs of Count N. Ignatyev", *Slavonic Review*, I, Dec. 1931; II, April; III, July 1932; I, p. 396.
[2] *Ibid.* I, p. 402.
[3] B.A., Elliot to Derby, 26 Sept. 1875, No. 596.

reports, but to their Governments and not to the Ambassadors
in Constantinople. As to the pressure to be put upon the Porte
for reforms, he could consent to it only after an agreement upon
these reforms was reached between the three Powers.[1] While
these conversations were going on, Ignatyev was active in
Constantinople pressing upon the Sultan to grant the Christians
some reforms and forestall further interference of the Powers.
On 2 October the Porte issued an *Iradé* in which certain reforms
were promised, the surtax of 2 per cent. was remitted and the
outstanding taxes up to 1873 were cancelled. Ignatyev proposed
immediately that the Powers should take note of the Sultan's
promises, record the refusal of the insurgents to follow their
advice and reserve liberty of action for any course which might
be imposed by the interests of humanity and the neighbouring
states. The Tsar approved this proposal and forwarded it to
Vienna. Andrassy accepted the first two points, but reserved
the right to complete the third one by some practical measures
for Bosnia and Herzegovina.[2] At the same time he warned
Russia against bringing the other Powers into the discussion
of further pacifying measures, as it would lead to no agreement
between them and would only hinder the action of the three
Powers. On 16 October he developed at length his views upon
the reforms to be introduced in the revolted provinces. Rejecting
the Turkish *Iradé* as insincere and likely to stimulate further
disturbance, he proposed that the Porte should be asked to
improve the moral and the material position of the Christians
by granting absolute religious equality, abolishing feudalism by
state purchase of the land and suppressing indirect collection of
taxes. Besides these fundamental reforms which could be undertaken immediately, the Porte should be also advised to proceed
to a general improvement of its administration.[3]

Ignatyev was not discouraged by the repeated rebuffs his
proposals received in Vienna. He was tireless in furnishing new
ones, which often contradicted each other, in order to frustrate
what he believed to be Andrassy's policy. Having at first asked
for an authorisation for the Ambassadors to press reforms upon
the Porte, and then induced the Turks themselves to announce

---

[1] A.A., Andrassy to Mayr, 2 Oct. 1875.
[2] *Ibid.* 10 Oct.   [3] *Ibid.* 16 Oct.

reforms in order to forestall the intervention of the Powers, he endeavoured now to separate Russia from the other Powers and settle the Herzegovinian question in direct agreement with the Porte. He started negotiations with the Sultan for a secret alliance between Russia and Turkey similar to that of 1833. With a draft of the treaty proposed by the Sultan, he went to the Crimea, where the Tsar was staying, to win him over for this policy. The Tsar refused this proposal; he wished to co-operate with his allies, and the danger of a dissolution of Turkey, which Ignatyev considered would result from Andrassy's policy, was for him an additional reason for joint action with the Powers.[1]

Ignatyev was, however, more successful in his criticism of Andrassy's "practical propositions". The Russian Government accepted them as a starting point for discussion only, and left the question open whether the Powers should formulate the reforms and request the Porte to introduce them, or whether they should only advise the Sultan to proceed with reforms, keeping him in fear of their further intervention. In the first case they would have to exert strong pressure upon the Porte, not even shrink from a military intervention like that in Syria, to force it into executing the reforms. Jomini proposed therefore that the Powers should return to Ignatyev's proposal to take note of the Turkish reforms and reserve liberty of action. Yet he had no confidence in the success of the Turkish reforms. He told the Austrian Chargé d'affaires that in that event the Powers should meet in a conference to decide upon further action, and if necessary entrust Austria and Russia with a military occupation of the revolted provinces under a European commission. If they failed to agree among themselves they should preserve absolute neutrality, but this would probably lead to further extension of the revolt and re-open the whole Eastern Question.[2]

Andrassy refused the proposal to leave Turkey to introduce reforms alone, as well as the idea of a European conference and a military occupation. Although himself opposed at the beginning to an intervention in favour of the Christians, he realised now that it was unavoidable and preferred to take the initiative in it and

[1] A. Onou, *op. cit.* I, pp. 401–2.
[2] A.A., Mayr to Andrassy, 15–27 Oct. 1875, No. 55 A–F.

thus gain the sympathies of the Christians, than to leave Ignatyev to pursue his plans. He no longer concealed his distrust of Ignatyev and his policy, which, in his opinion, would not only prevent pacification, but endanger European peace. He assured the Russian Government that he had no confidence in the success of the Turkish reforms and in their being able to appease the rising, and insisted therefore upon his programme of special reforms for Bosnia and Herzegovina which the Porte would execute at the request of the Powers.

It was surprising that Russia should place such a great confidence in the Porte and insist upon it being given a free hand to introduce reforms alone, much the more so as she not only did not believe in its capacity for reform, but did not even believe that administrative reforms could at all ameliorate the position of the Christians. Her plan, and the only one she had faith in, was autonomy. This apparent contradiction between her conviction and her proposals was due to the fact that Russia, knowing that a direct demand for autonomy would be met with resistance on the part of Turkey and the Great Powers, aimed at preparing a situation in which autonomy would impose itself as the only means for appeasing the rising and preserving European peace. She could not satisfy herself with Andrassy's reforms which, though radical in substance, were lacking all guarantee for their realisation, and the application of which would leave conditions in the Balkans unchanged while creating the conviction among the Great Powers that they had done all that was in their power for pacification. She wished to let Turkey show what she was capable of, and take the failure of her reforms as a pretext for a more efficacious intervention of the Powers. Since the Porte would have demonstrated its incapacity for reforms, the Powers could no longer request it to introduce them, but would be obliged to seek for more radical measures, such as autonomy or foreign occupation of the revolted provinces. Thus the Russian plan would have been accomplished, and the resistance of Austria overcome by the force of circumstances.

Meanwhile the attempt at leaving Turkey a free hand was resolutely opposed by Austria, and Russia felt herself compelled to yield to her insistence in order to preserve the community of the imperial league and make a joint action of the Great Powers possible.[1] Gortchakov, who returned to St Petersburg at the beginning of December, left Andrassy free to decide whether he would persist with his reforms or leave the Porte to pursue its own. He tried, however, to obtain some guarantees for the execution of Andrassy's reforms, but failed in this too.

On 30 December, having secured Germany's adhesion, Andrassy communicated to England, France and Italy his programme of reforms and invited them to support it with the Porte. He proposed full and entire religious liberty, abolition of tax farming, the employment of direct taxes for local needs, and state help in purchase of land from the landlords. These reforms were to be conducted under the supervision of a special commission composed of an equal number of Moslems and Christians. The Porte was to notify acceptance of his Note and at the same time confirm officially to the Powers the reforms promulgated in its *Iradé* of 2 October and its *Firman* of 12 December. He realised that this, indeed, would not give the Christians the guarantee which they appeared to be demanding, but he held that "they would find relative security in the fact that the reforms accorded would be recognised as indispensable by the Powers, and that the Porte would have pledged itself to Europe to carry them into action".[2]

In his negotiations with Russia Andrassy justified his reforms by the necessity of effecting real amelioration of the position of the Christians and removing the causes of future conflicts. His biographer Wertheimer says that "the reform note claimed a decisive influence in oriental affairs for the Monarchy, and stated as an incontestable dogma that she would not permit any Power to contest her first place there....". "In short, in its European character," he concluded, "adapted at the same time to the conditions of Bosnia and Herzegovina, lies the great meaning of Andrassy's Note, which was essentially to pave the way to a future acquisition of the two Turkish provinces by Austria-Hungary."[3] In January 1876 Andrassy expressed the hope to the Governor of Zagreb that his reforms should bring at least a

---

[1] B.A., Loftus to Derby, 24 Nov. 1875, No. 356, conf.
[2] A. d'Avril, *Négociations relatives au Traité de Berlin*, p. 109.
[3] Andrassy, II, pp. 272–3.

temporary appeasement of the rising and that the Powers could not prevent Austria from occupying these provinces if the Christians were compelled again to seek protection in Austria.[1] "We have no pretension to have worked for eternity," he said to the French Ambassador, "it is sufficient for the present to have patched up the situation and to have maintained the *status quo*."[2] There is no doubt that Andrassy had no illusion as to Turkish capacity for reforms, and that in proposing them he did not intend really to improve the lot of the Christians and remove the causes of future disturbances. Such a result would be, moreover, contrary to Austria's interests, as it would have deprived her of a pretext to occupy these provinces in the future. The reforms were for him a means only to prevent more serious changes in the Balkans, to frustrate Ignatyev's designs and preserve the leadership of the imperial league. Should the insurgents accept them and return to their homes, Austria would gain a moral advantage by establishing herself as their protector, and would leave the possibility open for annexing the two provinces in the event of renewed disturbances. Should they refuse these reforms, the Powers would have a reason for abandoning further intervention and leaving the Porte to suppress the rising by force.

Germany did not participate in the negotiations which led to the Andrassy Note. Having no direct interest in the East she left her allies to deal with it, prepared to support every measure they agreed upon. Bismarck realised from the outset that they would be able to act in common so long only as they were doing nothing, and that any change in the Balkans would bring their interests into conflict. Germany had an interest in maintaining their rivalry, for it compelled them to seek for her alliance and gave her the preponderant position in the Dreikaiserbund. But she did not wish an open conflict between them, as it would break up the imperial league and bring about new groupings of the Powers, which would inevitably weaken her position. By the beginning of 1876 Bismarck began to fear such a possibility. The divergent interests of his allies came to the fore already in the Consular mission and showed themselves clearly in their

[1] A. von Mollinary, *op. cit.* pp. 294–7.
[2] D.F., No. 25.

subsequent efforts to drive each other out of the Balkans. Andrassy's reforms were a temporary compromise, which could change nothing in the Balkans and would only postpone for a while an open disagreement. To overcome Austria's resistance Russia endeavoured to bring the other Powers into the discussion of the Herzegovinian question, thus forcing her to yield to her demands or to separate from her, neither of which solutions was in the interest of Germany. Andrassy, indeed, resisted Russia's pressure and succeeded in preserving the initiative in the Dreikaiserbund, but he had none the less consented to his programme of reform being presented to the Porte as the programme of all the Great Powers. He was a guarantee for Germany that Austria would not become too intimate with Russia behind her back, and his maintenance in power therefore of vital importance. But how long would he be able to resist Russia and the military party, who desired co-operation with her? If he were obliged to retire, the elements hostile to Germany would come into power, who would endeavour to settle their differences with Russia and in co-operation with her turn against Germany.[1]

All these considerations led Bismarck to the conclusion that he could no longer remain passive, but must take a part in events in order to prevent a conflict between his allies or their solving the Eastern Question without Germany and against her. The solution which best suited Germany was that aimed at by Andrassy, but it encountered great obstacles on the part of Russia. Bismarck realised that so long as the question of Bosnia and Herzegovina was dealt with separately from the complex of the whole Eastern Question, Russia and Austria could not agree among themselves, for neither would Russia consent to Austria annexing these provinces, nor would Austria allow reforms which would exclude her completely from the East. But he believed that their interests could be reconciled in a larger scheme, which would give Russia compensations for Austria's acquisitions. The realisation of this scheme presupposed a definite solution of the Eastern Question and could be carried out only in concert with all the Powers. He was prepared to let all

---

[1] B.A., Russell to Derby, 2 Jan. 1876, No. 8, secret.

the Powers take territorial compensations.[1] His plan was that Austria should take Bosnia and Herzegovina, Russia recover Bessarabia, England take Egypt, and France and Italy might compensate themselves in Northern Africa. Germany would ask nothing for herself, but she would gain very much by creating a constellation "in which all the Powers would need us, and be hindered as much as possible by their mutual relations from coalition against us".[2] Bismarck calculated that his plan would push Russian and Austrian interests and rivalries farther East and compel them to seek for Germany's alliance; that it would separate England from France by her acquisition of Egypt, and create for Russia and England a satisfactory *status quo* "which gives them the same interest in maintaining the present state of affairs as we have ourselves".[3]

Early in January 1876 Bismarck took steps to remove Russia's objections to Austrian pretensions, and win over England for his plan. He proposed to the Russian Ambassador that Russia should come to an agreement with Austria on the basis of mutual compensations in Turkey and offered his mediation with England to secure her consent to it.[4] But this proposal was rejected by Gortchakov, who suspected in it ulterior motives. Russia, he answered, wished no territorial conquest.

Before revealing his plan to Russia, Bismarck had offered England an understanding for close co-operation in Turkish affairs. Taking the Andrassy Note as a pretext, he visited the British Ambassador on 2 January and expounded to him his fears of a possible conflict between Russia and Austria or their intimate collaboration in the event of Andrassy's fall. Either of these events would be detrimental to Germany and might also bring European peace into jeopardy. The only security against these complications was an agreement between her and England. He had withheld an unqualified approval of Andrassy's Note as he wished to learn previously England's opinion and to conform his attitude accordingly. He was prepared to resist the annexationist pretensions of Austria and Russia if England wished it. But without her support he would not oppose them

---

[1] *Ibid.* and 3 Jan. No. 9, secret, and 19 Feb. No. 76, most conf.
[2] G.P., No. 294.   [3] *Ibid.*
[4] S. Goryainov, *Le Bosphore et les Dardanelles*, pp. 314–15.

because he did not think either of those Powers would be strengthened by such increase of territory, or the interests of Germany be affected by it. On this question he would, however, reserve his opinion until he knew that of Her Majesty's Government, and...he also hoped to know what the French Government might be disposed to do. He would be glad to see France take again a lively interest in Oriental matters which might turn her attention from brooding over a war of revenge against Germany. He would also welcome the co-operation of Italy. If he could thus obtain for Germany the good will of England and her friends he could look to the future with greater confidence.[1]

Bismarck's overture was received in London with mixed feelings. Derby replied that he too desired co-operation with Germany in Turkish affairs, but that he must consult the Cabinet before giving his definite answer. Distrustful of Bismarck ever since the war scare, Derby feared being drawn into a secret trap and wished to examine the proposal in greater detail before making up his mind.

Opinion differed in the British Government upon the answer to be given to Bismarck's overture. Disraeli favoured an agreement with Germany,[2] seeing in it a means of breaking up the Drei-kaiserbund and of recovering England's influence in European affairs. But Derby was still suspicious of hidden designs and delayed his answer for more than a month.[3] On 1 February Bismarck renewed his overture, insisting upon the danger of a conflict between Russia and Austria and stressing the necessity for "a timely understanding" to prevent it. It was only on 12 February that Derby sent his answer. He explained to Bismarck that he had hitherto abstained from discussing the question of the steps to be taken in the event of Andrassy's proposals failing to accomplish their purpose "solely because of the difficulties which he felt in laying down principles which were to guide the action of Her Majesty's Government where the future seemed so uncertain and when circumstances might vary from day to day". "I could only indicate in general terms the opinions of Her Majesty's Government, first that any disturbance of the territorial *status quo* would be inadvisable and

[1] B.A., Russell to Derby, 2 Jan. 1876, No. 8, secret.
[2] Queen Victoria, p. 444.
[3] Disraeli, p. 21.

dangerous, as one rectification of frontiers could not fail to lead to another, and when a policy of annexation was once entered upon, no one could foresee where it would end."[1] In another despatch of the same date he wrote to Russell "that England desires no exclusive alliances", that the maintenance of peace could be "materially promoted by a cordial understanding and by concerted action between Germany and England", but that this understanding, "desirable as it may be in principle, cannot be definitely adopted without a clearer knowledge than we now possess of the motives which have led to Prince Bismarck's recent overtures, and of the expectations which he, and the Government which he represents, may have formed of the results of the understanding proposed by him".[2]

Bismarck answered "that his reason for wishing for a frank and frequent exchange of ideas with England..." resulted from his conviction that England and Germany were the two Powers best able to prevent mischief if things took a threatening turn.

Austria and Russia, and even France and Italy, had special interests in the East about which they might some day quarrel, whilst Germany had none. England had a legitimate right to the road to India, which Germany cordially supported, and both wished for nothing but peace in the East, and so he believed that England and Germany were the two Powers naturally called upon to keep order among those whose interests were special and conflicting.

To prevent war there were, in his opinion, two ways of dealing with the Eastern Question. The first was that all the Powers should agree, as long as possible, to work cordially together to maintain the territorial "Status Quo"....

But circumstances might arise in Turkey unfavourable to a maintenance of our present peace policy.

If the insurrection continued, Montenegro might claim more territory with access to the sea, or union with Serbia. Russia might support these pretensions, and Austria oppose them, and other dangerous questions might ensue, to which even the combined influence of England and Germany might not find a pacific solution.

If then peace became impossible without territorial modifications the second way of dealing with the Eastern Question might come into operation.

It consisted equally in agreeing and working cordially together to

[1] B.A., Derby to Russell, 12 Feb. 1876, No. 115.
[2] *Ibid*. No. 117, conf.

maintain the peace of Europe, not by upholding the territorial "Status Quo", but by amicably settling what should be done with Turkey to satisfy the Powers concerned, instead of going to war about it....

To obtain the friendly co-operation of France in a pacific settlement of the Eastern Question, as also that of Italy, he would gladly, with the consent of Her Majesty's Government, meet their wishes half-way, whatever they were.[1]

This attempt to attract England to a scheme for the partition of Turkey, which would have prevented a war between Germany's allies and solved the Eastern Question to Germany's advantage, proved to be a failure. Bismarck was henceforth driven to seek for an understanding between Russia and Austria, confident that, if partition imposed itself by the force of events, England would not oppose it.

While Russia and Austria were fighting for supremacy in the Balkans, and Germany endeavouring to prevent a conflict between them, Great Britain remained isolated and reserved, unable yet to grasp the true meaning of their action and their real intentions. She was not opposed to an improvement of the position of the Christians, but she did not see any means of achieving it without weakening or even breaking up the Ottoman Empire. The pacificatory action of the three Powers seemed to be inadequate for this purpose, and therefore inspired her with fears of their secret designs. Derby did not believe in the possibility of reforms "in a country where everything was centred in an antagonism of religions and races". From the outset he was opposed to the policy of interference, which in his opinion only prevented Turkey from suppressing the rising. He considered Turkey strong enough to cope with it if only allowed to do so, and that Serbia and Montenegro would not move unless they secured the support of Austria or Russia. He was suspicious of Austria's annexationist pretensions, but he equally rejected the idea of autonomy, as both these solutions would open the door to further dismemberment of Turkey.[2]

Disraeli was particularly distrustful of Andrassy, who, he wrote, "changes his mind every week or day, and has half a dozen

---

[1] B.A., Russell to Derby, 19 Feb. 1876, No. 76, most conf.
[2] R.D., Shouvalov to Jomini, 2–14 Oct. 1875.

intrigues at work which will defeat each other".[1] Immediately after the insurrection broke out, he asked his Ambassador in Vienna "to see Andrassy at once and to ascertain his real wishes".[2] He believed that Austria and Russia had ulterior motives and that their reform plan was aimed at binding England's hand for the future, when events might render independent action necessary. He was against England supporting this plan for the sake of a simulated concert, which could not last long. Moreover, the proposal of reserving a certain percentage of the taxes for local use, and of state purchase of land were inconsistent with the principles upon which England was ruled herself, and could hardly be recommended by her to another country. Derby was also in doubt. He considered that most of the reforms demanded were already included in the *Firman* of 12 December and did not see why the Porte was asked "to grant the Christians what it has just decreed to them".[3] Before answering the Note he wished to know what the three Powers intended to do if either Turkey or the insurgents refused to accept it. Gortchakov replied that "this eventuality referred to the second phase of the question", and that acceptance of the Note did not imply any obligation for further co-operation.[4] Beust, the Austrian Ambassador, said that the insurgents would be left to the mercy of the Turks if they refused to cease hostilities.[5] None of these explanations was satisfactory, apart from their being divergent.

Meanwhile the Porte also urged the British Government to accept the Note. Whatever the objection against it, England was unable to offer any counter proposal, nor could she remain isolated with safety to her interests. She therefore gave the Note only her "general support", making reservations with regard to the local application of taxes and the state purchase of land, and refusing to ask a written reply from the Porte. "They look on the proposals", wrote Derby, "as being in the nature of suggestions or recommendations for adoption by the Porte in its endeavour to put an end to the insurrection, and were not prepared to do more than to offer such friendly advice as circumstances seemed to require."[6]

---

[1] Disraeli, p. 15.   [2] *Ibid.* 12.   [3] R.D. II, p. 658.
[4] B.A., Loftus to Derby, 7 Jan. 1876, No. 9.
[5] B.A., Derby to Buchanan, 18 Jan. 1876, No. 23.
[6] B.A., Derby to Buchanan, 24 Jan. 1876, No. 70.

France and Italy gave their consent at once to the Andrassy Note, seeing in their participation a means of asserting their influence in the European concert and preventing the three Powers from solving the Eastern Question without them. France regarded it even as an occasion for strengthening her connections with Russia, and endeavoured to persuade Italy and England to accede to it.

The Porte desired to forestall Andrassy's programme by its own reforms, which were to be applied to the whole Empire, and hoped that this would render European intervention unnecessary. In this endeavour it was strongly supported by the Russian and the British Ambassadors, both of whom wished to counteract Andrassy's designs. Elliot was at first somewhat puzzled by this divergence between Russia and Austria, who pretended to be working in concert; but he soon realised that Ignatyev genuinely desired to prevent further interference with Turkey and supported him warmly.[1] To Ignatyev the Turkish reforms were a means of attracting the Tsar into a separate agreement with the Sultan, and he tried again to win him over to this policy.[2] But his plan found no sympathy with Gortchakov, who considered co-operation with his allies to be indispensable for Russia. Ignatyev consoled himself with the hope that the Turkish reforms would give the Porte and the Powers opposed to intervention a pretext to refuse Andrassy's programme.

Andrassy tried to deter the Porte from its reforms, seeing in them a new move of Ignatyev against him. He assured the Turks that the insurgents would not be satisfied with the reforms coming from the Porte and that they would only be encouraged to resistance. Having failed with this, he endeavoured to induce the Turks to postpone their programme until he had produced his own. But the Turks remained obstinate. They argued that their reforms had nothing to do with the insurrection, which would be suppressed by force, but would be applied to the whole Empire. Even Andrassy's threat that in the event of further complications he would be guided exclusively by his own interests remained without effect. On

[1] B.A., Elliot to Derby, 17 Sept. No. 565, 15 Oct. No. 666, conf. 1875.
[2] *Revue d'Histoire Moderne*, Sept.–Oct. 1935, pp. 382–4; D.F. No. 27.

12 December the Porte issued a Firman which promised extensive administrative reforms for the whole Empire and considerable improvement in the position of the Christians. It made, however, no impression upon the insurgents, nor upon the Great Powers. England's hesitation in adopting the Andrassy Note induced the Porte to try to counteract joint action of the Powers. Before the Note was communicated to it, it declared to the Powers that it would refuse every collective or identic proposal on their part. But the Powers paid no heed to its protest. Thereupon the Porte urged England to accept the Note and considered this as a guarantee for its safety.[1]

On 31 January the Austrian Ambassador read the Note to Rashid Pasha and left him a copy of it, together with a copy of the answer the Porte had to send to the Powers. The other Ambassadors came afterwards and urged its acceptance by the Porte. But it was only after long negotiations and additional pressure that they succeeded in inducing the Sultan to accept the Note. On 13 February the Porte notified its acceptance of the proposed reforms, but made reservations with regard to the local use of the taxes, which was inconsistent with its fiscal system, and the state purchase of land, which she intended to solve in another way. The text of notification was entirely different from that proposed by Andrassy.

These reforms were publicly proclaimed in Bosnia and Herzegovina with a promise of a general amnesty for those who returned home, and two commissions were established to carry them out. But the Porte was without the financial means necessary for the execution of these reforms. Its officials proceeded to introduce them with reluctance. The Moslem population was opposed to them and resorted to new reprisals. The Christians remained distrustful of Turkish promises, and showed no wish to abandon their struggle.

Andrassy was determined to carry through his plan of pacification, and offered the Porte his help to induce the Christians to accept the reforms. He ordered Baron Rodić and General Mollinary to prevent further smuggling of arms and ammunition

---

[1] B.A., Elliot to Derby, 13 Jan. 1876, No. 45.

and arrest every insurgent crossing the frontier with arms.[1] They were also to advise the insurgents and the refugees to accept the reforms and return home. Similar instructions were received by the Austrian Consuls in Mostar and Trebinje. The latter was, besides, to threaten the refugees with expulsion from Austria, and the insurgents with being blockaded and left to their fate, if they refused to follow this advice.[2] Andrassy sent special agents "to buy off the chief men by offers of subventions if they returned to Turkey or of permission to remain on Austrian soil with a pension if they were afraid to go back to their old homes".[3] He suggested also that the Turks should try to win over the insurgent leaders by bribery.

Baron Rodić met the insurgents in Ragusa but failed to move them to submission. Early in March he was sent to Cetinje to ask for Nicholas's co-operation in the work of pacification. Rodić was to bring to the notice of the Prince certain advantages for Montenegro in case of the dissolution of Turkey if the Prince lent his assistance to Austria, but, in the event of his refusal, to threaten him with closing the frontier and with stopping the financial assistance which Austria was giving him.[4] Prince Nicholas, well aware of the importance of these considerations, promised to do all he could. Through his mediation a suspension of hostilities for ten days was established and an arrangement was made for a meeting between the insurgents and Baron Rodić in Sutorina. But the Prince was playing a double game. He told General Alimpić, who was sent by the Belgrade Government to conclude a treaty with Montenegro for common action against Turkey, that "nothing will come of the reconciliation. The insurgents will put forward such proposals that the Porte will not be able to accept them".[5] Together with the Russian Consul in Ragusa, with whom he was working in close co-operation, he worked out instructions for the insurgents, to serve as their answer to Baron Rodić. At the meeting in Sutorina the insurgents delivered to Rodić a memorandum containing the conditions upon which

---

[1] A.A., Andrassy to Rodić, 21 Feb., and to Mollinary, 24 Feb. 1876.

[2] D. Harris, *A Diplomatic History of the Balkan Crisis of 1875–1878*. "The First Year", p. 243.

[3] *Ibid.* pp. 246–7.

[4] V. Djordjević, *Crna Gora i Austrija*, p. 379.

[5] S.A., Alimpić's report of his mission to Cetinje, Feb. 1876.

they consented to stop fighting and return home. They demanded: (1) That the Christians should be given at least a third of the land as their property; (2) that the Turkish garrisons should be withdrawn from Herzegovina and concentrated in six towns; (3) that the Turks should rebuild the ruined houses and churches, give the Christians farm implements and food supplies for at least one year, and exempt them from taxation for three years; (4) that the Christians should not surrender their arms until the Moslems had been disarmed and until the reforms had been entirely accomplished; (5) that a commission of the Christians and the Turks should establish a constitution on the basis of the Andrassy Note according to which reforms should be carried out in Bosnia and Herzegovina; (6) that a European commission should receive money from the Porte to aid Christians and that it should prepare necessary supplies for them before their return; (7) that Austria and Russia should maintain their agents in the towns garrisoned by the Turks to supervise the execution of the reforms.

Thus all Andrassy's efforts to induce the insurgents to accept his reforms remained without result. They considered them insufficient for a real improvement of their position, and void of any material guarantee for their execution. They knew the Turks too well to be able to trust their promises. As they said in a manifesto of 26 February "only true liberty can disarm us...". "In these projects of reform there is not a word said as to real liberty—liberty, independent and securely guaranteed by the Powers of Europe."[1]

During all these negotiations the Turks continued to prepare themselves for further operations. They were determined to make an end of the rising if the Christians rejected their peace offers. At the beginning of March there came new conflicts, but the Turks were defeated and repulsed from Nikšić. The struggle was renewed in April both in Bosnia and Herzegovina. On the 13th Muktar Pasha tried to force his way to Nikšić, but he was met in the Duga Pass and forced to retreat after sustaining heavy losses. Muktar informed the Porte that 7000 Montenegrins had taken part in this battle.

The Porte was already dissatisfied with the conduct of

[1] *The Times*, 11 March 1876.

Montenegro, believing that the assistance the insurgents received from her as well as from Serbia and Dalmatia, enabled them to sustain the struggle. It began also to doubt the real intentions of Russia and Austria, who had failed to restrain the two Principalities from interference. At the request of the Sultan the Porte decided on the 20th to concentrate troops at Skutari and open hostilities against Montenegro. This decision alarmed the European Ambassadors and provoked irritation in St Petersburg. Without waiting for special instructions, Ignatyev directed a sharp note to the Porte warning it in the name of all the Ambassadors of the danger it was running if it attacked Montenegro.[1] Andrassy endeavoured to deter the Porte from this step, threatening to close the port of Klek and refusing all responsibility for the consequences.[2] Gortchakov proposed common action by the Powers for the maintenance of peace, declaring that Russia could not restrain the other Christians from revolt if Montenegro were attacked.[3] Meanwhile the Porte had abandoned its intention already after Ignatyev's note. England therefore refused to join the other Powers in pressing the Porte. But France, Italy and Germany associated themselves with Russia and Austria, making it clear to the Turks that Montenegro stood under their protection.

The interference of the Christian Powers with the rising and the special concessions the Porte was obliged to grant the insurgents under their pressure provoked great discontent not only at the Porte but among the Moslem population itself. In spring 1876 this discontent became widespread and resulted in more frequent conflicts with the Christians. One of them was particularly brutal—and symbolised the irritation and fanaticism which prevailed among the Turkish masses. A Christian girl from Bulgaria, refusing to accept Islam, had taken refuge in the American Consulate in Salonika. The fanatical Turkish mob, which was preparing an attack on the Consulate, got hold of the French and the German Consuls on 6 May and murdered them. This brutal act aroused public opinion in Europe to the real state of things in the Balkans. The Powers

[1] A.A., Zichy to Andrassy, 25 April 1876, No. 32A.
[2] A.A., Andrassy to Zichy, 23 April 1876, Tel. No. 368.
[3] Schweinitz, I, pp. 322–3.

immediately sent their warships to Salonika to prevent further massacres.

Simultaneously with the rise of Turkish fanaticism there was a growing dissatisfaction among the educated class against the Sultan himself, for his yielding to the Christians and his weakness in quelling the insurrection. Already in the previous autumn there had sprung up deep divergences at the Porte as to the policy to be pursued with regard to the insurgents and the Powers. Midhat and Avni Pasha advocated a forcible suppression of the rising, Midhat insisting also upon the introduction of radical reforms in the whole Empire and a constitution which would limit the powers of the Sultan.[1] This policy found no favour with the Sultan, and in December 1875 Midhat resigned in protest against the insufficiency of the proposed reforms, while Avni was soon removed to Salonika as a Governor. Midhat started a subterranean agitation against the Sultan and his ministers, throwing upon them the whole responsibility for the difficult conditions in the country, and demanding restriction of the Sultan's powers. As the dissatisfaction was spreading, his followers became more and more numerous, and he was soon looked upon as the leader of the reformists.

On 10 May 1876 the Softas and Ulemas demonstrated before the court palace and extorted from the Sultan the deposition of the Grand Vizier and of the Sheikh-ul-Islam. Mehmed Rushdi Pasha, who was appointed as new Grand Vizier, brought Midhat and Avni Pasha into the Government. Midhat succeeded in winning all his colleagues for the constitution and for the deposition of the Sultan if he refused to grant it. In the night between 29 and 30 May Abdul Azis was forced to abdicate in favour of Murad V, and arrested in Capa Tope, where four days later he was found dead.

The failure of the Powers to appease the rising and of the Porte to suppress it by force encouraged the other Christians to revolt. At the beginning of May an insurrection broke out in Bulgaria. Before it had time to develop, the Turks quelled it by ruthless massacre, in which, according to subsequent information, "some 12,000 innocent men, women and children have been massacred, hundreds of young women carried off or

---

[1] H. Elliot, *op. cit.* p. 228.

dishonoured, and some sixty villages more or less completely burnt...".[1]

The insurrection in Bulgaria had been prepared immediately after the rising in Herzegovina. On 12 August 1875 Bulgarian national leaders held a meeting and discussed the plan of action.[2] They dispersed afterwards to organise it, and some of them went to Serbia and Russia to ask for help. A premature attempt at a rising in September failed and created discord in the Committee of Action. A month later another Committee was founded under the leadership of Obretenov, which started arming and organising the people for revolt. In April 1876 the preparations were nearly completed, and the leaders met to decide upon the final measures, when the Turks discovered the plot and began massacres and plunder.

It is difficult to state how far Serbia and the Slav Committees participated in the preparation of the Bulgarian revolt, but there can be no doubt that they did lend their assistance. In the desire to win over all the Balkan peoples for common action, Serbia could not have overlooked the importance of a rising in Bulgaria. Indeed, already in August 1875 the Belgrade Government decided to facilitate the passage of the Bulgarian emigrants into Bulgaria, and to help them with money and arms.[3] After the first meeting of the Revolutionary Committee, "Panajot Chitov and two other delegates went to Belgrade to elicit from Serbia arms, monetary help and, above all, military support".[4] The Serbian Government maintained direct contact with certain of the Bulgarian leaders. An attempt was made to come to an understanding as to common action,[5] but the Bulgarian movement was discovered and crushed before Serbia was ready for action.

Immediately before the rising General Chernaev was sent by the Slav Committee to Serbia. According to reports of the Serbian Consul in Bucarest, he ought to have been in close contact with the Bulgarians.[6] One of the Bulgarian leaders,

---

[1] *The Journal of Modern History*, March 1932, p. 39.
[2] A. Hajek, *Bulgarien unter Türkenherrschaft*, p. 251.
[3] *Zapisi Jevrema Grujića*, III, p. 109.
[4] Hajek, *op. cit.* p. 252.   [5] *Zapisi Jevrema Grujića*, III, p. 151.
[6] S.A., Petronijević to Pavlović and Ristić, 19 March, 13 May, 1 and 14 June 1876.

Botjov, was sent to Odessa to collect money and arms. Sir Henry Elliot says in his reminiscences that "during the winter of 1875–6 Russian agents, directed by the Slav Committees of Moscow and Odessa, which were in close alliance with General Ignatyev, were busy organising a rising in Bulgaria".[1] In his reports on the suppression of that rising he constantly dwelt upon the action of the Russian and the Serbian agents, to whom he attributed the whole movement.[2] Though the Bulgarian insurrection was quickly suppressed, it had a fateful influence on future events. Aroused by its bloody suppression, public opinion in England and Russia clamoured for reparations and guarantees of security for the Christians.

[1] H. Elliot, *op. cit.* p. 257.
[2] B.A., Elliot to Derby, 7 May, No. 469, 9 May, No. 473, 17 May, No. 508, conf.

CHAPTER IV

✻

THE BERLIN MEMORANDUM AND THE REICHSTADT AGREEMENT

THE consent of Russia to the Austrian reform plan disguised temporarily their divergent aims, but they were revealed again as soon as these reforms had to be put into execution. Neither Austria nor Russia really believed that these reforms could remove the causes of conflict between the Christians and the Moslems, nor that Turkey was capable of putting them into effect. Both of them therefore regarded the reform plan as a means of counteracting each other's designs. Austria wished the success of her programme in order to prevent more radical measures, and asked the insurgents and the refugees to satisfy themselves with the promise of reforms and return home before they were introduced. Russia, who did not like these reforms and awaited their failure to bring forward more serious demands, insisted upon the Porte's introducing them before the insurgents returned.[1] It must give proof of its earnest intentions so as to enable the Powers to use their influence upon the Christians for reconciliation.

When the insurgents rejected the Austrian programme and put forward their counter-proposals, the disagreement between Austria and Russia became still deeper. Andrassy considered these counter-proposals unacceptable. He endeavoured to persuade Gortchakov that they were "unrealisable", and that the Powers should "decline every guarantee and every control other than those which they have pledged themselves before Europe to demand".[2] Gortchakov had quite a contrary opinion. He agreed with the insurgents' demand for guarantees and

---

[1] B.A., Loftus to Derby, 22 April 1876, No. 156.
[2] A.A., Andrassy to Langenau, 8 April 1876, Tel. No. 17.

considered that their other proposals could be discussed. The mere fact that they have been made, he argued, proved that the insurgents were willing to come to an understanding with Turkey.[1] In a conversation with the Austrian Ambassador he returned to his idea of autonomy as the only practical solution of the rising.[2] The Russian press began to attack Turkey and to support the wishes of the insurgents. *Golos* wrote in an article that the Powers "should continue their efforts...to improve the situation of the insurgent provinces. Autonomy of the Christian communities ought to be the solid basis of this improvement...."[3]

This disagreement with Russia and the renewed propaganda for autonomies created great embarrassment for Andrassy. He could in no way reconcile his interests with such views; but he felt it also impossible to separate from Russia at this stage of the question, when co-operation with her was indispensable. He hastened to correct the impression that he was absolutely opposed to the insurgents' demands and informed Gortchakov that his declaration to the Porte "prejudices absolutely nothing" and that he was ready to support the demands for concentration of the Turkish troops, and for the Christians' preserving their arms. Fearing a disagreement between his allies, Bismarck also adopted the view that the demands of the Christians should be taken into consideration. He explained to Andrassy that he believed "this course would be more agreeable to us than the creation of autonomous states".[4] He sounded Shouvalov, who visited him at the end of March, as to Austrian occupation of the revolted provinces and Russia's taking compensation in Bessarabia.[5]

Gortchakov also desired to continue collaboration with his allies, and the attitude of Andrassy and Bismarck inspired him with hope that some common ground would be found for further joint action. On 4 April he invited Andrassy to meet him at Berlin at the beginning of May "to exchange ideas in private conversation with regard to the eventualities which might have

[1] A.A., Langenau to Andrassy, 11 April 1876, No. 18A–C.
[2] A.A., Langenau to Andrassy, 21 March 1876, Tel. No. 23.
[3] B.A., Loftus to Derby, 1 April 1876, No. 126.
[4] A.A., Andrassy to Francis Joseph, 12 May 1876.
[5] *Ibid.*

to be envisaged for the maintenance of the general peace".[1]
The meeting took place on 12 May in an atmosphere clouded by
the Salonika murders and the disorders in Constantinople,
which was not without an influence on its decisions. Gortchakov
came to Berlin with a Memorandum in which he expounded
the measures hitherto taken by the Powers for pacification.
The chief cause of their failure was, in his opinion, the
lack of material guarantees for execution of the reforms. The
moral guarantees foreshadowed in the Andrassy Note had
proved to be ineffective and insufficient. The Powers would
therefore be compelled to adopt material sanctions similar to
those taken for Syria in 1861, i.e. to appoint an international
commission for the supervision of the reforms which would be
supported by a foreign occupation. He proposed that a conference
of the six Powers should be summoned to decide upon these
measures, and asked that his Memorandum should be delivered
to the Ambassadors of the Great Powers as a proposal of the
three Northern Powers.[2]

Gortchakov's proposal met with strong opposition from both
Andrassy and Bismarck. Material guarantees meant a European
tutelage over Turkey, which would exclude Austria as the most
interested Power, and bring about changes contrary to her
interests. A European conference would have deepened still
more the divergences between Russia and Austria and perhaps
dissolved the Imperial Alliance. By a series of amendments
Andrassy radically modified Gortchakov's Memorandum, striking
out both the idea of guarantees and of a conference, and reducing
it to a demand for a two months' armistice for direct discussion
between the Porte and the insurgents of the latter's proposals,
which he also modified. This new proposal, known later on as the
Berlin Memorandum, differed from Gortchakov's both in substance and in purpose. It could no longer serve as a basis of
discussion for the Great Powers, for it embodied the definite
decisions of the Dreikaiserbund which the other Powers were
invited to support. Andrassy and Bismarck succeeded in imposing it upon the Tsar, who, under the influence of the recent
events in Turkey, was inclined to believe in her imminent

[1] D. Harris, *op. cit.* p. 288.
[2] A.A., Gortchakov's original proposal.

dissolution, and was therefore all the more desirous to maintain the unity of the Dreikaiserbund.[1] Gortchakov submitted to the wishes of his Emperor, succeeding only in adding the final paragraph in Andrassy's project, which intimated the possibility of coercion by the Powers in the future if their present efforts brought no appeasement of the rising.

Thus for the third time Russia yielded to Andrassy's resistance to all real reforms and accepted measures which she did not believe in. If she had any illusion about Germany's support in case of divergences with Austria,[2] she must have realised at Berlin that Bismarck was more inclined to assist Austria in resisting Russian demands, than in supporting them with Austria. Andrassy's attitude also left no doubt as to the impossibility of overcoming resistance with the aid of the other Powers. If Russia wished to preserve the Dreikaiserbund, and this she regarded as the only guarantee for the maintenance of European peace, she could do so only by constantly retreating before Austria. Such an attitude would have been incomprehensible after the realisation that Russia was asked to sacrifice exactly those interests which she intended to protect through that alliance. But at Berlin the Russo-Austrian conflict was viewed from a new angle, and a solution was found which could satisfy both parties. Before accepting the Austrian project, an agreement in principle was reached between them as to their territorial annexations in the event of the break-up of Turkey.[3] Appeased by the conviction that the development of events, whatever course it took, would find the alliance of the three Emperors prepared, and realising that no manœuvres could induce Austria to consent to autonomies, Russia abandoned her demands for material guarantees.

That it came to such an arrangement was mainly due to Bismarck. He was well aware that Russia and Austria were pursuing opposite aims, and that they could not agree upon the question of reforms. To avoid a conflict between them he tried in January to win over England and Russia for the partition of Turkey. Having failed in this plan, he now endeavoured to bring his allies to agree upon the policy of mutual compensations and

---

[1] A.A., Andrassy to Francis Joseph, 12 May 1876.
[2] S. Goryainov, *op. cit.* p. 316.
[3] A.A., Andrassy to Francis Joseph, 12 May 1876.

to co-ordinate their action to that ultimate goal. He invited Andrassy to come a few days earlier to Berlin, an invitation which was readily accepted by Andrassy, who himself intended to reach Berlin before Gortchakov in order to secure Bismarck's support. In a conversation which lasted three hours Bismarck laid stress on the necessity of preserving the Dreikaiserbund and declared himself ready to support every arrangement between Austria and Russia.

"After I had pointed out to him the difficulties of the various solutions without drawing any conclusions," Andrassy reported to his Emperor, "he asked me if we considered an intervention, either alone or with Russia, acceptable. I answered, 'Neither of them'.... Thereupon Bismarck said that Germany, when another solution was impossible, had nothing against Austria's taking a portion [of the Turkish Empire] and Russia's doing likewise. He had already inquired in St Petersburg whether Russia would be satisfied with the return of Bessarabia.... The idea seems not to have been displeasing in St Petersburg, but as yet he has received no positive answer. He wished to know if your Majesty would accept it. I answered that I believed yes, but that we could not expose ourselves to a rejection, and would therefore have to await such a proposition rather than present it...."[1]

When Gortchakov arrived the question was discussed in greater detail. "I have talked with Gortchakov about plans for the future", wrote Andrassy again, "and have brought him round to declaring that he has no objection to the annexation of Turkish Croatia. Enough for the beginning."[2] These "plans for the future" referred to territorial annexations by Russia and Austria and the organisation of the Balkan peninsula in the event of the break-up of Turkey. Russia consented to Austria's taking a portion of Bosnia in that case and reserved Bessarabia for herself. They discussed in principle all the points which were two months later embodied in the Reichstadt Agreement. This understanding explains Russia's yielding on the question of reforms. It was the first success of the Bismarckian policy of partition. Soon after the meeting at Berlin the *Norddeutsche Allgemeine Zeitung*, which was closely in touch with the Chancellor,

[1] A.A., Andrassy to Francis Joseph, 12 May 1876.
[2] *Ibid.*

began openly to advocate the occupation of Bosnia by Austria.[1]

The Berlin understanding marked a departure from the original policy of Russia and Austria. It asserted their determination not to let the Balkan crisis bring them into conflict. Russia receded from her intention of barring the way to Austria's extension in the East by creating an autonomous Bosnia and Herzegovina, and consented to their being annexed by Austria. Austria, on the other hand, realised that she could not get hold of these provinces without re-opening the Eastern Question and without Russia's concurrence, and consented to her taking some territory for herself as compensation.

The Berlin Memorandum was communicated to the French, Italian and British Ambassadors on Saturday, 13 May. It proposed first that the Powers should concert among themselves upon the measures to be taken to prevent a repetition of such events as those of Salonika, and suggested that warships should be sent to the menaced points and that combined instructions should be given to the commanders to co-operate in preserving peace and order. Since the insurgents had refused to cease fighting without material European guarantees for the execution of the reforms, and since the Porte had declared itself incapable of introducing them before the rebels had laid down their arms, the three Powers proposed that the Sultan should be persuaded to grant a two months' armistice. During this time the Porte might enter into direct negotiations with the insurgents, taking their counter-proposals as a basis for discussion, but taking exception to their demands for land and the establishment of a constitution for the two provinces. Should the armistice expire without an arrangement being reached, the three Powers were of opinion that diplomatic action must be strengthened by "the sanction of an *entente*, in view of the efficacious measures which might appear necessary in the interest of general peace, in order to stop the evil and prevent its development".[2] In communicating this Memorandum to the foreign Ambassadors, Prince Gortchakov told them that he and Count Andrassy would remain in Berlin till Monday the 15th, and that they hoped that the three

[1] Andrassy, II, p. 296.
[2] A. d'Avril, *op. cit.* p. 121.

Powers would be able to inform them of their decision before their departure.

France and Italy gave their consent at once, but Britain refused this time to associate herself with the action of the Dreikaiserbund. When, on Monday the 15th, Derby returned to London he found Disraeli determined to reject the Memorandum, and on the same day informed the Ambassadors of the three Powers of England's objections to it. Both the British Government and public opinion were greatly offended by the manner in which the three Northern Powers had conducted their pacificatory action and the role of arbiter they had assumed in Eastern affairs. "I have nothing to answer to your proposals," said Disraeli to Shouvalov, "except that you treat us like Montenegro or Bosnia."[1] And in the Cabinet he exclaimed: "It is almost a mockery for them to talk of a desire that the Powers should act in common, and then exclude France, Italy and England from their deliberations and ask us by telegraph to say yes or no, to propositions which we have never heard discussed."[2] *The Times* gave expression to this feeling in a series of articles attacking the Dreikaiserbund's policy. "Those Emperors and Chancellors", it wrote, "had unconsciously come to believe that their authority was paramount."[3]

Disraeli considered that Turkey was incapable of carrying out the reforms demanded from her, and that even a mere attempt to do so would weaken her forces still more and deliver up the country to anarchy. He was particularly suspicious of the last paragraph of the Memorandum which hinted at the employment "of efficacious measures" if the armistice failed to bring about pacification. By promising them renewed intervention in their favour, the three Powers were openly encouraging the insurgents to reject all the conditions of the Porte. Disraeli feared that by supporting the Dreikaiserbund in this action England would be "drawn step by step into participating in a scheme which must end very soon in the disintegration of Turkey. ...It is asking us to sanction them in putting the knife to the throat of Turkey, whether we like it or not,"[4] he said in the

[1] R.D., Shouvalov to Gortchakov, 7–19 May 1876.
[2] Disraeli, p. 25.
[3] *The Times*, 24 July 1876.   [4] Disraeli, pp. 24–5.

Cabinet. In his opinion it was better both for Turkey and England that she should give up Bosnia and Herzegovina altogether rather than acquiesce in the new proposals. But before taking a definite decision upon this new programme of reforms, Disraeli wished to know the opinion of the Porte. He was ready, if Turkey agreed, "to recommend an armistice and a European Conference based upon the territorial *status quo*".[1]

It is interesting to note that the ideas of an armistice and of a conference were common to Disraeli and Gortchakov. Had his Memorandum been communicated to the Great Powers, as Gortchakov demanded, England could not have rejected it on the plea that she was not consulted in the preparation of the new reforms. In yielding to Austria, Russia was only estranging England from herself. The Berlin Memorandum was conceived in London as Russia's work and the whole attack of the British press was directed against her.

Like Disraeli his colleagues took the demand of the three Powers as an affront to Great Britain and resolved to reject it.[2] Even the proposal for an armistice and a European conference was omitted in the official answer Derby sent to the three Powers. He informed them on the 19th that Great Britain could not insist upon the Porte's accepting an armistice "without knowing whether the military situation admitted of its being established without prejudice to the Turkish Government.... The mere fact of the insurrection remaining unsuppressed would be likely to give it additional vitality, and the result of an armistice might therefore be to lead to the rejection of any demands which the Powers might fairly be expected to concede, and thus hinder rather than advance the prospect of pacification...." He doubted also the Porte's "being willing and able to come to an arrangement with the insurgents on the basis proposed", and considered an armistice "illusory" in face of the declaration that "if the insurrection continued after the armistice the Powers would intervene further".[3]

The rejection of the Berlin Memorandum on the part of

---

[1] Disraeli, p. 25; Sidney Lee, *King Edward VII*, I, p. 419.
[2] *Life of Carnarvon*, II, p. 330.
[3] B.A., Derby to Russell, 19 May 1876, No. 385.

England created some confusion within the Dreikaiserbund. Andrassy tried to induce her to revise her decision and accept at least the armistice. He argued that if the rising continued it would be very difficult to keep Russia within the limits of a moderate programme and to prevent Serbia and Montenegro from entering the war.[1] France endeavoured also to bring Britain back to the European concert, fearing lest her separation might encourage the three Powers to act alone in solving the Eastern Question. Bismarck was prepared to mediate between England and the other Powers for an understanding. He defended the Berlin programme to the British Ambassador as a basis of Russo-Austrian co-operation and as a guarantee for the maintenance of European peace. If it failed they might come into conflict, since Russia favoured more radical measures to which Austria was opposed. Germany did not wish for that conflict, nor did she think it could serve general peace. She therefore supported and desired Britain to support that programme.[2] But all these arguments failed to move Disraeli. His attitude was taken and he did not mean to change it.

Having failed to bring Britain back to the European concert, the five Powers decided to act alone. But events in Constantinople frustrated their intention. On 30 May when the Note was to be communicated to the Porte, the Sultan Abdul Azis was deposed, and there was no Government to receive the communication. At the proposal of France the Powers resolved to postpone their step until the new Sultan was recognised.

The intention of the five Powers to act without England created fresh embarrassment for the British Government. If, as was certain to be the case, the Turks refused the Memorandum, there was a danger that the five Powers might exercise pressure upon them. There was the still greater danger that Russia might use the resistance of the Turks as a pretext to enter the Straits with her fleet. Disraeli was informed that Ignatyev had suggested to the Sultan that he should invite the Russian fleet to protect him. To prevent a possible *coup de main* on the part of Russia, Disraeli ordered the fleet to proceed to Beshika Bay. He thought also of

---

[1] B.A., Buchanan to Derby, 17 May 1876, Nos. 299, 301.
[2] B.A., Russell to Derby, 26 May 1876, No. 234, very conf. and secret.

seizing the Turkish fleet himself.[1] On this occasion he wrote to
the Queen: "Your Majesty's fleet has not been ordered to the
Mediterranean to protect Christians or Turks, but to uphold
Your Majesty's Empire. Had Your Majesty sanctioned the
Berlin Memorandum, Constantinople would at this moment
have been garrisoned by Russia, and the Turkish fleet have been
placed under Russian protection."[2]

Suspicion of Russia was deeply rooted in England and was
now increased still more by the conduct of her Consuls and Slav
Committees. It was believed in London that the resistance of
the insurgents, the failure of the Andrassy Note and the rising
in Bulgaria were all due to the machinations of General Ignatyev
and the Russian agents. "We ought fully to recognise", wrote
The Times, "that there is a real antagonism between Russian
and English policy...there is a resolve that Russia shall not
tear up with impunity the Treaty of Paris and renew her policy
of aggression."[3] "It is Russia," it wrote again, "which has
armed the Serbians and the Montenegrins against the Turkish
authority and holds them ready to enter on the campaign. It is
Russia which pushed the late Government of Turkey to its
destruction, and has been foiled by the deposition of the Sultan.
Russian missionaries are despatched to kindle the zeal of the
Slavs, Russian society furnishes money for their equipment,
Russian journals proclaim the extent and power of the crusade."[4]

By 5 June the new Sultan was recognised by all the Powers.
The Porte immediately granted an armistice of six weeks and a
general amnesty, hoping thus to prevent the interference of the
Powers. Russia did not mean to let the Turks frustrate the
action of the Powers and proposed that they should proceed at
once with their note. But the Powers were no longer unanimous
as to further action. France considered that recent events
imposed a reconsideration of the whole situation.[5] She endeavoured to induce England to come back to the European
concert and was prepared to find some formula which might
satisfy her. All her efforts, however, remained unsuccessful, and
only estranged Russia from her. On 6 June Russia proposed

---

[1] *Life of Carnarvon*, II, p. 330. [2] Queen Victoria, pp. 455–6.
[3] *The Times*, 23 May 1876. [4] *Ibid.* 7 June.
[5] D.F., No. 61.

that the five Powers should declare to the Porte that they remained unanimous as to the pacification of the revolted provinces, but that in view of the reforms the Porte had announced they consented to adjourn the communication of their note. England refused even such a moderate declaration, but the other Powers accepted it. Meanwhile on 15 June a guard officer killed Hussein Avni Pasha and Rashid Pasha in the Cabinet room. This event left the impression that Turkey was breaking up from inside and shattered all hopes of reform.

Immediately after the decision of the British Cabinet to reject the Memorandum, Russell was instructed to express to Bismarck the sincere wish of the British Government "to act in concert with the German Government in all matters, so far as it may be possible to do so, since they believed that the interests of Germany and England are equally directed to the maintenance of the *status quo* and the preservation of European peace".[1] At that moment Disraeli had in mind a European conference, "on the basis of the *status quo*, admitting the creation of new vassal states, but *sine qua non*, no increase of the territory of any existing vassal state".[2] Profiting by the overture for co-operation with England Bismarck had made in January, he desired now to win him over for a European conference. "Nothing must be hurried," he wrote to the Queen, "and before the Congress meets the policy of England and Germany should be decided and the same."[3] "I feel convinced it is the only practical solution in the long run", he stated in a letter to Derby...."If Bismarck agrees to this, the affair is finished and for a generation."[4]

At first Bismarck left Disraeli's overture for co-operation without an answer. When it was repeated on 26 May he told Russell that German interests would not be affected by the ultimate destiny of Turkey, but that "Germany like England was most interested in the preservation of peace, and peace, as matters now stood, depended on the continuance of the friendly understanding existing between Austria-Hungary and Russia, which the general concert of the Great Powers tended to confirm and conciliate, but which the withdrawal of the support of

[1] B.A., Derby to Russell, 17 May 1876, No. 381.
[2] Disraeli, p. 30; Queen Victoria, p. 455.
[3] Queen Victoria, p. 454.
[4] Disraeli, p. 30.

England might weaken and disturb". He confessed to the British Ambassador that Gortchakov came to Berlin with a broader plan for pacification, which was "based on the establishment of the autonomy of the revolted provinces under Turkish governors", and that Andrassy refused to consent to it. He expressed the hope that England might be able to lend her moral support to Austria "because he looked upon the independence and strength of Austria as essential to the peace of Europe".[1]

The invitations to the conference were never sent. Later on Disraeli was very much reproached for having rejected the Berlin Memorandum without making an alternative proposal. Defending himself in Parliament he urged the probability that the three Powers "in their self-love and just pride" would have rejected any proposal from England. In his opinion, "it was not a wise thing for a country, and a country like England, to make proposals which it had not the means to carry into effect".[2] In fact Disraeli had thought of a conference only as a means to counteract the separate action of the five Powers. It was not his intention to take the initiative in the solution of the complex Herzegovinian question. His purpose was to preserve the Ottoman Empire and restore British prestige. It is probable, therefore, that the cold reception which his overtures for co-operation found in Berlin, and the subsequent events in Constantinople, induced him to abandon all idea of a conference.

On the same day that Bismarck assured Russell that "the withdrawal of the support of England might weaken and disturb" the existing understanding between his allies, Andrassy told the British Ambassador in strict confidence that although he regretted the separation of England, he considered it "fortunate" that she had rejected the Memorandum. "He looks forward to the independent attitude of Her Majesty's Government", reported Buchanan, "being most useful in promoting Austrian as well as English interests, as circumstances are sure to arise when Her Majesty's Government will be able to exercise greater control over the course of events than if they were embarrassed by the stipulations of the memorandum."[3] Andrassy made this declara-

---

[1] B.A., Russell to Derby, 26 May 1876, No. 234, very conf. and secret.
[2] Disraeli, p. 27.
[3] B.A., Buchanan to Derby, 26 May 1876, No. 324, secret.

tion for Derby's private information and under the condition
that it "must never appear in a Blue Book". It was probably
this sudden change of opinion that induced Derby to think that
Andrassy "did not know his mind for a week together".[1] But
Disraeli was inclined to believe that his "policy of determination"
had not only frustrated the designs of the Dreikaiserbund, but
had broken up that alliance itself. "I look upon the tripartite
confederacy to be at an end", he wrote to Lord John Manners.[2]
When the five Powers decided to suspend further action, he
considered that he had achieved his purpose, and that the
"unnatural alliance" was "as extinct as the Roman Trium-
virate".[3]

On 10 June Disraeli approached the Russian Ambassador and
in a long conversation endeavoured to persuade him that he had
complete confidence in Russia's policy, both in Asia and Turkey.
"It seems to me that if Russia tells us now what she wants", he
said, "we could still come to an agreement; but she should tell
us directly, and not through the mediation of Harcourts,
Münsters and Beusts." But though he showed his readiness
"to examine in the spirit of conciliation and good will" every
proposal coming from Russia, he did not believe that anything
could be done at the moment to pacify the rising.

"The insurgents are not fighting for reforms," he observed to
Shouvalov, "and nothing will satisfy them, because they are fighting
for independence. In this state of things the struggle and the shedding of blood is inevitable: neither you nor we can prevent it. You
have been wrong to restrain Montenegro and Serbia, since the conflict was imminent and its solution depended upon its issue. We
believe that a bleeding is necessary and we will consider it together.
If it is the Christians who get the upper hand, then we shall only
have to register accomplished facts; if it is Turkey who crushes the
Christians and if repression becomes tyrannical, it will be the turn
of all the Great Powers to interpose themselves in the name of
humanity, and then the interference of Europe will be legitimate."[4]

Lord Derby gave the same assurance to Count Shouvalov,
adding that it would be necessary to allow the Sultan two or

[1] Disraeli, p. 33.
[2] *Ibid.* p. 31.
[3] Queen Victoria, p. 458.
[4] R.D., Shouvalov to Gortchakov, 10 and 11 June 1876.

three weeks to come to a direct arrangement with the insurgents. He professed to know that the Porte would offer them an organisation analogous to Crete, but as the Christians would accept nothing less than independence, which the Sultan could not now accord, the struggle would be renewed. If the insurgents vanquished the Turks they would obtain their independence; if not they would have to accept a situation analogous to Crete, which Europe would secure to them even in case of their defeat.[1]

Shouvalov found it difficult to explain the real motives and intentions of the British proposal. He did not know whether Disraeli wanted to separate Russia from Austria, or expel Austria from the Dreikaiserbund and take a place there, or simply to draw nearer to Russia in order to impose her own will in future decisions, or whether he really desired to assure European peace through an *entente* with Russia.[2] Gortchakov suspected Disraeli of intending to break up Russia's *entente* with Austria and France; he had information that a similar attempt had recently been made in Vienna. Nevertheless he instructed Shouvalov to try to win him over to the idea of the establishment of tributary autonomy for Bosnia and Herzegovina, and some territorial concessions for Serbia and Montenegro. He especially emphasised the necessity of urgent action by the six Powers for that purpose, in order to prevent the impending catastrophe.[3]

Shouvalov made great efforts to induce Disraeli and Derby to consent to autonomy, and at one moment he believed that they were not opposed to it, but that they were unwilling to intervene with the Porte. But Disraeli and Derby began to retreat as soon as they were acquainted with the Russian views. They asked him to explain what the consequences would be if the Porte refused to concede autonomy and what meaning Russia attached to the phrase "*autonomie vassale et tributaire*".[4] He assured them that Russia did not mean to intervene, but only to give unanimous advice as a last effort for pacification, and that she had in mind an autonomy like that of Serbia and Roumania; but he failed to satisfy them. The deliberations dragged on up to the end of June, Shouvalov making vain efforts to convince the two

[1] R.D., Shouvalov to Gortchakov, 11 June.
[2] *Ibid.*
[3] R.D., Gortchakov to Shouvalov, 14 June 1876.
[4] R.D., Shouvalov to the Tsar, 22 June 1876.

Englishmen that, since they accepted the Cretan status for the revolted provinces, it would be better to press it upon the Porte and thus prevent further bloodshed, than to wait for the result of the struggle.

The hesitation of England to adopt the principle of autonomy and its final rejection was largely due to the resolute resistance Andrassy showed against autonomy. Andrassy was informed by both Gortchakov and Beust of the British proposal and the negotiations between Russia and England. England's readiness to accept the autonomy created great embarrassment for him. He had only with great difficulty dissuaded Russia from that plan and induced her to consent to his programme of reform; if she were supported by England, he would be unable to prevent the formation of autonomous states if Turkey consented to them. His only hope was to prevent an understanding between England and Russia, and he used all his energy to achieve that object. He warned Derby strongly against the idea of autonomy and independence, pointing out the dangers they presented for European peace. Against the autonomy he expounded his old arguments: the mixed population of the two provinces, religious and racial hatred between the Moslems and the Christians, and the inevitability of the other Christians asking for the same concessions and therefore of the revolt's spreading further instead of being quelled. Were the insurgents aware that they would obtain independence if they vanquished the Turks nothing would stop them fighting, and if war ensued the Russian Government would be unable to resist any longer the pressure of its public opinion.[1]

This campaign against autonomy was not without some influence in London. Although at first refusing to commit himself to any clear course of policy, as he was asked to by Andrassy, and professing still to believe in the possibility of self-government, Derby finally adopted Andrassy's views. In a conversation with Shouvalov on the 28th he used the same arguments against autonomy.[2] On the 29th he informed him in a letter that so long as the insurrection lasted all plans for the improvement of

[1] A.A., Andrassy to Beust, 15 June, Tel. No. 19, and 25 June, No. 24, 1876. B.A., French to Derby, 22 June 1876, No. 412.
[2] B.A., Derby to Loftus, 22 June 1876, No. 393.

administration in the revolted provinces would be fruitless, that
the British Government did not "clearly understand what is the
political plan which the Russian Government have in view",
and that Serbia should be warned "in a tone which did not admit
of misconstruction" that she would not be protected "from the
consequences of failure and defeat" if she entered the war.[1] "The
only thing they admit here", wrote Shouvalov to the Tsar, "is
that the oriental crisis arose too soon for our liking, and that we
may wish to adjourn it in order to prepare a solution more in
our favour."[2]

In fact Disraeli had no settled opinion about autonomy. In
October 1875 he wrote to Lady Bradford: "Fancy autonomy
for Bosnia...autonomy for Ireland would be less absurd."[3] In
May he was ready to propose autonomy and considered it as a
solution which would settle the affair for a generation.[4] But
when Russia proposed autonomy he refused it. Speaking about
the Eastern Question in the House of Lords in February 1877,
he said that he had refused the Russian plan "for establishing a
chain of autonomous states", because it would have weakened
Turkey and brought her slowly to dissolution.[5] Disraeli was
equally contradictory in the question of the maintenance of
Turkey. Although extolling it as the purpose of his policy, he
was more than once ready to acquiesce in partition, and even to
take the lead in it. Autonomy or non-autonomy, the maintenance
or the break-up of Turkey, were for him the means of policy
only, the purpose of which was to enhance the influence and
prestige of Great Britain.

While the Great Powers discussed further measures for
pacification Serbia and Montenegro were making last preparations for war. The incapacity of the Turks to overcome the rising
and the disorders in Constantinople convinced them that
the Ottoman Empire was breaking up and that it could not
offer serious resistance to an attack from outside. This conviction prevailed also in Russia. When it became evident that
war was imminent Russia appealed to the Powers to maintain
absolute neutrality, hoping that the Christians would vanquish

---

[1] B.A., Derby to Shouvalov, 29 June 1876.
[2] R.D., Shouvalov to the Tsar, 20 June and 2 July 1876.
[3] Disraeli, p. 13. [4] *Ibid.* p. 30. [5] *Ibid.* p. 121.

the Turks.[1] This proposal was accepted by Italy, France and Germany. England accepted it too, with reservations in the event "of a different course being pursued by other Powers".[2] Austria could not, however, consent to absolute neutrality as she feared lest Serbia and Montenegro should occupy Bosnia and Herzegovina. Concealing his real motives from Gortchakov Andrassy argued that if the Powers declared absolute neutrality they would not be able to prevent the reprisals which would ensue if Turkey were victorious.[3]

Such an attitude on the part of Austria again provoked disagreement between St Petersburg and Vienna. Gortchakov was already discontented with Andrassy's having opposed autonomy, which, he believed, all the other Powers were prepared to accept. He wrote two memoranda on the Eastern Question and the Tsar read them to William I. According to Manteuffel, who was acquainted with their contents later on, these memoranda "contain only the ideas of protection of the Christians, without any mention of the Russian aims or of intention to break up Turkey".[4] William and Bismarck advised moderation and agreement with Austria. These circumstances, indeed, imposed an exchange of views with Austria. The Tsar proposed that Andrassy and Gortchakov should meet together on the occasion of his interview with Francis Joseph on his return from Germany —the interview which had been already arranged in May. The necessity of a direct contact was felt also in Vienna and the Russian proposal was readily accepted.

The meeting between the two Emperors and their Ministers took place at Reichstadt on 8 July. Gortchakov still hoped to succeed in winning over Andrassy for some form of autonomy and for the principle of non-intervention. He read his two memoranda to Andrassy, but the latter refused to discuss them. Andrassy produced his own proposal that the two Powers should take into consideration the possibility of both the victory and the defeat of Turkey, and concert among themselves for both these eventualities. The result of their deliberations was an agreement upon a common attitude of Austria and Russia during and after

[1] R.D., Gortchakov to Shouvalov, 27 June 1876.
[2] B.A., Derby to Loftus, 1 July 1876, No. 396.
[3] A.A., Andrassy to Novikov, 7 July 1876.
[4] G.P., No. 231.

the war. It was decided to remain neutral during the war, in consequence of which Austria had to close the ports of Klek and Cattaro. If the Turks defeated the Christians the two Powers would intervene to prevent sanguinary reprisals and secure some reforms for the revolted provinces. Serbia and Montenegro should preserve their territorial *status quo*. If the Christians were victorious the creation of a great Slav or other state was excluded, but Serbia and Montenegro should obtain some territorial aggrandisement: Serbia an adjacent part of Bosnia, and Montenegro a part of Herzegovina and a port on the Adriatic; they were also to divide between themselves the Sandjak of Novipazar. In that event Austria would annex the rest of Bosnia and Herzegovina, and Russia Bessarabia and some parts of Turkey in Asia. Constantinople might be set up as a free city, Thessaly and Epirus could be united to Greece, and Roumania, Bulgaria and Albania erected into autonomous principalities.

This agreement was verbal. Andrassy claimed later on that he had dictated its substance to Novikov immediately after the meeting and had asked him to send a copy of it to St Petersburg together with a map of the territories allotted to Austria.[1] Gortchakov stated that he had never received that copy. He wrote on his part a précis of the agreement for his Emperor's use which differed on several points from Andrassy's text. These differences gave rise later on to some discussions as to what was actually agreed.

The main points of difference are the following: In case of defeat of the Christians Russia proposed that Bosnia and Herzegovina should be organised on the basis " of the programme marked out by the despatches of 30 December and the Memorandum of Berlin, or at least according to the Cretan Statute". In the *pro memoria* which was sent to the Tsar together with the text of the agreement, Gortchakov mentioned also that they should be organised "if possible on a larger basis of administrative autonomy". Andrassy said nothing about autonomy. He mentioned only the liberties and reforms which had been demanded

[1] The Austrian version is published by A. F. Pribram in his *Secret Treaties of Austria-Hungary*, 1879–1914, II, p. 188. The Russian version is published in the *Krasnyi Archiv*, vol. I, p. 37, and in N. W. Tcharykov's autobiography, *Glimpses of High Politics*, p. 103.

from the Porte and granted by it. This difference is not accidental. It shows that in the question of autonomy Andrassy and Gortchakov stood by their own views.

In the event of the victory of the Christians the Russian text contemplates two eventualities: (1) the mere victory, and (2) the complete dissolution of Turkey. The Austrian text makes no difference between the two eventualities. Russia foresees the formation of independent principalities only in the event of "complete downfall of the Ottoman Empire in Europe"; whereas in case of victory she admits only of territorial increase for Serbia and Montenegro and annexations for herself and Austria. Again Russia talks of independent principalities, while Austria mentions the autonomous ones only. They differ also in the question of territorial increase for Montenegro: Russia gives her the whole of Herzegovina, but Austria only a part of it. As to the territory which was to be annexed by Austria, the Russian text allows for "Turkish Croatia and some parts of Bosnia contiguous to her frontiers according to a line to be agreed upon". According to Andrassy, Austria was to take "the rest of Bosnia and Herzegovina".

The difference between the two texts proceeds probably from the fact that they were both written from memory after the meeting, but it discloses also the divergence of tendencies between the two parties. This is particularly clear in the question of territorial aggrandisement for Serbia and Montenegro, which Russia desired to enlarge, and Austria to restrict as much as possible—and in the question of reforms for the revolted provinces, to whom Russia wished to secure autonomy, while Austria did not mean to go further than her reforms. It is interesting, however, that both the Austrian and the Russian texts differed from what was later on inserted in the Budapest Convention as being agreed upon at Reichstadt.

Both Russia and Austria were content with their achievement at Reichstadt. Russia had secured Austria's neutrality in the war and her support for the maintenance of *status quo* of Serbia and Montenegro in case of their defeat. Austria had succeeded in removing the idea of autonomy which threatened to embroil her with Russia, and in obtaining the guarantee that Bosnia and Herzegovina should not be occupied by Serbia and Montenegro.

But the essential point of the Reichstadt Agreement was Russia's consent to Austria's taking Bosnia and Herzegovina, in return for which she was to take Bessarabia, in the event of the dissolution of Turkey. The basis was thus laid for their co-operation in the future, which was of decisive importance for the further development of the Eastern Question. The latent antagonistic interests which divided Russia and Austria in Bosnia found satisfaction in the break-up of Turkey. The two Powers subordinated their divergences to a higher common interest—the maintenance of their alliance—the alliance which could be maintained only at the expense of Turkey. This same interest would compel Russia later on, when after the defeat of Serbia the question of Bosnia came again to the fore, to take upon herself the task of breaking up the Ottoman Empire.

CHAPTER V

*

THE SERBO-TURKISH WAR

THE result of a year's effort by the Great Powers to appease the rising was the recognition of their inability to agree upon any programme of reform which would reconcile their divergent interests and improve the position of the Christians. The attempts to reach an agreement had only revealed their divergences and strained their relations still more. Further estrangement among them was averted only by the entry of Serbia and Montenegro into war, which the Powers regarded now as the only solution of the deadlock to which their pacifying action had brought them. Russia hoped that the war would inflame the whole Balkan peninsula and enable a definite solution of the Eastern Question to be reached. Austria saw in the war a means of preventing an understanding between Russia and England to her detriment and of getting hold of Bosnia and Herzegovina. England preferred war to a separate action by the three Northern Powers. Having rejected both the Berlin Memorandum and the idea of autonomy, she expected that the war would clear up the situation and enable her to decide her policy. After a year's endeavour to quell the rising, the Powers came to wish for its further spreading and to seek in it a means to avoid a conflict among themselves.

The Powers had not only failed to pacify the rising, but had actually helped the revolutionary forces in the Balkans to develop. Although warlike, Serbia and Montenegro were not prepared in 1875 to go into action. The Bulgarians had begun their preparations only after the outbreak of the rising in Herzegovina. By preventing the Porte from suppressing the movement by force, the Powers had prolonged it and given time to the other Christians to complete their armament and organise other revolts. On the other hand, the repeated defeats of the Turks in Herzegovina and the disorders in Constantinople created the conviction that Turkey would fall to pieces at the first shock and encouraged the Christians to take up arms. They were able to do so now without fear of being prevented by the Powers.

Prince Milan was opposed to the war, believing that the Powers would not allow it and that it would inevitably lead to a disaster. He had overthrown the "Ministry of Action" in order to avoid being forced into war, and created a Cabinet of younger Liberals and Conservatives with Kaljević as President. Although personally an autocrat, he consented to the introduction of some liberal reforms in the municipal and press law, hoping that these might divert public opinion from war.[1] But these measures produced quite opposite results, for they only facilitated the agitation of the nationalist and revolutionary elements. With the coming year the Liberal press redoubled its efforts to prove that Serbia was bound by her duty to her subjected nationals and her own interests to go to war and that an abstention from it would be fatal for her future. The clamour of this agitation silenced the more moderate Conservative elements, many of whom sided with the Liberals. Much more important and dangerous was the·revolutionary activity of the Radicals who preached war in the hope that it would destroy the whole bureaucratic system. They took advantage of the difficult situation of the country and the weakness of the Government to incite the peasants against the regime and stirred up public opinion all over the country. A series of student revolts took place, plots were discovered by the police and threatening letters were sent to the Prince. On 15 February 1876 a conflict between the Radicals and their opponents took place at Kragujevac. A red flag was carried through the town by the mob crying: "Long live the Republic", and order was restored only after the army was brought in. This incident was considered both in Belgrade and abroad as the beginning of an internal revolution. "The internal situation was almost as serious as the external. It was difficult to say which was worse—the anarchy which threatened from within, or the war from without."[2]

The agitation in Serbia found an echo among the insurgents in Bosnia and Herzegovina and the Serbs in Austria. They criticised Prince Milan and the official policy as treachery to

[1] S. Jovanović, *Vlada Milana Obrenovića*, I, p. 264.   [2] *Ibid.* p. 278.

the highest interests of Serbdom, contrasting it with the heroic sacrifices of Prince Peter Karadjordjević who fought among the insurgents in Bosnia. The Bosnian insurgents issued a memorandum in which they openly attacked Serbia for not coming to their help. The peaceful policy of Prince Milan was thus disavowed by both his own people and the insurgents, and he could find support for it neither in the army nor in the political parties. However dangerous the war might seem to be, opposition to it in such circumstances was almost impossible.

Under the pressure of public opinion Milan began to think of the possibility of a war and to prepare himself for it. Indeed, although overthrowing the "Ministry of Action" he dared not stand openly against the aspirations of his people. He accepted the war loan, reducing it only to two million ducats, and endeavoured to realise it on the foreign market. This loan was to be used partly for military preparations—and he insisted upon their being ready before the spring—and partly for the support of the insurgents.[1] During the winter the Government sent no more volunteers across the frontier, but assisted the rising with money and war materials. At the same time steps were taken for getting into touch with the Balkan peoples with a view to securing their co-operation in the event of war. In October 1875 Filip Hristić was sent to Cetinje to sound the views of Prince Nicholas for joint action. The Prince was disposed to co-operate with Serbia, but it was decided to postpone action till the next spring and in the meantime to assist the insurgents to hold on.[2] In February 1876 General Alimpić was sent to Cetinje with a draft treaty of alliance and a military convention to be concluded with Montenegro. But Nicholas prolonged negotiations and finally refused to sign the treaty. He was indeed pressed from various sides and encouraged by the prospect of territorial concessions to remain quiet. Russia made strong remonstrances to both Belgrade and Cetinje against the conclusion of the treaty. General Ignatyev advised the Porte to make some territorial concessions to Montenegro and thus put an end to the insurrection.[3] This idea was favourably received at St

---

[1] *Zapisi Jevrema Grujića*, III, pp. 152–6.

[2] S.A., Hristić's report of his mission to Montenegro, 24 Nov. 1875.

[3] B.A., Elliot to Derby, 20 Feb. 1876, No. 221, conf., and 19 March 1876, No. 294, conf.

Petersburg, and it seemed that the other Powers were not opposed to it.[1] Ali Pasha, the Governor of Bosnia, sent his secretary, Dr Koetschet, to the Prince asking for his assistance in the work of pacification.[2] At the same time Andrassy sent General Rodić to Cetinje to ask for Nicholas' mediation with the insurgents to accept his reforms, telling him that this service would much strengthen his own claims on the Great Powers. The whole idea of territorial concessions for Montenegro was abortive from the outset, for the Porte never seriously intended to make them. But for the moment it made an impression on the Prince and influenced his action. Pressed by Russia and Austria, and with the prospect of enlarging his country without any sacrifices, he prolonged the negotiations, made various objections to the project of the treaty and sent Alimpić back without signing it.[3]

An attempt was also made to come into connection with the Greek Government and renew the alliance which was concluded in 1867. In autumn 1875 the Serbian Government intended to send an agent to Athens, but the Greek Government refused to receive him. In February 1876 they tried again to send an agent, but were refused once more.[4] Prince Milan told Doskos, the Greek Agent, that war with Turkey was inevitable and invited his Government to join Serbia and Montenegro.[5]

Despite obstinate refusals from Greece, the Serbian Government resolved in March to send Milutin Garašanin as a private person, to inform himself whether Greece considered herself bound by the Treaty of alliance of 1867, what was her probable attitude towards the situation in Turkey and what was the disposition of public opinion towards Serbia. Garašanin reported to his Government that in his opinion no support could be expected from the Athens Government, for King George was opposed to any action. Public opinion was greatly distrustful toward Serbia, reproaching her for her neutrality in 1867 and for having profited by the Cretan rising to drive the Turks from her fortified towns. They regarded her as a tool of Panslavism which

---

[1] D. Harris, *op. cit.* pp. 402–5.
[2] J. Koetschet, *Aus Bosniens letzter Türkenzeit*, p. 31.
[3] S.A., Alimpić's report of his mission to Cetinje, 15 April 1876.
[4] M. Lhéritier, *Histoire diplomatique de la Grèce*, III, p. 385.
[5] A.A., Andrassy to Wrede, 14 March 1876, No. 28.

they feared as much as Turkey. Garašanin believed therefore that no support could be expected from Greece, but that she would wait to see the development of events and take advantage of a favourable situation to extract concessions from the Porte.[1]

But in Salonika Garašanin came into contact with the members of the "War Committee" which was established by some opposition leaders. Its president was the ex-Premier Leonidas Bulgaris. Its purpose was to prepare an insurrection in the Greek provinces of Turkey and open a press campaign to win public opinion to its cause and thus force the Government into action. Garašanin recommended his Government to give monetary assistance to this Committee and use it as a means for forcing the Athens Government into action. "In this way", he wrote, "Serbia would hold all the threads of the insurrection in her hands."[2] This proposal was accepted by the Belgrade Government and 20,000 dinars were sent to Salonika.[3] Bulgaris informed Ristić that he was preparing volunteer detachments to rouse the population in Macedonia and occupy the Rodope mountains, that Thessaly was ready to rise and that another detachment would be directed to Ohrid.[4]

Some attempts were also made to make contact with Albania and Roumania. The northern tribes in Albania seemed to be disposed for common action; their leader Bib-Doda was in communication with Serbian agents and received some monetary help.[5] But no result was reached. Roumania began to arm at the end of 1875, but when approached by Serbia refused to take any part in a war.

The conduct of Russia and Austria made Milan suspicious of their real intentions and encouraged him to continue the preparations. While pressing peace upon Serbia, they secretly supported the insurgents, or allowed their agents to do so. The correspondence between the Russian Consul in Dubrovnik (Ragusa) and the Prince of Montenegro leaves no doubt that the Slav Committee of Moscow not only assisted the insurgents but directed in fact the whole action in Herzegovina.[6] The

[1] S.A., Garašanin's report of his mission to Greece, March 1876.
[2] *Ibid.*   [3] *Zapisi Jevrema Grujića*, III, p. 166.
[4] S.A., Bulgaris to Firmalion. No date.
[5] *Zapisi Jevrema Grujića*, III, p. 150.
[6] S.A., Correspondence between Prince Nicholas and Yonin, 1875–6.

rivalry of Russia and Austria for the sympathy of the insurgents, while at the same time they were co-operating in appeasing the movement, where, it was no secret, their views widely differed, made it impossible for Serbia to remain inactive. Milan "believed that Austria could have prevented the entry of Peter Karadjordjević into Bosnia, and that she had not done so because she favoured his pretensions to the Serbian throne. At the same time that she advised a peaceful policy to Prince Milan, which undermined his popularity, she encouraged Karadjordjević to popularise himself by participation in the insurrection."[1]

The attitude of Russia was still more puzzling. She strongly insisted upon the maintenance of strict neutrality. In January she frustrated the plan of Serbia and Montenegro to address themselves to the Great Powers by a memorandum in which they would expound the difficulties of their position. She also prevented Serbia from asking the Porte to transfer the administration of the orthodox schools and churches in Bosnia to the Serbian Metropolitan.[2] Meanwhile at the same time Gortchakov recommended the Belgrade Government not to stop its armament since nobody could foresee what the spring might bring about.[3] There was nothing accidental in this communication, for he also told the French Ambassador that his policy would have been quite different had the rising broken out two years later,[4] and the German Ambassador that his present policy was in harmony neither with his inclinations nor with his habits. "I was always for clear and decided measures", he said, "but what can I do when the Minister of War hangs on one arm and the Minister of Finance on the other?"[5] Yet when Serbia, encouraged by this communication, hastened her military preparations, he joined Andrassy in protesting against it and asked her to give a clear declaration for peace.[6] He intervened also in Belgrade and Cetinje to prevent the conclusion of an alliance between them. Completely disconcerted by such conduct, Milan told the Russian Consul "that he found it strange that

[1] S. Jovanović, *Vlada Milana Obrenovića*, I, p. 293.   [2] *Ibid.* p. 283.
[3] A. N. Kartsov, *Iza kulisami diplomacyi*, p. 21; S.A., Pavlović to Magazinović, 2 Feb. 1876.   [4] A.A., Langenau to Andrassy, 17 March 1876.
[5] Schweinitz, *op. cit.* I, p. 320.
[6] S.A., Pavlović to Cukić, 20 Feb. 1876.

one thing was spoken in St Petersburg, another in Constantinople and yet another in Vienna, and that it would have been more natural to speak and work openly and not to resort to this unstraightforward manner."[1]

This vacillating and contradictory attitude of Austria and Russia, with whom Milan hoped to find support against the warlike elements in his own country, compelled him to lean more and more on his own people. He was fully conscious that if he took the lead of this movement he would recover all his popularity and become a national Prince.

Meanwhile conviction was ripening in Serbia that a war was inevitable. At the beginning of May 1876 the Cabinet of Kaljević resigned and the Stevča Mihailović's "Ministry of Action" was returned to power. This Cabinet considered it its task to prepare the country for war. They undertook at once to work out a war plan, hastened the armament and renewed negotiations with Montenegro for joint action. On 10 June the treaty of alliance and a military convention were signed, which provided for the co-operation of the two states in both the diplomatic and military fields for the purpose of liberating the Balkan Christians, and especially the Serbs, from the Turkish yoke. Serbia promised to make every effort to win over Greece and Roumania for common action and to work together with Montenegro to prepare the other Christians for a general rising. Serbia further consented to give Montenegro a subsidy of 40,000 ducats. The military convention delimited the territorial command of the two armies and formulated the purpose of their action, but indicated no detailed plan of operation, since their fields of action were too remote from each other.[2]

Events in Constantinople and Bulgaria left the impression that Turkey had begun to dissolve from within and that the moment for action had come. The agents of the Slav Committee and the Slavophil press encouraged Serbia to go forward and assured her that Russia would not abandon her. From the beginning of the insurrection they preached a crusade against Islam for the liberation and union of all the Slavs. After the failure of the Berlin Memorandum they opened a vehement

[1] S.A., Pavlović to Cukić, 16 March 1876; S. Jovanović, *op. cit.* p. 296.
[2] *Zapisi Jevrema Grujića,* III, pp. 170–4.

campaign against the Powers who were incapable of solving this question, and advocated an independent action of Russia and the Balkan Slavs. *Novoe Vremja* wrote that the Slavs would not soon have such a favourable opportunity to free themselves from the slavery of four centuries.[1] "Serbia has the right to go to war against Turkey", wrote *Golos*, "in order to solve the Eastern Question in a natural way. Russia will not allow her kinsmen in the Balkans to be crushed in their struggle, even if the whole of Europe had to burn in flames for it."[2]

By the end of April the Slav Committee sent General Chernaev to Serbia. The hero of Tashkent and the editor of the *Ruski Mir*, one of the most militant Slavophil papers, he came now to Serbia to carry out their plans on the spot. "He surveyed our frontiers, saw our troops, and returned 'full of enthusiasm'. Our prospects in case of war seemed to him 'bright'. He advised us to go to war and that as soon as possible."[3] He asked only that the war should be fought for the "Slav Idea"—for the liberation of all the Balkan Slavs. Serbia was not expected to defeat the Turks, but only to sustain the struggle for two months. Within that time Russia would be prepared to enter the war herself.

General Ignatyev, who had a policy of his own, favoured the plan of the Slav Committee, and indeed acted more as their agent than as the Imperial Ambassador. "To our men he spoke in the language and tone of a Slavophil—but in fact our war in 1876 was necessary to him for that diplomatic struggle which he had for years led with England for supremacy in Constantinople."[4] Through his Consul in Belgrade, Kartsov, he asked Ristić: "How long will Serbia delay to take in her hands the defence of the Christians, who looked upon her only for protection from further massacres?"[5] Kartsov was himself a Slavophil, but he had to obey orders from St Petersburg which bade him advise peace. Placed between Ignatyev and Gortchakov, he endeavoured to satisfy both of them. "Officially he recommended peace; privately, as our friend, he instigated us to war, assuring us that Russia would follow...."[6] "In the course of 24 hours he urged

[1] S. Jovanović, *Vlada Milana Obrenovića*, I, p. 305.   [2] *Ibid.*
[3] *Ibid.* p. 307.   [4] *Ibid. op. cit.* p. 306.   [5] J. Ristić, *op. cit.* I, p. 83.
[6] S. Jovanović, *Vlada Milana Obrenovića*, I, p. 293.

upon us by turns both peace and war.''[1] At the end of June the
Tsar sent a message to Prince Milan asking him to preserve
peace at any price and threatening to leave him to his fate if he
entered the war. By then it was too late to stop.

The efforts of Serbia to revive the Balkan alliance and to
prepare a general rising of the Balkan peoples remained fruitless.
Neither Greece nor Roumania believed in the capacity of the
Balkan peoples to fight the Turks without the support of some
Great Power, and refused to take the risk involved in an independent struggle. The attempt to force the Greek Government
into action by the aid of a revolutionary nationalist propaganda was
unsuccessful, for the number of those who carried out this action
was very small and their means very limited. Serbia was unable
to supply them with money, since she herself failed in realising
the war loan and was obliged to rely on her own resources.
For the same reasons the attempt to organise an insurrection in
Macedonia and Albania failed. Serbia and Montenegro alone
were willing to enter the war and prepared to sustain the sacrifices.

It was clear, however, that these two Principalities were too
weak to measure themselves against the Ottoman Empire, and
that in their desire to liberate Bosnia and Herzegovina they
risked losing their own liberty. Yet they were too much engaged
towards the insurgents by their propaganda before and their
support during the insurrection to be able to abandon them now.
Their inaction hitherto was justified by the efforts of the Great
Powers to appease the rising. Since the Powers failed in this
undertaking, the Turks were now free to suppress the movement
by force. In that event Serbia would have lost all her influence
in these provinces and incurred great responsibility in the future.
It was not unlikely that such an attitude would have provoked
an internal revolution and brought about a change in the throne
itself. Thus considerations of both internal and foreign policy
combined to push her into action. But in going to war Serbia
remained faithful to her mission of Piedmont, and even if she
succumbed in the struggle, her sacrifices would cement the feelings
of union among the South Slavs and impel them to new efforts
for complete liberation.

The Serbian Minister of Foreign Affairs, Jovan Ristić, believed

[1] S. Jovanović, *Vlada Milana Obrenovića*, I, p. 295.

that Russia could not remain a passive onlooker in this struggle. She had from the outset taken an active interest in the fate of the insurgents and endeavoured to ameliorate their position. If she were unable to abandon these two provinces, she could still less abandon Serbia and Montenegro if they were defeated in the war. Therefore, even if they failed in liberating their brethren, they would preserve their possessions and their influence in Bosnia and Herzegovina. There was, moreover, the possibility of the Slavophils compelling Russia to take an active part in this struggle. The war which Serbia and Montenegro were about to start would give them a strong weapon of propaganda. In that event Serbia would achieve all her aims with the aid of Russia. Indeed the Government of St Petersburg dissuaded Serbia from war, and even told her that if she entered it Austria would be free "to take against her the measures which she considered necessary". But Ristić trusted Ignatyev and the Slavophils more than official declarations. He did not wait for Russia's approval, for he considered it unwise for a young state to ask in advance the assent of diplomacy for its deeds. They would never obtain it. Success belonged to those who were able "to see through the disposition of diplomacy and knew how to draw her with them".[1] This calculation was based on Russian interests in the Balkans and the probable influence the Slavophils would be able to use on her foreign policy. In so far it proved to be correct. But it overlooked the international difficulties which Russia had to overcome before she was free to wage a war on Turkey. In order to neutralise Austria she was obliged to cede Bosnia and Herzegovina—the two provinces for which Serbia fought. In entering the war Serbia was in fact fighting a lost battle, for she was doomed to lose these provinces irrespective of the result of the struggle. All that she could still hope for were some compensations in the South.

Although convinced that war was inevitable, Ristić tried at the last moment to settle the matter by peaceful ways. He intended to send a letter to the Grand Vizier asking him to convey the administration of Bosnia to Serbia and that of Herzegovina to Montenegro under the payment of a yearly tribute.[2] But Prince

---

[1] S. Jovanović, *op. cit.* p. 311.
[2] J. Ristić, *Diplomatska istorija Srbije*, I, pp. 90–1.

Nicholas rejected this proposal, and Milan himself desired to
open hostilities as soon as possible. Nevertheless the Serbian
Government sent the letter to the Grand Vizier. Bosnia was not
demanded, but the Porte was informed of Serbia's decision to
enter Bosnia in order to restore peace, and was asked to order
its troops not to oppose the Serbian army.[1] The letter was
delivered on 29 June; on the next day war was declared without
waiting for an answer.

The original plan of operations was based upon an offensive
in the South, at Nish, where most of the Turkish army was
concentrated. But this plan was altered later on because of the
fear of a Turkish attack from the East and the West. It was
decided therefore to form four army corps and advance on all
fronts. Apparently this was the worst of all plans, for the Serbian
army amounted to 130,000 men only, and could hardly defend,
still less attack, on a frontier line of over 180 kilometres. Yet
during the first few days they crossed the Turkish frontier at
all points and began to advance. But they were soon stopped
and forced to retreat to their own soil. At the end of July the
Turks attacked with much superior forces and captured Knjaževac
and Zaječar.

These first defeats completely discouraged Prince Milan. He
thought the war lost and proposed to the Government to ask for
an armistice. But the Government did not share this opinion
and succeeded in dissuading him from this step. The war plan
was now changed and the bulk of the army was directed to Nish,
where the Turks threatened to break through to Belgrade. In
defending their own soil the Serbian army proved much better.
They successfully repulsed the incessant attacks of a much
stronger enemy and maintained their positions for another
month. But despite this stubborn resistance the Serbian army
was melting away, and being without reserves it was incapable
of resisting the Turks much longer. When, therefore, in the
middle of August, France, Italy and England offered their
mediation for an armistice, the Belgrade Government accepted
it. Ristić considered that the war was finished and endeavoured
only to save what he could. He was very much disappointed
with the bad response the Balkan peoples made to the Serbian

[1] J. Ristić, *op. cit.* I, p. 94.

call, and with the passive attitude of Russia. Prince Milan, fearing lest the Porte might request his abdication, hastened to ask for Russia's and Austria's protection. Andrassy promised to support him but advised him to change the Cabinet. "The Ministers", he said, "must be sacrificed in order to save the dynasty."[1]

Montenegro operated in Herzegovina, where she met with little Turkish resistance and succeeded in occupying the greater part of the province. But the defeat of Serbia endangered her position too and forced her to accept the mediation of the Powers.

The Great Powers demanded from the Porte an armistice of one month for both Serbia and Montenegro. The Turks consented to the armistice but insisted upon their preliminaries of peace being accepted at the same time. They intended to impose such terms as would prevent the recurrence of similar attacks in the future. Their preliminaries for Serbia presumed the abolition of national militia and the fortresses, the payment of war indemnity and the right of the Porte to construct and exploit the railway line from Belgrade to Nish. They insisted also upon Prince Milan coming to Constantinople to pay homage to the Sultan.[2] But the Powers refused to discuss conditions of peace before the armistice was established, and as the Porte insisted upon the acceptance of its preliminaries, a suspension of arms was established for ten days, beginning from 15 September.

Meanwhile at this moment the situation in Serbia suddenly changed. The Slavophils had skilfully exploited the massacres in Bulgaria and the Serbian war to awaken Slav feelings in their countrymen and create a strong movement in favour of war. Slav Committees were established all over Russia and a wholesale propaganda started in favour of the Balkan Slavs. The Crusade was preached in churches and patriotic speeches delivered at the ball of the Slav Committees. Distinguished persons were seen in the streets begging help for the Christians. The press glorified General Chernaev and appealed for the assistance of Russian volunteers. The excitement permeated all classes and reached even the throne itself: the Empress Marie and the Heir Apparent Alexander patronised this action and took an active part in it.[3]

[1] A.A., Andrassy to Wrede, 23 Aug. 1876.
[2] S. Jovanović, *op. cit.* p. 336.
[3] Schweinitz, *op. cit.* pp. 340–1.

"The whole of Russia", wrote the Russian historian, Tatiščev, "was united in a magnanimous *élan*: to come to the help of her Slav brethren and co-operate in their liberation."[1]

Neither the Tsar nor the Government could remain indifferent to this movement, much the less so as the Slavophils were the only support of the autocratic regime. The Russian Government was conscious of the difficulties of a war for the Slav Idea, but they realised also the impossibility of leaving Serbia to the mercy of Turkey. Without identifying themselves with the Slavophils, they did not refuse such assistance as was in their power. They gave leave to officers who desired to go to Serbia and facilitated the passage of volunteers. The effect of this agitation on the Tsar soon found expression in a speech he addressed to his guard officers after the army manœuvres, in which he told them that he had endeavoured and wished to preserve peace, but if the honour of the country were attacked he would know how to vindicate it. Gortchakov was also affected by it. "Were it not for the Tsar", wrote von Schweinitz, "Gortchakov would soon give expression to his ideas in a circular to the Powers."[2]

At the beginning of September, Russian volunteers began to pour into Serbia. Among the men who came to fight for the Slav cause there were some of the highest social standing. The Slav Committees sent men and money without stint. Supported by these volunteers, who came under his command, General Chernaev obtained an almost omnipotent influence in Serbia: the Prince and the Government looked on him as the last hope. Chernaev desired to continue the struggle until Russia should be brought into action. On 16 September he proclaimed Milan as King of Serbia, hoping that this might afford a pretext for continuing the hostilities. This incident, however, remained without effect and was quickly disposed of. But when the suspension of arms expired without the Powers obtaining a regular armistice, and the Porte prolonged it for another seven days, Chernaev advised the Serbian Government to reject it unless the Porte consented to a regular armistice of six to eight weeks. Hostilities were therefore resumed on the 28th. Chernaev

[1] S. S. Tatiščev, *Imperator Alexandar*, II, p. 317.
[2] Schweinitz, I, p. 346.

hoped he would be able to rout the bulk of the Turkish army, which was massed on the left bank of the Morava and was exposed to an attack from three sides. A bloody battle causing great casualties on both sides lasted two days, but the Turks kept their positions. The situation remained practically unchanged for the next three weeks, when the Turks took the offensive, broke the Serbian line and occupied Djunis, which gave them a commanding position and free access to Belgrade. The Serbian army was defeated and began to retreat in disorder. Complete disaster was averted only by the immediate intervention of Russia, who sent an ultimatum to the Porte requesting it to cease hostilities in forty-eight hours and accept an armistice of six to eight weeks. The Porte accepted the Russian demands at once. The war was over, and a European conference was summoned in Constantinople to decide upon the conditions of peace.

When the Serbs entered the war they had hoped that it would be the signal for the other Balkan peoples to rise, and that the Slavs would consider it as their own work and give every assistance. The Slavophils had sent General Chernaev with a quarter of a million roubles and had promised their further help.[1] Among the Serbs in Austria the enthusiasm for the insurgents was even greater than in Serbia. Svetozar Miletić was tireless in urging upon Prince Milan the necessity of war. It was on his initiative that money and material had been collected and sent to the insurgents, despite the prohibition of the Hungarian authorities. In case of war he asked his countrymen to prepare themselves for further sacrifices, sacrifices which "nature, blood and humanity imposed upon them".[2] Opinion in Croatia was divided. Starčević and his followers favoured the annexation of Bosnia and Herzegovina by Austria, hoping thereby to unite all the Croats under the Habsburg's rule and transform the dual into a triple monarchy. But Strossmayer and Rački realised that the destiny of Croatia was tied up with that of Serbia and that Austria was their common enemy. They fought for an independent South Slav state and regarded the union of Serbia with Bosnia and Herzegovina as a first step towards that goal. Already

[1] *Zapisi Jevrema Grujića*, IV, p. 172.
[2] *Spomenica o herzegovačkom ustanku*, 1875, p. 18.

in August 1875 Strossmayer was invited by the Serbian Government to prepare detachments of volunteers and thus let Croatia participate in the liberation of Bosnia.[1] He used all his influence to induce the Bosnian Catholics and even the Moslems to collaborate with the Serbs, and helped Serbia in placing her war loan.[2] It seemed as if in case of war Serbia might reckon upon considerable help from her kinsmen in Austria, and that such a war, if coupled with an insurrection in Bulgaria, would make it impossible for Greece and Roumania to remain passive onlookers.

But these hopes were soon shattered. The insurrection in Bulgaria had been quelled before Serbia declared war. A detachment sent to incite the population had been met with indifference, and "the Bulgarians threw down or delivered to the Turks rifles distributed to them by the Serbian army".[3] Like Bulgaria, the Greek provinces in Turkey remained unmoved. Bulgaris informed the Serbian Government four days after the outbreak of hostilities that he had failed to organise a revolution owing to lack of funds. The response of the Slavs in Austria was almost insignificant. The war had only deepened the gulf between the two opposite parties in Croatia, and provoked a press campaign and some regrettable manifestations against Serbia.[4] The Catholic priests in Bosnia signed a memorandum against the union with Serbia and began to work against her.[5] Bishop Strossmayer indeed acquired a whole hospital with equipment and material and placed it at the disposal of the Serbian Government, but nis work was disapproved in Vienna and his action was paralysed by the anti-Serbian agitation. In Vojvodina the enthusiasm proved to be more platonic than real. The Hungarian Government arrested Miletić and some other prominent members of the Omladina, and the people showed little initiative. At first Russian help was scarce. The volunteers came in greater number only after Serbia had been obliged to ask for an armistice, and then their strength amounted to 2718 men only.[6] Roumania refused to let any war material for Serbia cross her frontier,

---

[1] F. Šišić, op. cit. p. 372.   [2] S.A., Orešković to Ristić, 25 May 1876.
[3] J. Ristić, op. cit. p. 124.
[4] S. Jovanović, Strosmajer i Rački, pp. 97–8.
[5] S.A., Cukić to Ristić, 18 July 1876.
[6] Zapisi Jevrema Grujića, III, p. 243.

despite the protest of the Serbian Minister and his reference to the Treaty of 1868, and Greece declared null the Treaty of 1867 and refused Serbia's invitation to join her.

In defence of the Christian cause Serbia and Montenegro stood alone, and even they were not in accord. Montenegro operated in Herzegovina, which was practically denuded of Turkish troops, and persistently refrained from directing her forces towards Serbia, when she was threatened by the Turkish invasion, despite repeated requests from Belgrade.[1] On the eve of the war Nicholas sent a letter to Francis Joseph expressing his regret at being obliged to diverge from the line of policy hitherto recommended to him, and his belief that in case of disaster his nation would find a protector in Austria.[2] Andrassy promised the Prince his protection but warned him that he would not accept any accomplished fact and that the ultimate issue of the struggle must be with Austria. At the same time he sent him a subsidy of 30,000 florins, which was being given him under the disguise of building roads, and dispatched von Toemel to Cetinje to prevent Montenegro from co-operating with the Serbian army and from doing anything that might be against Austrian interests.[3] In obedience to Andrassy's wishes, Nicholas sent back 600 volunteers who came from Boka, and recalled his army from Mostar.[4] He managed thus to remain victorious with his small army, while Serbia, with much greater forces, was defeated.

Serbia had sustained enormous sacrifices both in men and materials. One-sixth of her total population was mobilised and every tenth man was killed or wounded. "The war was conducted on our soil, Eastern Serbia was downtrodden and devastated; the number of men who abandoned their homes and lived without shelter approximated to 200,000."[5] The Government failed to conclude a loan abroad and was obliged to revert to an internal forced loan, requisitions, reduction of salaries, etc. They obtained a loan in Russia of 3,750,000 roubles, but one million only of this sum was sent to Serbia during the war. "Four-fifths of the whole war burden Serbia covered alone from her own resources."[6]

[1] S. Jovanović, *Vlada Milana Obrenovića*, I, p. 325.
[2] V. Djordjević, *op. cit.* pp. 386–7.   [3] *Ibid.* pp. 391–4.
[4] S.A., Belimarković's report from Cetinje, 25 Sept. 1876.
[5] S. Jovanović, *op. cit.* I, pp. 350–1.   [6] *Ibid.* p. 315.

Despite all these sacrifices, Serbia was not able to liberate her brethren. She was too weak and too unprepared to conduct the war with Turkey with any prospect of success. Even if she had overcome Turkey, she could not have obtained Bosnia and Herzegovina, since they had already been allotted to Austria. But the significance of her entry into war lay not in its immediate result, but in the moral influence it had on the South Slavs, and in the further events it conditioned.

Serbia was the first among the South Slav provinces to free herself from a foreign domination. As the most militant among them, and placed between Austria and Turkey, where her nationals remained still under foreign rule, she became naturally the bearer of their aspirations for liberation and union in an independent state. In going to war to help her brethren in Bosnia and Herzegovina, she showed that she was conscious of her national mission and ready to sustain all sacrifices to fulfil her rôle of Piedmont. These sacrifices cemented the feeling of union among the South Slavs and gave them the force to continue the struggle. Although Bosnia and Herzegovina were ceded to Austria at the Congress of Berlin, they never ceased being Serbian and never abandoned the struggle for complete liberation.

The Serbian War, on the other hand, had a decisive influence upon the further development of the crisis. It compelled Russia to enter the war, which though greatly disappointing Serbia, contributed undoubtedly to promote the aim for which she fought herself. For if Russia did not break up the Ottoman Empire, her victories none the less paved the way to its final liquidation. It is only when looked upon in that light—as a factor which strengthened the ties among the South Slavs, which weakened the Ottoman Empire and strengthened its enemies, the Balkan peoples—that the Serbian War acquires its real meaning and its full importance.

CHAPTER VI

✱

THE CONSTANTINOPLE CONFERENCE

THE defeat of Serbia presented again the question of Bosnia and Herzegovina in its original complexity. The Powers had failed to come to an agreement upon it, and hoped that Serbia would facilitate its solution. But her intervention had only complicated the matter still more. Beside Bosnia and Herzegovina, there was opened now the question of Serbia and Montenegro, whom Turkey desired to put under her own control. On the other hand the bloody suppression of the rising in Bulgaria made it impossible for the Powers to maintain her longer under the Turkish rule. This new situation, and the reaction which the events in the Balkans had upon public opinion in Great Britain and Russia, compelled the Powers to change their attitude. Russia was driven into a war against Turkey, which she entered in agreement with her allies, while the other Powers preserved neutrality. Thus the policy of partition, which Bismarck advocated from the outset, imposed itself by the force of circumstances.

At the same time while the wave of Slavophilism was spreading over Russia a deep indignation against the Turkish massacres in Bulgaria swayed the British people and created a movement which, though failing to impose itself upon the Government, had a powerful influence on their conduct up to the end of the crisis. The news of these massacres provoked a series of demonstrations and public meetings throughout the country. Lord Derby was flooded with petitions asking the Government to punish the wrongdoers and denouncing the policy of support of Turkey. Lectures and pamphlets on the Eastern Question helped to enlighten the public on the real character of the Turks and the sufferings of the Christians under their domination. The feeling of resentment and indignation permeated all classes and sections irrespective of political colour, and moved some of the most notable politicians and churchmen. On 6 September Gladstone published his pamphlet, *Bulgarian Horrors*, in which he attacked the British Government for its indifference and its tendency to "mitigate and soften as much as possible...the whole devilish enginery of crime....I entreat my countrymen," he wrote, "upon whom far more than perhaps any other people of Europe it depends, to require and insist that our Government which has been working in one direction, shall work in the other, and shall apply all its vigour to concur with the other States of Europe in obtaining the extinction of the Turkish executive power in Bulgaria. Let the Turks now carry away their abuses in the only possible manner, namely by carrying off themselves."[1]

Gladstone's pamphlet was followed by his speech at Blackheath, in which, after telling the story of the massacres, he declared: "It is the duty of Europe to stop what we now denounce. Honour be to the Power, whatsoever its name, that first steps in to stop them."[2]

Bulgarian atrocities gave Gladstone an opportunity to raise a general question of morals in international politics. Can a state seek the protection of its interests by maintaining the oppression and sufferings of other peoples? As a rule this question has little influence on the actual conduct of foreign policy, and in disregarding it Disraeli did nothing that Bismarck, Andrassy and the others were not doing. Disraeli considered British interests as identical with those of Turkey and defended the integrity of the Ottoman Empire in order to protect these interests. Gladstone rejected the idea that British interests were "the sole measure of right or wrong". Were they recognized as the only guidance of policy for Great Britain, then the other states could equally put forward their own interests, which would create a permanent conflict among them and a chaos. He asked his countrymen to follow "an established tradition older, wider, nobler far—a tradition not which disregards British interests but which teaches you to seek the promotion of those interests in obeying the dictates of honour and justice."[3]

Gladstone was not opposed to Disraeli's policy solely because he was supporting the Government which had committed these

---

[1] W. E. Gladstone, *Bulgarian Horrors*, p. 61.
[2] W. E. Gladstone, *Speech in Blackheath*, p. 19.
[3] J. Morley, *The Life of William Ewart Gladstone*, II, p. 175.

atrocities, but considered it wrong even from the point of British interests. England resisted the emancipation of the Balkan Christians and defended the integrity of Turkey in order to prevent Russia dominating in the Balkans. But such an attitude compelled the Balkan peoples to seek the Russian alliance and become the pillars of her influence in the East. It was precisely the protection of her interests that directed England to separate the Christians from Russia by promoting their emancipation. For a chain of free Christian states constituted a much stronger bulwark against Russia than Turkey. In Gladstone's opinion the interests of Britain were identical with those of the Christians and not with those of Turkey, as Disraeli believed. By taking the side of justice and liberty she promoted at the same time her own interests.

Gladstone's views found great support among his countrymen. But in putting himself at the head of this movement, essentially humanitarian though it was, he unintentionally gave it a political character and provoked a strong reaction among his opponents. "The Bulgarian atrocities became...a burning issue between the two great parties in the state, with the result that for the next two years major issues of foreign policy came to be considered not on their merits, but from the angle of party prejudice and with such passion and bias as is almost unequalled" in British history.[1]

The British Government was not indifferent to the trend of public opinion, much the less so as it was shared by their own followers and threatened to break up the party itself.

"The Bucks election shows that the agitation has not been without effect on our party", wrote Salisbury to Disraeli. "It is clear enough that the traditional Palmerstonian policy is at an end. We have not the power, even if we have the wish, to give back any of the revolted districts to the *discretionary* government of the Porte....

"I should like to submit for your consideration whether the opportunity should not be taken to exact some security for the good government of the Christians generally throughout the Turkish Empire. The Government of 1856 was satisfied with promises.... We must have something more than promises...."[2]

[1] R. W. Seton-Watson, *Disraeli, Gladstone and the Eastern Question*, p. 57.
[2] Disraeli, p. 70.

This was indeed a unique occasion for England and Russia to listen to the voice of their peoples and unite in a common endeavour to secure a better government for the Christians. Had Disraeli adopted Salisbury's proposal the whole crisis would have ended in a different way. This co-operation would have undoubtedly paved the way to a definite solution of the Eastern Question, and in so far changed the whole history of Europe. But Disraeli interpreted the feelings of the British people as a momentary aberration and believed that "the country will soon come to its senses".[1] The question of atrocities was for him a political duel with Gladstone, whom he believed to have taken the lead of this movement in order to drive the Conservatives from power. He could not adopt the policy advocated by Gladstone, and so confess that he had hitherto pursued a wrong course. He realised, however, that this agitation was depriving him of the support of the country at the moment when he most needed it. Encouraged by it, Russia might take an aggressive attitude which he would be unable to resist and which might put him in a humiliating position. To meet this eventuality it was most important for him to check the agitation and to restore his position. A counter-attack came soon from the Conservative ranks, and Disraeli himself, in his speech at Aylesbury, denounced the agitation as being worse than the atrocities themselves.[2]

It was in such an atmosphere that the Powers again approached the question of reforms, which they had in vain tried to solve for the last twelve months. Their views and their interests remained the same, while the anti-Turkish agitation in Russia and England, far from uniting these two Powers, came to complicate their relations still more. Hitherto Russia and Austria were the chief rivals in the Balkans; England stood aside waiting for an opportunity to break up the Dreikaiserbund. Henceforth the centre of conflict moved to Russia and England, whose antagonism dominated the crisis up to the end.

The first question the Powers had to decide was the establishment of a regular armistice for Serbia and Montenegro. On 1 September the Powers asked the Porte to grant an armistice of not less than one month. Disraeli hastened to press upon the

---

[1] Disraeli, p. 62.   [2] Ibid. p. 66.

Porte the necessity of peace, hoping "that the leading part, which England may take in obtaining an armistice, and afterwards in preliminaries, will make the excited 'Public' forget, or condone the Elliotiana". [1] He was most anxious, however, lest this "new point of departure", as he called it, should not be interpreted by his opponents as a concession made under the pressure of popular outcry. "The first and cardinal point at the present moment", he wrote to Stafford Northcote, "is that no member of the Government should countenance the idea that we are hysterically 'modifying' our policy, in consequence of the excited state of the public mind. If such an idea gets about, we shall become contemptible." [2]

The Russian Government believed that the British Cabinet would now be compelled to take a more active part in favour of the Christians. Pressed by a similar agitation at home, they saw in a close co-operation of the Powers the only way to a peaceful solution. By the end of August Gortchakov suggested that they should meet in a conference to decide upon the future organisation of the Balkans. He considered that a conference alone could provide a speedy and satisfactory solution and avert possible dangers. He hoped that the Powers, aroused by the Turkish atrocities, would unite in common action to protect the Christians. He was confident of the support of France and Italy, and considered also that the consent of England to autonomy was assured. The only opposition might come from Austria, but if Germany joined the other Powers, Austria could hardly resist their pressure. He therefore asked Bismarck, who often assured him of his readiness to return the services rendered in 1864–70, to take the initiative in proposing a European conference. [3]

This idea met with strong resistance from Bismarck. He considered the conference dangerous both to European peace and Germany's relations to her friends. It would bring the existence of the Dreikaiserbund into question, as it would inevitably deepen the divergences between Russia and Austria. Germany would be compelled to take sides, which she could not do without hurting one of her allies. Even if the Powers came to an agreement he doubted the success of their action in Constantinople. He refused to propose a conference, and even

---

[1] Disraeli, p. 51.   [2] *Ibid.* p. 61.   [3] G.P. No. 231.

to attend it without a fixed programme and a previous under-standing among the Powers which would guarantee its success.[1]

Great Britain and Austria were confidentially sounded as to their disposition towards a conference, but they refused it too. Andrassy argued that the war had not brought about a new situation and that the conference lacked a practical basis. The chances of a definite arrangement were now less than before the war, when it was still possible to ask from the Porte such reforms as would give some guarantees of stability; now this argument could no longer be used, and all that was left in favour of the Christians were the agreements which had been reached in Vienna, Berlin and Reichstadt. "I have believed from the outset", wrote Andrassy to Novikov, "that a replastering was the only possibility. Now even a temporary solution was more difficult than before the war. The order of things which would come out of the present situation would satisfy neither Mussul-mans nor Christians, neither Russia nor us."[2] All these arguments were calculated to show that if Russia wished to create a satis-factory arrangement, a conference was not the means of attaining it. This intimation was undoubtedly understood in St Petersburg. Gortchakov told Schweinitz that an agreement with Austria would be easily reached if the programme of "away with the Turks" were to become a reality.[3] In fact, it was not his disbelief in a possibility of a satisfactory solution, but his fear of it, that made Andrassy oppose the idea of a conference. Swayed by the atrocity agitation Britain might easily go far enough to meet Russia's wishes, and an arrangement might be reached contrary to the interests of Austria, yet such as she could neither oppose nor prevent. All the same Andrassy did not reject the conference altogether. If Russia were to insist upon it he would not oppose, but he requested that the programme should be fixed by the three Powers in advance. He suggested as the basis: *status quo* for Serbia and Montenegro with some territorial rectification for the latter, and for Bosnia and Herzegovina the reforms proposed in his Note with the guarantees contained in the Berlin Memo-randum. In short, Andrassy did not mean to go beyond his

[1] G.P. No. 228.
[2] A.A., Andrassy to Novikov, 6 Sept. 1876.
[3] Schweinitz, I, p. 345.

earlier proposals for Bosnia and Herzegovina, despite the fact that the whole of the northern half of European Turkey was in revolt, and that the question was no longer one of amelioration of conditions of one or two provinces, but of the whole system of Turkish rule.

The plan of a European Conference was thus frustrated from the outset. The negative attitude of Austria and Germany induced Russia to clarify her relations with her allies and see whether a common action with them was possible, or whether she would be obliged to seek for other means to achieve her aims. To this Bismarck himself soon gave an occasion. At the beginning of September he advised his Emperor to send a special envoy to the Tsar, who attended the manœuvres at Warsaw, in order to learn his real intentions and his relations with Austria and England, and to assure him that whatever be his decision Germany would preserve the same friendly attitude towards him which he had preserved towards her in 1864, 1866 and 1870. In proposing this visit, Bismarck pointed out that the Tsar was in a difficult position owing to the Slavophil agitation, and that Germany's refusal to propose a conference might have created the feeling with him that he was treated coolly. In such a situation the feeling of isolation. might easily overcome the Tsar and give the anti-German elements, to whom, Bismarck believed, Gortchakov was not unsympathetic, an opportunity of influencing his decisions. It was necessary therefore to persuade the Tsar that he could count upon Germany. Gortchakov's arrival at Warsaw indicated that some political move was meditated. He was now more inclined "to make front with England against Andrassy" than to come to an understanding with him. He might even enter into closer contact with Andrassy's enemies, especially Prince Albrecht, and try to bring Andrassy down. It was necessary therefore to lend the Tsar a trustworthy channel which would enable him to disclose his more intimate intentions of which he would perhaps not like to write.

On the other hand there were also possibilities of a rapprochement between Britain and Russia. The popular excitement in England and the haste with which Derby proposed an armistice made Bismarck fear lest he might seek an understanding with Russia in order to escape more serious consequences. He did not believe they could agree to anything more than an armistice. But if an understanding were in prospect which would influence future relations with the friendly Powers, Germany would help it and mediate to give it the form acceptable to Austria. For this reason she must be informed of the relations of Russia with England and Austria and of their influence upon the position of France. Germany could accept all that Russia and Austria agreed upon, she could also accept all that Russia and England agreed upon, under the condition of her mediating to bring Austria into it. In the event of a more permanent understanding between England and Russia, Germany's participation in it would have been perhaps more natural than her presence in the Dreikaiserbund. There was little probability of such an understanding, but he thought it advisable to give Russia assurances even for such an eventuality.[1]

Bismarck had reason perhaps to fear Anglo-Russian co-operation in Eastern affairs, for it would have brought Austria into a very difficult position. But it was doubtful whether it would have been possible to give this co-operation a form acceptable to Austria, as he desired. Russia and England could have acted together, for they were both inspired by the desire of ameliorating the lot of the Christians. The position of Austria was a different one: she could not consent to reforms which would have deprived her of Bosnia and Herzegovina; and such were all serious and real reforms. All these difficulties and dangers could be avoided if Russia went to war. Bismarck's desire to convince her that she could count upon Germany whatever be her decision, could have had one purpose only: to encourage Russia into action.

It was in this sense that Bismarck's declaration was understood by the Tsar and Gortchakov. But they wanted Germany's support against Austria, who opposed Russian demands, and not against Turkey. The Tsar expressed the hope to General Manteuffel, who was sent as a special envoy owing to the personal favours he enjoyed at the Russian Court, that in case of a conflict with Austria Germany would act in the same manner as he did in 1870. He believed that if Germany sided with Russia in the question of reform, Austria would not push her resistance so far as to risk a war. Gortchakov,

[1] G.P. No. 229.

on his part, endeavoured to learn whether Bismarck was prepared to help Russia in her efforts to arrive at a pacific solution. He told Manteuffel that although a war against Turkey would be very popular, the Government was strong enough to resist the popular stream and pursue a policy dictated by Russian interests. These interests demanded peace and the Tsar would exert all his forces to solve the Eastern Question in a peaceful way. Russia demanded real guarantee that the Christians would be treated well and enjoy protection and security. This was for her a point of honour, and only if it were contested would war become unavoidable. Germany could help Russia to avoid this war if she adopted her views and supported them openly. "Russia has a firm resolve to maintain the Dreikaiserbund", he said to Manteuffel, "but hitherto she has made concessions to Austria in all negotiations with her, without thereby improving the matter, and he, the Prince, has the conviction that if Germany supported the views of Russia in any positive form, Austria would join him completely."[1]

Manteuffel's mission proved to be a *faux pas*, which brought home quite unexpected results. It made clear to Bismarck that a platonic declaration of friendship was not sufficient to remove the feeling from Russia that his reserved attitude had hitherto in fact enabled Austria to resist or counteract all Russia's efforts for reforms. The Tsar's question as to the attitude of Germany in the event of war with Austria, and Gortchakov's invitation to prove his friendship in practice by supporting Russia's endeavours for a peaceful solution, caused great embarrassment to Bismarck. He could not reject these demands without showing that his declaration of friendship was a mere farce, and strengthening the already prevalent conviction that he was in fact on the side of Austria. But neither could he accept them without abandoning Austria and probably bringing the Dreikaiserbund to an end. All his efforts to maintain that alliance by imposing co-operation upon his allies became inadequate at the moment when Russia refused to make further concessions to Austria and desired to take a course dictated by her own interests. The question of choice, which Bismarck had made in his heart much earlier, had to be faced now in all its complexity.

[1] G.P. No. 231.

At first Bismarck pretended that no questions were directed to him through Manteuffel and sent no answer. But Gortchakov wished to force him to declare himself one way or the other, and instructed his Ambassador to inform him whether an answer was to be expected from Berlin as to the attitude of Germany in the event of Russia being compelled to take a separate position, and as to what Bismarck proposed instead of a European conference.[1] Bismarck refused to give an answer. He ignored the second question, and replied to the first that an answer to it was given in the personal letters exchanged by the two Sovereigns at the occasion of Manteuffel's visit.[2] But the Tsar pressed him through Werder, the German military attaché, to obtain an answer. On 1 October Werder wired: "The Emperor of Russia has said verbally in his answer to his Majesty the Kaiser and to Field-Marshal von Manteuffel, he hoped that if it should come to a war with Austria, his Majesty the Kaiser would act in the same manner as he did in 1870. The Emperor of Russia speaks of it to me almost every day, and desires an urgent confirmation."[3] Bismarck denied that such a question was transmitted by Manteuffel and the Tsar's letter, and pretended that the "separate position" mentioned in the Tsar's letter was understood by him as a war against Turkey, and not Austria.[4] It is easy, however, to see from Manteuffel's report and from the Tsar's letter that in asking Germany as to her attitude in the event of a war with Austria, Russia did not intend to attack her unprovoked, but desired solely to be certain whether Germany would support her programme of reforms, which Austria was opposed to, and which therefore might provoke a conflict with her. It was believed in Russia that if Germany supported her demands Austria would accept them too, and in that way a peaceful solution could be arrived at. Had the Tsar by the "separate position" meant a war with Turkey, how could he have talked of satisfying his honour without disturbing the peace? Besides, why should he ask about Germany's attitude in that event after Manteuffel's communication?

Bismarck considered that the whole affair was a trap designed by Gortchakov to compromise him with the Tsar, or to estrange

[1] G.P. No. 234.   [2] G.P. Nos. 234–5.
[3] G.P. No. 239.   [4] G.P. Nos. 240–1.

him from Austria and England. He had undoubtedly reason to be discontented with Gortchakov, but he could hardly expect that the Russians would remain blind for ever to the fact that his attitude was not friendly to them and that it helped the Austrians to frustrate their plans. It was only natural that Gortchakov should take the first opportunity offered to him to learn the real intentions of Germany. That this inquiry placed Bismarck in an awkward position was due only to his double policy.

Bismarck advised his Emperor not to answer the Werder question. Should it be repeated in an official form, he intended to ask previously to what purpose Gortchakov needed this declaration and what use he would make of it.[1] In order to hide his responsibility, he ordered that all the documents relating to this affair should be removed from the Foreign Office.[2] He could pretend that the reports of the military attachés were sent to the War Office and were decided on by it. But his Emperor was deeply impressed by the Tsar's question, and desired to help him. He found it difficult to remain passive in the Eastern troubles, and thought it his duty to take a more pronounced attitude against Turkey. He insisted upon a verbal answer being given to the Tsar through Werder.[3]

It was only a month later that Bismarck answered the Tsar's question. Schweinitz, who was returning to St Petersburg, was told that Germany could not discuss this question before it was officially formulated, and even then not *in abstracto*, without its concrete conditions. At any rate, before answering it Germany would intervene to prevent a conflict between Russia and Austria. Should this prove to be impossible and a war ensue, she would remain neutral. But if the war provoked intervention of the other Powers, she might be compelled by her own interests to abandon that neutrality. It was not in her interest to see a substantial and lasting reduction of the power of Russia; neither could she consent to the independence or position of Austria as a Great Power being endangered. Schweinitz was instructed to make use of these ideas so far as the situation required. He had to assure the Tsar that the Emperor William assented completely to his expectations. This was to serve as an answer

[1] G.P. No. 241.   [2] G.P. No. 242.   [3] G.P. Nos. 243, 245.

to the Tsar's question and was therefore to be made verbally, and in reference to his latest declaration regarding his decision to wage a war against Turkey if the conference failed. He was also to be assured that in case of such a war, Germany would use her good offices to keep Austria and England neutral.[1]

By delaying his answer for more than a month Bismarck gained in time and let events develop and create a situation in which it lost much of its importance. He thus succeeded in avoiding the dangers which he had brought upon himself by his declaration of friendship. But his silence and the ambiguity of his answer indicated clearly that he did not mean to abandon his attitude of reserve and that no help could be expected from him for Russia's reform plans. This meant that Austria would continue to obstruct all real reforms.

Meanwhile the Turks were in no mood to listen to the advice of the British Government. They believed that despite all the anti-Turkish agitation England could not fail to defend her interests in the East if they came into jeopardy. On 30 August the Sultan Murad V was deposed and replaced by Abdul Hamid. Midhat Pasha, who was the chief actor in this plot, obtained an almost omnipotent influence with the new Sultan. He intended not only to take full advantage of the victory, but also to get rid of the interference of the Powers. He refused to grant the armistice unless his preliminaries of peace were accepted simultaneously.

Derby was indignant at the behaviour of the Porte. He asked his Ambassador to tell the Porte that "in the extreme case of Russia declaring war against Turkey, H.M.G. would find it practically impossible to interfere in defence of the Ottoman Empire".[2] But he found little support from his Ambassador for this policy. Elliot wrote to him on 4 September that his

conduct here has never been guided by any sentimental affection for them, but by a firm determination to uphold the interests of Great Britain to the utmost of my power; and that those interests are deeply engaged in preventing the disruption of the Turkish Empire is a conviction which I share in common with the most eminent statesmen who have directed our foreign policy....We may and must feel indignant at the needless and monstrous severity with which the Bulgarian insurrection was put down, but the necessity

[1] G.P. No. 251.   [2] R. W. Seton-Watson, *op. cit.* p. 62.

which exists for England to prevent changes from occurring here which would be most detrimental to ourselves, is not affected by the question whether it was 10,000 or 20,000 persons who perished in the suppression. We have been upholding what we know to be a semi-civilised nation, liable under certain circumstances to be carried into fearful excesses: but the fact of this having been just now strikingly brought home to us all cannot be a sufficient reason for abandoning a policy which is the only one that can be followed with a due regard to our own interests.[1]

Convinced that British interests demanded the preservation of Turkey, Elliot endeavoured to preserve the unrivalled influence he had wielded in Constantinople ever since the deposition of Abdul Azis. While advising the Porte to grant the armistice he endeavoured to find a formula acceptable to it. He asked Lord Derby to inform him of the conditions of peace which he would be prepared to support so as to be able to calm the Turks.[2]

Beside Elliot the Porte was also supported by the Austrian Ambassador, and in fact by Andrassy himself. Although joining the Powers in demanding an armistice from the Porte, Andrassy instructed his Ambassador "to ask at the same time that the Porte should make known the conditions of peace to which it pretended".[3] Already by the end of August Andrassy warned the British Government against too radical reforms. He feared lest Derby, in his desire to prevent war, should go too far in meeting the wishes of Russia, which would place Austria in an awkward position. The situation, as he represented it, was such that the Powers could not exceed the limits set up by his Note, without abandoning the principle of the integrity of the Ottoman Empire. There was no alternative between his Note and partition, and if the Powers were not prepared for partition, they could not ask for more than had already been asked and granted, without affecting their own interests.[4]

The attitude of Elliot and Andrassy was not without influence on the British Government. On 11 September Derby proposed the following bases of peace: (1) Virtual *status quo* for Serbia and Montenegro; (2) administrative reforms in the nature of local autonomies for Bosnia and Herzegovina; (3) some similar

[1] B.A., Derby to Salisbury, 20 Nov. 1876.
[2] B.A., Elliot to Derby, 6 Sept. 1876.
[3] B.A., Elliot to Derby, 5 Sept. 1876.
[4] A.C., Andrassy to Wolkenstein, 17 Sept. 1876.

guarantees against future abuses in Bulgaria; and (4) no changes in the Treaty of Paris[1].

These bases were at once accepted by Russia, but they were refused by Turkey and strongly criticised by both Elliot and Andrassy. The Turks therefore gave only a suspension of arms for ten days. Elliot objected to autonomy as being impracticable and inacceptable to the Porte. Andrassy objected to both autonomy and the reforms for Bulgaria. He marshalled once more his old arguments against the autonomy, trying to prove that it would break up the Ottoman Empire. In a dispatch to his chargé d'affaires in London, Count Wolkenstein, he asked Lord Derby whether he was prepared to impose autonomy upon the Porte, and whether he could do so and yet maintain the Ottoman Empire. "Unless we are prepared to say that the Turkish Empire must fall", he wrote, "we cannot go beyond certain limits, and must confine ourselves to such conditions as can be imposed upon the Porte by pacific means."[2] To the British Ambassador he said that "in any proposal made to the Porte some reference should be made to the reforms already agreed upon in order that the Christians may understand that it is only such reforms that it is intended to obtain for them".[3] Andrassy's opinion that autonomy would break up the Ottoman Empire is interesting as proving indirectly that that Empire could be preserved only by maintenance of the system of oppression. But what he really feared was not that Turkey would refuse autonomy, but that she should accept it, for in that event the road to Austria's expansion in the East would be closed. His arguments against the impracticability of this organisation and the dangers of Turkey rejecting it could not conceal the real reasons of his opposition.

Although ready at the beginning of September "to dictate to the Porte", Disraeli did not believe in the success of this policy.

"I cannot help doubting," he wrote to Derby, "whether any arrangement...is now practicable. I fear affairs will linger on till the spring, when Russia and Austria will march their armies into the Balkans, either simultaneously and with a certain understanding, or one following the other's example from jealousy and fear.

[1] B.A., Derby to Elliot, 11 Sept. 1876.
[2] A.C., Andrassy to Wolkenstein, 17 Sept. 1876.
[3] B.A., Buchanan to Derby, 20 Sept. 1876.

"As Count Andrassy observed to Sir Andrew Buchanan, 'there is no alternative between the notes of this year and the solution of the Eastern Question.'

"I think the probability is that it will be 'the solution of the Eastern Question', and, if so, it is wise that we should take the lead in it. Our chance of success will be greater because from us it will be unexpected....

"Whatever the jealousies of Austria and Russia, they would prefer a division of the Balkan spoil under the friendly offices of England to a war between themselves certainly, and perhaps with others."[1]

But Andrassy's opposition to radical changes calmed Disraeli's fears and encouraged him to fall back on his former line of policy. He proposed now that an understanding should be reached with Austria and Germany for a common resistance to Russia's pretensions. Within a month he entertained both the idea of partition of Turkey, in which he desired to take a lead, and of a coalition to defend her against Russia. During the whole crisis he vacillated between these two extremes without ever knowing which one of them he was really pursuing. And the lack of any clear policy left his colleagues at the mercy of Gladstonian agitation and divided the Cabinet into "seven parties or policies", as he wrote to the Queen a year later, making it impossible for him to take any decided measure for the protection of British interests. These divergences in the Cabinet began to be felt already at this moment. On 23 September Salisbury wrote to propose an understanding with Russia for the settlement of this question—a policy which was diametrically opposed to Disraeli's newest plan of a common action with Austria and Germany against Russia.

"Our best chance of coming to a peaceful issue of these perplexities", wrote Salisbury, "is—in my belief—to come to an early understanding with Russia. Our danger is that we should make that result impossible by hanging on to the coat-tails of Austria. Austria has good reason to resist the faintest approach to self-government in the revolted provinces. Her existence would be menaced if she were hedged on the south by a line of Russian satellites. But her existence is no longer of the importance to us that it was in former times. Her vocation in Europe is gone. She was a counterpoise to France and a barrier against Russia; but France is gone, and the development of Russia is chiefly in the regions where Austria could not, and if she

[1] Disraeli, p. 52.

could would not, help to check it. We have no reason, therefore, for sharing Austria's tremors: and if we can get terms from Russia that suit us, it would be most unwise to reject them because they are not to the taste of Austria.

"I venture to press this point, because I see that Austria is urging a return to a state of things in which the lives and property of the Christian populations of the three provinces will be dependent on the promises of the Porte: and that in this policy she will be backed by the advice of Buchanan and Elliot. I feel convinced that such an arrangement, though comfortable to the pure Palmerstonian tradition, is not suitable for the exigency; and that it would not be supported in Parliament."[1]

Salisbury's proposal was not accepted by Disraeli, who was now occupied with thoughts of resisting Russia. Derby explained to Andrassy that by autonomy he meant an "administrative autonomy which would give the population some control over their own local affairs". On the 25th the Powers communicated to the Porte the following bases of peace: (1) Virtual *status quo* for Serbia and Montenegro. (2) That the Porte should undertake in a protocol to be signed at Constantinople by the representatives of the Mediating Powers to grant to Bosnia and Herzegovina a system of local administrative autonomy, by which is to be understood a system of local institutions which shall give the population some control over their own local affairs, and guarantees against the exercise of arbitrary authority. There is to be no question of the creation of a tributary state. (3) Guarantees of a similar kind to be provided against maladministration in Bulgaria.[2] But Russia was not satisfied with Derby's interpretation of autonomy and reserved her definite opinion on it. Andrassy, on the other hand, remained hostile even to the word "autonomy". He instructed his Ambassador to ask the Porte to omit the words "autonomy" and "protocol" in its reply.[3] The Porte not only omitted them, but protested against such demands. On the 28th hostilities were resumed, as Serbia refused to consent to further suspension of arms.

After a month of futile deliberations the Powers failed to induce the Porte to grant a regular armistice or to agree among

---

[1] Disraeli, pp. 70–1.   [2] D.F., No. 78.
[3] B.A., Elliot to Derby, 29 Sept. 1876, No. 1079, conf.

themselves as to the bases of peace. The conviction was growing in Russia that a satisfactory solution could be reached by a war only. But before having recourse to arms she made one more effort to come to a peaceful arrangement. On 26 September Gortchakov proposed to the Great Powers that in the event of Turkey refusing to grant an armistice or accept the peace conditions of the Powers, Russia should occupy Bulgaria and Austria Bosnia, and the other Powers send their fleets to Constantinople.

This proposal was communicated to the Vienna Government by a special envoy, Count Sumarakov, who took with him an autographed letter from the Tsar for Francis Joseph. The Tsar drew the attention of the Austrian Emperor to the difficult conditions in the Balkans and the danger of their creating complications in Europe. Russia and Austria were directly interested in the East and "ought to come to an agreement or to take separate ways", wrote the Tsar. In his opinion the Powers should endeavour to obtain previously a regular armistice. He accepted the bases proposed by England, which were in fact but "an enlargement of the principle of communal, district and municipal autonomies the germ of which was laid in the Note of 30 December". He understood Austria's repugnance to a great Slav State, and rejected that idea too. But he considered that "some piecemeal autonomies, without cutting off political ties, would not have the same inconvenience". As a neighbour Austria would always be able to influence and control their development. He wished to be certain whether this result could be achieved "quickly and efficiently through an *entente* of the Great Powers", and whether in case of its being frustrated "by lack of accord among the Cabinets, or by loss of time, or finally by the obstinacy of the two parties to refuse every arrangement", Austria was prepared to co-operate with Russia in imposing it by force. In that event he proposed that Austria should occupy Bosnia and Russia Bulgaria. "If at the same time", the Tsar added, "the Great Powers could be induced to enter the Bosphorus with their fleets to protect the Christians, a similar demonstration would probably be sufficient to crush the arrogance of the Turks and force them to submit to the decisions of Europe." Should these hopes be frustrated, however, and the force of events push

Turkey towards complete dissolution, the provisions of the Reichstadt Agreement, so far as they provided for compensations for Austria, would remain in force. The Tsar was ready to examine the views of Francis Joseph with a sincere wish to come to an understanding, and prayed him to have regard to his position, which obliged him to take a clear and decided course and to pursue it energetically.[1]

Francis Joseph answered that he agreed with communal and administrative autonomies, but that he could not accept the political ones. He could not consent to the proposed occupation of Bulgaria and Bosnia, because this would incite the other Christians to revolt. Besides, such an occupation could not be temporary, for neither Russia nor Austria could abandon these provinces to the mercy of the Turks after having pacified them; while their establishment there would provoke the protests of the other Powers. He suggested that a European commission should be summoned to work out the details of peace and that the fleets of the Great Powers should be used as a coercive measure to impose them upon Turkey. Should she refuse them, the impossibility of maintaining her domination would become clear to the world. Her resistance would probably be followed by new massacres. "At that moment our intervention, which certain Powers oppose at present, would be accepted, even desired by the whole of Europe." The purpose of this intervention would be the realisation of the programme of Reichstadt, and the definite occupation of territories designed in that agreement. But if the Tsar desired to precipitate the process of the dissolution of Turkey, he would not oppose it, but would occupy the territories necessary for the protection of his own interests. In this case as in every other he would remain faithful to the Reichstadt agreement as regards the definite organisation of the Balkan Peninsula.[2]

Andrassy believed that Sumarakov's mission was the consequence of Manteuffel's visit to Warsaw. He did not know the purpose of Manteuffel's mission, but he was informed that the Emperor William had promised his nephew to stand by him "under all circumstances".[3] Fearing unpleasant eventualities,

---

[1] R.D., the Tsar to Francis Joseph, 23 Sept. 1876.
[2] A.A., Francis Joseph to the Tsar, 30 Oct. 1876.   [3] Andrassy, II, p. 357.

he visited the German Ambassador on 13 September and communicated to him "one point" from the Reichstadt Agreement
which had not hitherto been communicated to Germany. He
informed him specifically about the organisation of the Balkans
in case of victory of the Christians, which he had proposed at
Reichstadt. Gortchakov did not wish it to be communicated to
Germany, fearing lest England should learn of it, and Andrassy
asked therefore that the strictest secrecy should be observed.[1]
Sumarakov's visit induced him to send a special envoy to
Bismarck to learn his views and intentions. On 3 October
Baron Münch went to Varzin on a secret visit, with copies of
the Tsar's letter and the Austrian answer. Apart from fears
of a Russo-German understanding, to which he attributed
Russia's latest proposals, Andrassy apprehended also the hostility of Italy, whose press exposed Austria's manœuvres to get
hold of Bosnia and Herzegovina and had started a sharp campaign
against her. He instructed Münch to draw Bismarck's attention
to the danger of an attack from Italy and to propose to him a
defensive alliance in the event of Germany being attacked by
France and Italy, or Austria being attacked by Russia and
Italy.[2]

Bismarck told Münch about the Tsar's question and his
reasons for avoiding an answer, which would have had a point
against Austria. For the same reason he could not enter into an
alliance with Austria, as it would have a point against Russia.
He did not believe Italy could wage a war against Austria,
but if this should happen, it would provoke indignation in
Germany, and the goodwill of her Chancellor would give good
chances for Germany's support. He could, however, conceive
of an alliance with Austria, but it must be an organic one
and sanctioned by the Parliaments. It could come only as
the result of more critical times, and the starting-point for it
must be the regulation of the question of North Silesia by
the suppression of the clauses relating to it in the Treaty
of Prague. For the present Germany must endeavour in her
own interest to prevent her neighbours from ceasing to be

[1] G.P. No. 233.
[2] A.A., Bericht des Baron Münch über seine Unterredung mit Fürst
Bismarck. Wien, 8 Oct. 1876.

Great Powers, for she could not put herself between the two revengeful peoples of France and Russia.

Bismarck had nothing against Austria accepting Russia's proposal for occupation. The fear of Russia establishing herself in Bulgaria seemed to him to be unjustified, for this would have weakened her, and besides, the Tsar had no such pretensions. England would not allow this, and Austria was in a favourable position, which she should not lose, to be on this point at one mind with England, and she should therefore avoid embroiling herself in the natural antagonism between Russia and Britain. Münch noticed that Britain played an important part in Bismarck's calculations, and concluded from his utterances that he counted upon the later phase of the Eastern crisis putting Russia, France and Italy on one side, and Germany, Austria and England on the other.[1]

Russia's proposal for occupation and a naval demonstration was rejected by all the Powers. Austria refused the occupation, but accepted the naval demonstration; England on her part refused the proposal altogether. Disraeli considered it as a "false move" to which Gortchakov was encouraged by Gladstone. His distrust towards Russia was only increased by the arrival of the Russian volunteers in Serbia and the renewal of hostilities. Both he and Lord Derby considered that the Tsar and his Government were playing a double game, and "while ostensibly promoting peace, are by indirect means making it impossible".[2] "The position of affairs never was more critical or more difficult", wrote Disraeli to Lady Bradford. "I don't believe the Russians have any money to make war, but they cannot resist what, according to their own language, 'they never had before': England on their side. Is it?"[3]

The fear of a Russian invasion of Turkey induced the British Government to take one more step to put an end to hostilities. On 5 October they requested the Porte to grant an armistice and suggested that the conference should meet to deliberate on the terms of peace. Elliot was instructed "to tell the Porte that the recommendation of the armistice by England was England's last

---

[1] A.A., Bericht des Baron Münch über seine Unterredung mit Fürst Bismarck. Wien, 8 Oct. 1876.
[2] Disraeli, p. 75.   [3] *Ibid.* p. 78.

step; that, if refused, she should attempt no longer to arrest the destruction of the Turkish Empire, but leave her to her fate; and that our Ambassador would leave Constantinople".[1]

Disraeli believed, however, that Gortchakov wanted war and that he would strike if Turkey refused the armistice. He was informed of a plan of General Fadeef, laid before the Russian Government, "in order to settle the fate of European Turkey in spite of the maritime Powers...". "From this and from other documents...I conclude the invasion of Turkey and conquest of Constantinople may be rapid", he wrote to Derby. "Constantinople occupied by the Russians, while the British fleet was in Beshika Bay, would be the most humiliating event, that has ever occurred to England."[2] He pressed upon Derby the necessity of making military preparations to come in time to the help of Turkey, as he feared "that Turkey, feeling she is utterly deserted, may make some mad compact with Russia, opening the Straits, and giving her complete control over the Asiatic shore".[3] He also asked the War Secretary and the First Lord of the Admiralty to consider the question of sending a British force and fleet to Constantinople, and to present this proposal to the Cabinet.[4] At the same time he suggested to Derby to "negotiate a treaty with Germany to maintain the present *status quo* generally. Not an alliance offensive and defensive", he wrote, "but a treaty for the maintenance of the *status quo*. This would make us easy about Constantinople, and relieve Bismarck of his real bugbear, the eventual alliance of England and France, and the loss of his two captured provinces."[5]

There is no trace of such an overture being made to Bismarck, probably because Derby was sceptical of its success. He only expressed in Berlin his "earnest wish" to act in concert with Germany. But the Queen used her connections with the German Court to influence the Emperor in favour of an understanding with England. Her efforts remained, however, without result, for Bismarck, whom Derby believed "would probably not be sorry to see England and Russia quarrel",[6] strongly dissuaded his Emperor from interfering in Russian affairs, even by advice.[7]

[1] *Ibid*. p. 80.   [2] *Ibid*. p. 99.   [3] *Ibid*. p. 100.
[4] *Ibid*. pp. 98–9.   [5] *Ibid*. p. 81.   [6] Queen Victoria, p. 490.
[7] G.P. No. 248.

The Tsar was resolved to have recourse to arms if the Powers failed to provide an efficacious solution. As this war would bring about a definite solution of the Eastern Question, which was one of the conditions of Austria's co-operation, he hoped that she would not refuse to join him. In a letter of 10 October he proposed the rupture of diplomatic relations with Turkey if she refused the armistice. In that event he would mobilise his troops and concert further steps with Austria. But even if Turkey accepted the armistice he feared the break-up of the Conference. He could not accept an inefficacious solution and feared that an agreement among the Powers, whose interests were divergent, would be difficult to achieve. He foresaw also that Turkey would refuse any clear programme. If he remained in a minority at the Conference—which was possible—he would recall his Ambassador and retain his liberty of action. Such an attitude might have as its final result the realisation of the programme of Reichstadt, since Austria considered a definite solution to be more in her own and the Russian interest. He supposed that Austria had in view the possibility of the dissolution of Turkey and a common war against her. The coming spring would be most suitable for military operations and he was therefore ready to come to an agreement about it.[1]

Austria was not inclined to precipitate the break-up of Turkey. She stuck to "natural dissolution" and the "conviction of Europe" of the impossibility of the preservation of Turkey as the conditions of her co-operation. Francis Joseph reminded the Tsar in his letter of 23 October, that it was not his intention nor his interest to precipitate the downfall of the Ottoman Empire. He foresaw it and therefore had at Reichstadt concerted with Russia as to what should come in its place, but he could admit of a joint intervention only when Europe became convinced of its necessity and desired it. He believed this moment would come soon, for Turkey would dissolve of herself. He held this to be the best way of protecting their common interests, but if Russia chose to act on her own, he would not oppose it, and was ready to regulate the details in a treaty to be concluded.[2]

[1] A.A., the Tsar to Francis Joseph, 10 Oct. 1876.
[2] A.A., Francis Joseph to the Tsar, 23 Oct. 1876.

The Tsar expressed his regret at Austria refusing co-operation, but he could not wait for a natural disruption of Turkey and leave the Christians unprotected. He did not believe Europe would make an end to Turkish misrule. He was resolved to accomplish alone what was considered right and necessary by the whole world.[1]

Negotiations soon opened between Vienna and St Petersburg with a view to regulating their mutual relations in the event of war. Before the Conference of Constantinople opened, Austria secured Russia's promise—which was inserted later in the convention itself—not to ask an autonomy for Bosnia and Herzegovina going far beyond the reforms proposed by the Andrassy Note and the Berlin Memorandum. Thus Russia went to the conference with her hands bound. She could not demand serious reforms for Bosnia and Herzegovina but only for Bulgaria, where she was sure to meet with an equally determined opposition on the part of England.

Meanwhile the Turks flatly rejected all the proposals in spite of the pressure put upon them by the British Government. That they dared to oppose the united action of the Great Powers was undoubtedly due to their belief that the latter were not really united, an opinion which the attitude of the Austrian and British Ambassadors helped to confirm. Elliot was consulted by the Sultan both *à propos* of the first and the second proposal of the Powers.[2] Derby's warnings to the Porte lost much of their vigour and meaning when they had to be communicated by Elliot, who could not help feeling that the objections of the Porte were based upon too good grounds, and actively assisted the Porte in providing a form which would avoid all that was prejudicial to Turkish interests.[3] The Porte, eager to avoid European intervention, found in him not only a good adviser, but an encouragement to go farther in opposing the Powers than perhaps he himself intended. Even the threat of Elliot leaving Constantinople was without effect. It finally consented to grant an armistice, but not less than six months. The idea of so long an armistice was to gain time and introduce some reforms

---

[1] A.A., the Tsar to Francis Joseph, 3 Nov. 1876.
[2] B.A., Elliot to Derby, 24 Sept. No. 1058, very conf.
[3] B.A., Elliot to Derby, 29 and 30 Sept. 1876, Nos. 1081, 1086.

E

which would make European intervention unnecessary. Six months later feeling in Europe would be calmed and the Powers who had an interest in maintaining Turkey would satisfy themselves with renewed promises on her part, while the general situation would be more in her favour.

The British Government at once accepted the armistice of six months, and asked Germany to press Russia to accept it too. Disraeli considered that the Porte had done very wisely in extending the armistice, hoping that it would give time for the British public to calm and "shut up" Gladstone.[1] France and Austria also accepted the armistice, but Germany reserved her opinion. Russia rejected it altogether on the ground that she could not press it upon Serbia and Montenegro, and that the commercial and financial world of Europe would suffer by it. In fact Gortchakov knew that the six months' armistice was a manœuvre inspired by Elliot, to evade the action of the Great Powers.[2]

Russia's refusal of the Turkish proposal brought the matter to a deadlock. The British Government declared itself unable to withhold its consent and unwilling to take any further step, though not opposed to a shorter term of armistice if granted by the Porte itself. On Shouvalov's suggestion, Derby invited Bismarck to take the initiative and make proposals for further action such as might be accepted by all the Powers. This Bismarck refused, saying that he knew of nothing that could be accepted by London, Vienna and St Petersburg alike. In his opinion European peace depended upon mutual concessions of interested Powers, which at present they were not disposed to make. He did not refuse, however, to tell the British Ambassador his private view on the Eastern Question. In his opinion the whole of Turkey, including all its various races, was not, as a political institution, worth great wars between the Great Powers. With no Power, continued Bismarck, does solicitude for the fate of the Balkan Christians weigh more than the fear of the formations that might replace the present conditions, and of the repercussion that these new formations might have on the security and the balance of power of the most interested states.

[1] Disraeli, p. 80.
[2] R.D., Gortchakov to Shouvalov, 17 Oct. 1876.

Austria is therefore quite right in desiring to remain neutral in the event of a Russo-Turkish war, and reserving the power to occupy Bosnia and Herzegovina in order to protect herself against all future formations. England would be wise to do the same with regard to her weak spot, namely to take Suez and Egypt and come to an agreement with Russia as to the preservation of Turkey in Constantinople and Adrianople. France could be also given some concessions in Syria.[1] In short, Bismarck did not think the Powers could settle the present crisis and preserve European peace otherwise than by partitioning Turkey —the plan for which he had tried to win England already at the beginning of that year.

The idea of partition was not strange to Disraeli. As I have pointed out before, at the beginning of September he had even thought of England's taking the lead in its realisation. He discussed that question now more fully with Lord Barrington. His chief difficulty was, however, to find compensations for England which could give her a real protection from Russia, as he believed that Egypt was not sufficient. "If the Russians had Constantinople," said Disraeli to Barrington, "they could at any time march their army through Syria to the mouth of the Nile and then what would be the use of our holding Egypt? Not even the command of the sea could help us under such circumstances....Our strength is on the sea. Constantinople is the key of India, and not Egypt and the Suez Canal."[2]

Meanwhile the defeat of Serbia compelled the Tsar to send an ultimatum to the Porte requesting an immediate suspension of arms and an armistice of six weeks. The Porte yielded to Russia and thus closed further discussion about the term of armistice.

On 4 November Derby proposed to the Great Powers a Conference in Constantinople on the basis of his proposals of 25 September, but adding a declaration reserving the independence and territorial integrity of the Ottoman Empire, and a declaration that the Powers did not seek any territorial advantages, any exclusive influence or commercial concessions. This proposal was at once accepted by the Great Powers, but it was still resisted by the Porte and received with apprehension and reluctance on the part of Austria. The Grand Vizier asked

[1] G.P. No. 250.   [2] Disraeli, p. 84.

the British Ambassador to inform him in advance of the measures the Powers intended to propose, adding that he could "grant all and perhaps more than was demanded" and thus render the Conference unnecessary. He yielded only after Derby told him that the Conference was the only alternative to war and threatened to withdraw all his support from the Porte if it refused the Conference.[1]

Andrassy was apprehensive lest England should make concessions to Russia to which he could not assent. He told Buchanan that

he feared little resistance to Russian views is to be expected from the other Powers and unless Austria-Hungary is supported by England, she would stand alone and proposals would be made to the Porte which it could not accept and war would be inevitable. He has been alarmed by reports from Berlin of the confidence which Her Majesty's Government are said to place on the views of Russia, in consequence of assurances given by the Emperor Alexander to Lord Loftus, as, he said, the Emperor has been giving similar assurances for the last year, but Prince Gortchakov has been acting in direct opposition to the declared policy of His Majesty—and in His Excellency's opinion, if such institutions are given to the Turkish provinces, as His Highness, it is believed, will advocate, a declaration to maintain the independence and integrity of Turkey will be entirely nugatory.[2]

Derby assured Andrassy that he did not intend to go beyond the bases of 25 September.[3]

While Russia was preparing herself for war, England began to prepare herself to prevent it. Russia's aggressive attitude —her volunteers and her ultimatum to Turkey—revived the deep suspicion which always existed against her in England. The Conservatives, who regarded the atrocity agitation as Liberal political propaganda, exploited this situation to launch an attack upon both Gladstone and Russia. Their press sounded the alarm against Russia, and the cry of Russian danger drowned that of Turkish atrocities. Already in October Gladstone wrote to Madame Novikov that "there was an undoubted and smart rally on behalf of Turkey in the Metropolitan press".[4] This change in public opinion, as well as Andrassy's resistance to all serious

---

[1] B.A., Derby to Elliot, 16 Nov. 1876.
[2] B.A., Buchanan to Derby, 5 Nov. 1876, No. 780, most conf. and secret.
[3] A.A., Beust to Andrassy, 7 Nov. 1876, No. 123.
[4] J. Morley, op. cit. II, p. 165.

reforms, improved the position of the Government and encouraged them to retreat to their former lines.

More than anybody else, Disraeli was convinced of Russia's warlike intentions and suspicious of her acts. "I foresee endless chicanery on the part of Russia, who is, at present, somewhat baffled and mortified", he wrote to Derby.[1] "The whole affair has been a conspiracy of Russia from the beginning", he wrote to Lady Bradford, "and she has failed in everything—even in active warfare the Porte has defeated her. I don't think she can stand it, and she will rush to further reverses."[2] He doubted the sincerity of Russia's desire to come to a peaceful settlement, and dreaded "that Russia will secretly encourage and invite the Porte to refuse the Conference, and then privately arrange with her".[3] In his Guildhall speech on 9 November Disraeli found an opportunity of assuring the Turks of his friendship and warning Russia. He told his audience that the great object of British policy during these critical circumstances was to maintain the general peace of Europe, and that peace could be best maintained by an observance of the Treaties in which all the Great Powers had joined.

"Those Treaties were not antique and dusty obsolete documents", he said. "It is hardly five years since—in 1871—the Treaty of Paris was revised. And that Treaty lays it down as the best security for the peace of Europe that we should maintain the independence and territorial integrity of the Turkish Empire. There is no country so interested in the maintenance of peace as England. Peace is essentially an English policy....But although the policy of England is peace, there is no country so well prepared for war as our own. If she enters into conflict in a righteous cause...her resources, I feel, are inexhaustible....She enters into a campaign which she will not terminate till right is done."[4]

The Tsar felt that British suspicion rested upon mere prejudice, and believing that it prevented natural co-operation between the two states, he resolved to explain his real intentions more plainly. On 2 November he told the British Ambassador that the story of the testament of Peter the Great was pure phantasy. He dismissed the idea of a Russian conquest of India, and pledged his word of honour that he desired no conquest, aspired to no

---

[1] Disraeli, p. 88. [2] Ibid. p. 86.
[3] Ibid. p. 90. [4] The Times, 10 Nov. 1876.

aggrandisement, and had no designs on Constantinople. "All he required was the amelioration of the position of the Christians, not however resting on Turkish promises, but on real efficient guarantees." He desired that Russia and England should come to an understanding and work together.[1] In the same sense Gortchakov wrote to Shouvalov: "It is really painful to see two great states, which united could regulate European affairs to their mutual advantage and to the advantage of all, troubling themselves and the world by an antagonism resting on prejudices and misunderstandings.... The Eastern Question is not a purely Russian Question, it affects the peace and prosperity of Europe and Christian civilisation."[2] "But to conquer English prejudices, absurd as they may be", he wrote in another letter, "is a task beyond human power."[3]

Gortchakov was informed of an attempt made by England "to organise, if not a coalition, at least a combined resistance against Russia".[4] The Tsar also suspected Disraeli of intending to occupy Constantinople and to keep the Straits permanently in his hands.[5] This induced him to strengthen the ties with his allies more closely. He hoped that a firm and pronounced attitude of the Dreikaiserbund would restrain England from hostile action. He asked the German Emperor for his friendly support "in removing distrust and preventing hostilities likely to disturb general peace".[6] And Gortchakov wrote to Bismarck asking for his "moral assistance expressed publicly and clearly".[7] Bismarck refused to declare openly that "Russia has a right, as a European mandatory, to make an end to the unbearable conditions",[8] as Gortchakov desired. But he lost no opportunity of expressing his confidence in the Tsar's pledge and dissuading England from hostile action. He tried to impress these views upon Salisbury, and ordered his Ambassador in Constantinople to use his influence in that sense.[9] On 5 December, answering a question in the Reichstag, he stated once more his confidence in the Tsar's disinterestedness and his good faith.[10]

[1] P.P., Turkey 2, No. 835.
[2] R.D., Gortchakov to Shouvalov, 3 Nov. 1876, No. 91.
[3] *Ibid.* No. 92.   [4] *Ibid.*   [5] G.P. No. 253.   [6] G.P. No. 254.
[7] G.P. No. 255.   [8] *Ibid.*   [9] G.P. No. 261.
[10] *Bismarck, Die Gesammelten Werke*, Bd. XI, pp. 471–9.

The Tsar's declaration to Lord Loftus was received in London with satisfaction. The Queen wrote a letter to him expressing her wish for co-operation in the maintenance of peace. But it brought no change in the attitude of the British Government. Gortchakov's desire that the Tsar's declaration should be published in order to reassure public opinion was refused. Disraeli regarded it as a "sentimental ebullition" and paid no heed to it. He believed in the warlike intentions of Russia and doubted the success of the Conference.

It is possible that Russia may wish to avoid, honourably, a struggle, which the state of her finances, the unpreparedness of her armies, and her want of naval power, may make her desirous to postpone.... Nevertheless, 1st, the bankruptcy of the Porte; 2ndly, the assumed alienation of England from the Turks, partly produced by the Bulgarian outrages, and partly by the non-payment of Turkish dividends, have prevailed on her, apparently, to take a step at which she first hesitated....It is wise, however, to assume that there will be an invasion of Turkey by Russia.[1]

He believed that the continental Powers would not oppose Russia's invasion of Turkey, but rather seek compensations for themselves.

"Generally speaking, the situation is very similar to the state, which preceded the partition of Poland", he wrote to Salisbury, "...It is highly probable that Austria will assemble a powerful force in Transylvania, and I believe that, in so doing, her object is to coerce Russia, but it will end by Russia having her own way, and Austria seeking consolation not only in the possession of Bosnia, which she will have previously occupied, but in Herzegovina, and, not unlikely, in Servia....It is a most critical moment in European politics. If Russia is not checked, the Holy Alliance will be revived in aggravated form and force. Germany will have Holland; and France, Belgium and England will be in a position I trust I shall never live to witness."[2]

With all these fears in his mind, Disraeli devoted his time and energy to preparing himself for war. He considered it of vital importance for England to prevent Russia from occupying Constantinople and the Straits. A commission under Colonel Home was therefore sent by the War Office to Constantinople to examine the positions on both sides of the Straits, to see how they could be best defended, what were the forces necessary for

---

[1] Disraeli, p. 103.   [2] *Ibid.* p. 104.

their defence and in what time they could be mobilised and transported to the spot.[1] On the basis of information from the War Office he came to the conclusion that "to attain her object, England would have to seize both the Bosphorus and the Dardanelles, and to hold the land approaches to each", that she "could at once dispatch an army sufficient to occupy and hold both positions", and that this army could reach Constantinople within twenty-one days.[2] These conclusions were presented to the Cabinet in November, and in view of an eventual conflict, it was decided to detain in England eight guns "of hitherto unprecedented size and power, which were being built...to the order of a foreign Government".[3]..."If we act in the manner I have generally indicated we shall probably, in the conclusion, obtain some commanding stronghold in Turkey from which we need never recede", he wrote to Salisbury. "It will be for the interest of the Porte itself that we should; and if they would sell to us, for instance, Varna, the supremacy of Russia might for ever be arrested."[4] In the Cabinet he said that "although partition has not been intended, it will come, and in that case offers will be made to us. Constantinople not likely to be offered, nor would it be desirable to accept. He would like to buy a port in the Black Sea from the Porte, as Batoum...or Sinope....He said Egypt would be offered as before, but he did not see what we should gain....What he wants is a Malta or Gibraltar, which would prevent the Black Sea being a constant threat to our maritime power in the Mediterranean."[5]

These war preparations had a triple aim: first of all, they were to enable England to prevent an occupation of Constantinople and the Straits by Russia; secondly, they aimed at persuading Turkey that she was not isolated and at restraining her from making a separate arrangement with Russia; finally they were to secure England's share in case of partition, which he considered would be a logical consequence of the situation. Bismarck's proposal that England should take Egypt was not to his taste. "I am surprised that Bismarck should go on harping about Egypt", he wrote. "Its occupation by us would embitter France,

[1] Disraeli, pp. 98–100, 117.
[2] *Ibid.* pp. 101–2.   [3] *Ibid.* p. 102.
[4] *Ibid.* pp. 103–4.   [5] *Ibid.* p. 102.

and I don't see it would at all benefit us, if Russia possessed Constantinople. I would sooner we had Asia Minor than Egypt."[1]

These warlike preparations provoked great dissension in the Cabinet. Even Derby became "stiff" and refused to sanction the order to the fleet to pass the Dardanelles in case of Russia threatening to force the Straits.[2] Carnarvon, Northcote and Cairns were alarmed at such proposals. "His mind is full of strange projects," wrote Carnarvon of Disraeli, "and if he had been ten years younger he might have risked splitting the Cabinet in order to achieve them."[3]

Beside military measures, Disraeli wished also to come to an understanding with some Great Power with the view of resisting Russia's designs. The idea of concluding a treaty with Germany for the maintenance of the *status quo* having met with many obstacles, he endeavoured to come to an agreement with France and Austria, as the signatories of the Treaty of 1856.

"It is not only our right," he wrote to Derby, "but, in my opinion, our duty, to enquire of France and Austria, what, in the event of the failure of the Congress, are their views and feelings with reference to their engagements under the Tripartite Treaty? This will give Austria, if she wishes it, an occasion to unburthen or unbutton herself—and may lead to important consequences....I have no hesitation myself in saying, that it would be most desirable to arrive at a clear agreement with Austria for joint action, and that, if the Conference fail, and Russia is arrogant and menacing, it should at once be intimated to Russia that the integrity of the Turkish dominions should not be violated."[4]

At the same time while proposing this plan to Derby, Disraeli used his secret channels to ascertain the possibility of an agreement with Austria. On 4 November his private secretary, Corry, entered into conversation with Graf Montgelas, secretary of the Austrian Embassy, telling him that this time he did not speak privately but "with authorisation". He told Montgelas that the crisis was approaching, that Germany was endeavouring to force England and perhaps Austria to a war with Russia in order to be free to fall upon France. Austria and England had the same vital interest in keeping Russia far from

[1] *Ibid.* p. 104.   [2] *Ibid.* p. 100.
[3] *Life of Carnarvon*, II, p. 348.   [4] Disraeli, p. 88.

the Danube, and they ought to come to an agreement before the Conference met. If they were united, Russia would not dare to break the peace.[1]

Montgelas answered that any proposal on the part of England would be gladly received in Vienna. They knew that the interests of England and Austria were identical, but had some doubt as to England's resolution to work in the sense of her interests. Corry told him that "his chief would be glad to have a written project" which would serve as a basis of an understanding. The next day Montgelas produced a "draft of a secret agreement", proposing that the two Powers should concert before the Conference upon the means for the maintenance of peace on the basis of the *status quo amélioré*. Should the present crisis lead to war, both Powers were to guarantee the territorial *status quo* of each other and of Turkey. If Russia provoked the conflict, war would be conducted both in Europe and Asia. Austria was to receive a yearly subsidy from England so long as the war lasted. She engaged to coerce Serbia and Montenegro, and, with the Sultan's approval, such of the revolted provinces as might be deemed necessary, in order to keep them neutral. In a separate document England was to engage not to oppose "if in case of war or otherwise the Sultan should think it to be his advantage that the provinces of Bosnia and Herzegovina (or parts thereof) be ceded to Austria".[2]

Corry considered this project as too far-reaching. England could not now conclude a formal offensive and defensive alliance. He objected especially to subsidies and the cession of Bosnia and Herzegovina to Austria. On 13 November he asked Montgelas to go to Vienna and inform Andrassy of their conversation before Salisbury's arrival there. As Montgelas was not able to leave his post, he asked permission to write to Andrassy about it, which Corry granted him. Consequently, on the 15th he laid before Count Beust the whole conversation and correspondence with

---

[1] A.A., Verhalten des K.u.K. Legationssecretär Grafen Montgelas in London. Eigenmächtige Verhandlungen mit Lord Beaconsfield, 1876–8. Montgelas, X, dossier B. Henceforth cited as "Montgelas". Montgelas's report of his conversation with Corry, dated 4 Nov. 1876, Belgrave Square, Privatim.

[2] *Ibid.* Montgelas to Corry, 5 Nov. 1876, inclosure "Draft of a secret agreement".

Corry. In an accompanying letter he told Beust that Disraeli pressed for an agreement before the Conference, but not so far-reaching, and that he desired Andrassy to send a special envoy to Constantinople. Montgelas's personal impression was that Disraeli "held the moment favourable to weaken Russia and was decided to take advantage of it". He prayed his chief not to tell Derby of it.[1] When Andrassy learned of this overture he approved of Montgelas's conduct, but did not encourage further conversations, as he feared being compromised with Russia.

In such an atmosphere of mutual distrust and war preparations the Powers assembled at Constantinople to discuss the question of the fate of the Christians. What was there that, after more than a year of unsuccessful attempts, could unite them now in a common effort to secure a better life for the downtrodden Rayahs? On the principal question of the organisation of the revolted provinces their interests and their views remained as divided as ever. Russia was convinced that autonomy alone offered sufficient protection to the Christians, but she realised that she could not accomplish it in co-operation with the Powers, and was therefore resolved to take separate action. Her chief aim at the Conference, if she failed to obtain the minimum of what she considered to be indispensable, was to maintain the united front of the Powers against Turkey, so as to have a pretext for war and to be able to present herself as a European mandatory. Austria, assured by Russia that no serious reforms would be demanded for Bosnia and Herzegovina, regarded the Conference as a preliminary phase to the war, and was careful only to avoid eventual surprises. Bismarck was content with the Russo-Austrian relations being directed in the right way, and endeavoured now to dissuade England from interfering prematurely. England seemed to be nearest to Russia, for she too desired an amelioration of the conditions of the Christians, but she spoke with two voices, one of which, at least, was decidedly anti-Russian.

The British delegate at the Conference was Lord Salisbury, one of those Ministers who disagreed with Disraeli's Turkophil policy. He considered that "the true intent and meaning" of the agitation was that "this time promises of better government of Christians won't do alone", and that "some kind of reliable

[1] A. A., Montgelas, Montgelas to Beust, 15 Nov. 1876.

machinery must be provided for seeing that the promises are kept". He had already written in September of the necessity of coming to an understanding with Russia to that effect. Now he doubted the possibility of "Russia being content with any terms to which Turkey can reasonably be expected to submit."[1] He had, however, no great confidence in Turkish reasonableness, and believed his mission to be a futile effort. His misgivings were only increased by the impressions he received in Paris, Berlin, Vienna and Rome, which he visited on his way to Constantinople.

Bismarck told Salisbury that he did not interfere in the Eastern Question because he considered "that what we were trying to do in Turkey was hopeless", and because interference on his part would amount to a threat which "would be remembered against him by Russia".

"His view of the prospects of peace was very gloomy", wrote Salisbury from Berlin. "He did not think it possible that Russia after doing so much should draw back.... He encouraged us to take Egypt as our share; failing that he thought it would be very useful for European civilisation that we should occupy Constantinople. But in any case he urged, two or three times, that if a decision became necessary, we should not take it at the first movement of Russia; that events would very likely bring her enterprise to an end; that when she began to feel the exhaustion of men and money, she would be accessible to reasonable terms; and that no Power not having command of the sea could hold Constantinople; and that therefore we should well afford to wait, and not commit ourselves to war with Russia till it became absolutely necessary.... I think he will help us in the Conference to any solution that seems practical. But he does not believe in a solution; and is only occupied with settling what shall be done when the Turkish Empire comes to pieces. Bosnia and the Herzegovina for Austria: Egypt for us: Bulgaria possibly for Russia: the Turks in Stamboul with some of the surrounding country like the Eastern Empire in its latest days: and the rest for Greece. That I take to be his new map of Europe."[2]

In Vienna Salisbury learned that Andrassy like Bismarck did not expect a successful issue to the Conference, and that he thought more of what would follow its failure than what should be done for its success.

---

[1] Salisbury, p. 90.   [2] *Ibid.* pp. 96–7.

He feels quite easy on the side of Germany, but he professes considerable apprehension of Russia. For this reason he objects to any policy for the settlement of the provinces which would be only illusory, and would give Russia a good opportunity of interfering two years hence; for her force would be much greater then, and her railways would be more complete. Bismarck was also of opinion that Russia was strengthened by delay. For this reason, Andrassy, though still opposing occupation and declining to give it the slightest sanction, is inclined to look upon it as perhaps not the greatest of possible evils. But he was very anxious to know whether, if Russia occupied Bulgaria, and he occupied Bosnia, we would occupy Constantinople.... He was very anxious for definite statement of intentions of England on this head, as he must otherwise coalesce with Russia.[1]

What struck Salisbury most was the almost complete identity both in views and arguments between Bismarck and Andrassy. He believed that they were in "active communication and tolerably close concert between them".

"Assuming then that Bismarck and Andrassy are for the moment partners", wrote Salisbury, "I think they rather wish than not that the Conference may fail and that Russia should waste her strength on a sterile effort, which may exhaust her present store of strength—hoping that it may require years of rest for her to secrete another store. But they do not mean her to establish herself south of the Danube.... Nor does either wish England to be dragged into the fray."[2]

The impressions from these visits confirmed Salisbury's doubts in the success of the Conference. "In the course of my travels I have not succeeded in finding the friend of the Turk", he wrote from Rome. "He does not exist. Most believe his hour is come. Some few think it may be postponed. No one has even suggested the idea that he can be upheld for any length of time".[3] He was all the more surprised to find in Constantinople, instead of extreme demands from Russia, a conciliatory and moderate attitude on the part of General Ignatyev. He was soon convinced that Ignatyev was genuine in his endeavour for a peaceful solution. They established good personal relations which helped negotiations very much.

Russia indeed sincerely desired an *entente* with England. Her Ambassador in Constantinople was instructed to demand autonomies and a military occupation for carrying the new organisation

---

[1] *Ibid.* pp. 100–3.   [2] *Ibid.* p. 102.   [3] *Ibid.* p. 107.

into life, but he was also to accept other adequate guarantees if occupation were refused. He was furnished with a maximum and the minimum project of reforms, but he was also to accept *ad referendum* every other project offering serious guarantees. "Even if our minimum prevails," wrote Gortchakov to him, "it would be a great result which would spare us the military campaign, which would be risky both politically and materially and would above all bear heavily on our financial position. If we can avoid it, while maintaining intact the honour and dignity of the Empire, I should applaud loudly and our country will gain."[1]

Lord Salisbury was not furnished with the "minimum of security for the Christians and the maximum of interference with Turkey", for which he had asked, but his instructions aimed at creating adequate securities for the Christian populations.

"Pacification cannot be attained by proclamations," wrote Derby to him, "and the Powers have a right to demand in the interest of the peace of Europe, that they shall examine for themselves the measures required for the reform of the administration of the disturbed Provinces, and that adequate securities shall be provided for carrying those measures into operation.... It should be understood by the Porte that Great Britain is resolved not to sanction misgovernment and oppression, and that if the Porte by obstinacy or apathy opposes the efforts which are now making to place the Ottoman Empire on a more secure basis, the responsibility of the consequences which may ensue will rest solely on the Sultan and his advisers."[2]

Russia having promised Austria not to ask for autonomy for Bosnia and Herzegovina, the problem reduced itself mainly to the organisation of Bulgaria, where the interests of England and Russia seemed to be opposed. The success of the Conference seemed to depend upon an agreement between them, and it was, therefore, the first question dealt with at the preliminary meetings of the delegates. Ignatyev proposed the creation of an autonomous big Bulgaria stretching from Bourgas on the Black Sea to Dedeagatch on the Aegean, then to the Lake of Ohrida and along Albania up to Nish and Vidin. The province was to be ruled by an irremovable Vali and a provincial Assembly. The

---

[1] R.D., Gortchakov to Shouvalov, 24 Nov. 1876.
[2] B.A., Derby to Salisbury, 24 Nov. 1876.

organisation was to be carried out under the supervision of a foreign army, which was to occupy the province temporarily. To this proposal both the Austrian and the British delegates objected. Austria, though secured with regard to Bosnia and Herzegovina, endeavoured to prevent the creation of an autonomous large Bulgaria, fearing lest it should make Russia preponderant in the Eastern half of the Balkans, and attract to her the other Slav provinces.[1] Salisbury considered a large Bulgaria to be "fatal to independence of the Porte", as it would give predominance to the Slav element, which would hold "the most important strategic position" and, with the magnitude of its resources, would become practically independent of the Sultan.[2] He proposed therefore division into two parts, of which "the Eastern would remain in the hands of non-Slav population" and constitute a strong barrier against any invasion. Ignatyev yielded on this point, having obtained satisfaction in the question of autonomy, despite the opposition of the Austrian delegate. The southern frontier was removed from the Aegean to Adrianople and Monastir, and the whole province was divided into two parts. It was agreed that each of these provinces should be governed by a Vali, nominated by the Porte for a term of five years with the consent of the Guaranteeing Powers. A provincial Assembly was to assist him in administration. The Turkish army was to be concentrated in the fortresses and principal towns. A national militia and gendarmerie were to be created. An international commission was to supervise the execution of these reforms with the assistance of a European gendarmerie.

The other questions presented little difficulty. Bosnia and Herzegovina were united in one province, and were deprived of a national militia. They were to be governed by a Vali nominated by the Porte with the assent of the Powers, who retained also the right to establish an international commission to supervise the execution of the reforms for one year. With these exceptions, the provinces remained practically under the complete control of the Porte. With Serbia and Montenegro peace was to be concluded on the basis of the *status quo*, but Serbia was to obtain

---

[1] B.A., Buchanan to Derby, 11 Dec. 1876, No. 866, conf.
[2] B.A., Salisbury to Derby, 13 Dec. No. 22, secret and conf., 14 Dec. 1876, No. 25 and 4 Jan. 1877, No. 84.

Mali Zvornik, and Montenegro some districts in Herzegovina and a free navigation on the River Bojana and the Lake of Skutari.

These proposals were formulated at the preliminary meetings of the Great Powers, from which Turkey was excluded. At the last meeting Ignatyev declared that the programme of reforms agreed upon represented "an extreme and irreducible minimum" for Russia, that it was no longer the wish of any single Power but "the common work of united Europe", and that therefore their complete accord was necessary to ensure its acceptance by the Porte.

The plenary sessions were opened on 23 December, when the proposals of the Powers were read to the Turkish delegates. But on the same day the Porte promulgated a new constitution, which provided for large reforms for the whole Empire. The Turkish delegates represented this constitution as the dawn of a new era, which made the reforms proposed by the Powers unnecessary. The conference was consequently adjourned. A week later the Turks presented their counter-proposals, rejecting all the principal points of the Powers. They criticised them as being in excess of the basis proposed for the Conference, and as encroaching upon their independence and integrity. To meet this criticism the Powers decided to reduce their proposals. On 15 January they presented to the Porte a greatly reduced résumé, declaring at the same time that if they were rejected, their Plenipotentiaries and Ambassadors would leave Constantinople. But the Turks were not intimidated by this threat. They summoned the Great Council, instituted by the new constitution, which, on 18 January, rejected the new proposals entirely.

Salisbury foresaw the danger of the Turks wrecking the Conference by their obstruction and asked permission in advance from his Government "to make use of the strongest means of pressure" against them.[1] He considered that the terms proposed were in the interest of Turkey, sparing her a ruinous war, and in the interest of England, as they furnished her the necessary security against Russia. In his opinion Russia had "given up most of the points to which objection was felt in England", and could not "concede more without danger to the Emperor's

[1] Salisbury, p. 115.

position".[1] He pointed out both to the Sultan and the Grand Vizier that, if they rejected the proposals, they could not count any longer on the support of England, and that, if they were attacked by one or several Powers, England would leave them to their fate. But the effect of his energetic pressure was greatly weakened by Elliot's Turkophil attitude and the contradictory conduct of the British Government. Elliot was convinced that the policy of supporting Turkey was the only way of preserving British interests, and that Russia aimed at undermining it by all means in her power. "Russia perhaps has no fixed plan of going to war with Turkey", he wrote, "but there can be at least no doubt of her determination not to lose the present opportunity of fatally weakening her. This object will be attained sufficiently for her purpose, if special privileges, supported by European guarantees or control, are secured for the revolted Slav provinces."[2] He was therefore opposed to the Conference, which would inevitably give Russia an opportunity to achieve her purposes on the shoulders of Europe. Russia in his opinion aimed at uniting the Great Powers upon a programme of reforms which would be presented to the Porte as the collective will of Europe—a programme which "if consented to by Turkey would have the effect of permanently weakening her, or, if rejected, would afford the wished-for excuse for declaring war".[3] He considered the proposals of the Powers as "impossible demands" and criticised them severely to his Government. He did not hide his views even from the Porte. "He allows it to be seen that his sympathies are with the Turks, and against the proposals of the Powers," wrote Salisbury. "I have no doubt he let Midhat clearly see that he agreed with him."[4]

Realising that Elliot frustrated all his work and that his "power of negotiation with the Turks is almost nil so long as he stays", Salisbury asked for Elliot's removal from Constantinople. But in London not only was his request refused, but all his conduct was disapproved. Both Disraeli and Derby were opposed to any pressure being put upon the Turks. Derby told the foreign Ambassadors that in case of Turkey refusing the proposals

[1] Salisbury, p. 115.
[2] P.P., Turkey, No. 2, Elliot to Derby, 23 Oct. 1876.
[3] H. Elliot, *op. cit.* p. 277.   [4] Salisbury, pp. 118–19

England would leave her an "entirely free hand and that there could be no word of any pressure on her part".[1] A day before the Conference opened he informed Salisbury and the Turkish Ambassador that in that event England would not "assent to, or assist in coercive measures against Turkey".[2] The Porte received this communication with "deep gratitude" and expressed its hope of England's support.[3] Odian Effendi was sent to London to work against Salisbury and try to get a loan and the neutralisation of Roumania in the event of war.[4]

Instead of facilitating and supporting Salisbury's efforts at Constantinople, the British Government put obstacles in their way and directly counteracted them. Disraeli was in fact quite discontented with his attitude, and asked Derby to "take him in hand". He considered that Salisbury had "unnecessarily bullied the Turks", and feared that he was "much duped by Ignatyev". "Salisbury seems most prejudiced", he wrote to Derby, "and not to be aware that his principal object in being sent to Constantinople is to keep the Russians out of Turkey, not to create an ideal existence for Turkish Christians...."[5] "I think we cannot deny that our policy preceding the Conference, and our efforts in it, were to maintain the integrity and independence of the Ottoman Empire."[6] In the Cabinet he spoke "of the difficulty of distinguishing between British interests and support of Turkey".[7] Carnarvon believed that he intended "to take part in the war, and on behalf of Turkey. He hardly indeed makes any secret of this."[8]

It was no mystery to the Porte that the Powers were not equally interested in the realisation of their reforms. Their attitude convinced it that it had nothing to fear if it rejected their proposals. The utterances of the British Government and the military preparations for defence of Constantinople, carried out by the British War Office, inspired it moreover with hope that it would not be abandoned in the event of war. Like England, Germany was indifferent to the fate of

[1] G.P. No. 268.
[2] P.P., Derby to Salisbury, 22 Dec. 1876.
[3] P.P., Safvet to Muzurus, 24 Dec. 1876.
[4] R.D., Ignatyev to Shouvalov, 2 Jan. 1877.
[5] Disraeli, p. 111.
[6] Ibid. p. 117.
[7] Life of Carnarvon, II, p. 347.
[8] Ibid.

the Christians. Austria had been opposed to radical reforms throughout the crisis, and had maintained that attitude during the Conference by refusing or taking *ad referendum* most of Ignatyev's proposals, even those already accepted by Britain.[1] Germany supported her by taking *ad referendum* the same points.[2] Russia had foreseen the failure of the Conference and her supreme aim was to preserve the united front of the Great Powers against Turkey. She therefore made concessions far beyond her earlier demands, which made the Turks believe that she was weak and desired to avoid war. Even the threat of the Ambassadors leaving Constantinople was not applied entirely, for the British and the German Ambassadors were sent on leave.[3]

Encouraged by Britain to resistance and inspired with hopes of her support, having no pressure to fear from the part of the other Powers and believing that Russia was weak and peaceful, the Turks saw no reason for accepting the proposals. They considered that Russia would not risk a war in opposition to the other Powers. But even if she plunged into it, they believed that this would provoke a general European war and that Britain would come to their help.[4]

It was strongly believed by both Salisbury and Disraeli that Bismarck worked for the rupture of the Conference.[5] Derby was informed that Andrassy boasted of having "privately propped up the Turks".[6] Gortchakov also considered that Andrassy did not wish the success of the Conference.[7] Ignatyev told the French delegate, Chaudordy, that "the Government of Berlin pushed Russia to warlike decisions".[8] The Tsar complained to the German Ambassador that "the German and the Austrian Ambassadors had always been without instructions when they had to support a Russian proposal".[9] Gortchakov required that Germany should give her support to Russia by accepting all the points agreed upon between her and England, and that she

---

[1] B.A., Salisbury to Derby, 13 Dec. 1876, No. 19; Salisbury, pp. 108–12.
[2] G.P. No. 267; Schweinitz, I, p. 403.
[3] B.A., Russell to Derby, 27 Dec. 1876, No. 568, and 29 Dec. No. 573.
[4] B.A., Salisbury to Derby, 7 Jan. 1877, No. 88; Salisbury, p. 117.
[5] B.A., Salisbury to Derby, 8 Jan. No. 90; Disraeli, pp. 112–13; D.F. No. 138.
[6] B.A., Derby to Russell, 11 Jan. 1877, No. 25.
[7] Schweinitz, I, p. 370.
[8] D.F. No. 126.   [9] Schweinitz, I, p. 403.

should use her influence in Vienna in the same sense.[1] Bismarck
refused both these demands under the plea of the impossibility
of taking any side without alienating his friends.[2] When Bismarck refused to consent to a further reduction of the proposals
of the Powers, the Russian press attacked him with accusations
of leaving Russia in the lurch.[3] The Tsar complained bitterly
to Schweinitz of the merely "platonic" support he was receiving
from Germany. In the course of this conversation he got so
excited that he left the Ambassador without offering him his
hand.[4] Shouvalov added fresh oil to this excitement by reporting
the lack of support he received from his German and Austrian
colleagues and the bad effect this made on the British Cabinet.[5]
The Russian papers, even the semi-official ones, accused Bismarck
of encouraging the Turks to resistance. "A few journals only
advised war against Turkey", wrote Schweinitz, "but many
openly said that peace must be preserved, in order to be so much
stronger later on against other enemies, and against false friends."[6]

Bismarck believed that all this campaign was inspired by
Gortchakov, who desired to throw upon Germany the responsibility for the difficulties to which his own policy had brought
Russia. He excused himself by saying he had never been informed
of Russian intentions and by declaring the impossibility of
giving support to proposals the content and the portent of which
he did not know. The lack of support in London he explained
by Gortchakov's equivocal and unfriendly attitude towards
Germany, which compelled him not to estrange his other
friends by an unreserved support of Russia.[7]

The conflict between the two Chancellors was largely due to
their personal animosity, which made Bismarck resent the manner
in which Gortchakov treated him and suspect him of desiring
to compromise him with the Tsar. But Gortchakov's complaint
of lack of support on the part of Germany despite her declared
readiness to pay Russia back for the services rendered in 1864–70
was not unfounded. Although Bismarck did not wish to choose
between his allies, he did not remain neutral in their conflict.

---

[1] G.P. No. 267.   [2] Schweinitz, 1, p. 372.
[3] *Ibid.* p. 378.   [4] *Ibid.*
[5] R.D., Shouvalov to Gortchakov, Jan. 1877; Schweinitz, 1, p. 380.
[6] Schweinitz, 1, p. 382.   [7] G.P. No. 273.

While refusing any support of Russian policy, he used all his influence to promote that of Austria. At Berlin he mediated with Russia to obtain her consent to the occupation of Bosnia and Herzegovina by Austria; he refused to propose a European conference, which was to discuss the reforms to which Austria was opposed; he supported Austria at Constantinople by taking *ad referendum* all the points objected to by Austria. He endeavoured not only to keep Andrassy in power, but also to obtain for him the sympathy and the support of Britain.[1] The maintenance of Andrassy in power was a guarantee for him that Austria and Russia would neither go to war nor become too intimate behind Germany's back, and that no military party, inspired with revenge against Germany and friendly to Russia, should direct Austrian policy. But his preservation in power demanded the furtherance of his policy, which was detrimental to Russian interests. Such an attitude was neither impartial nor friendly to Russia.

The Russian press campaign and the unfriendly utterances of the Tsar seemed to Bismarck to indicate a new departure in Russian policy. He believed that Gortchakov had endeavoured for two years to awake the Tsar's distrust towards Germany, to estrange him from her and bring about an alliance with France and Austria in which Russia would play the principal rôle. Neither Gortchakov nor Ignatyev made any secret of their preference for the French alliance. An attempt to discredit Bismarck with the Tsar was made in September by Werder's question as to Germany's attitude in case of a conflict with Austria. Gortchakov was pursuing the same object now by blaming Germany for the mistakes of his own policy. All this led Bismarck to the conclusion that "there were in Russia influential people who would rather go against Germany together with the Paris Government, than fight for the Eastern Christians in Turkey". "...I fear particularly", he wrote to Schweinitz, "that Prince Gortchakov's exertion is aimed at destroying the sympathy of the Emperor Alexander for his nephew and for Prussia, breaking off our *entente* with Austria and England as much as possible, and perhaps through diplomatic pressure in Vienna, perhaps through threatening Austria, by awakening her mistrust towards

[1] B.A., Russell to Derby, 27 Dec. 1876, No. 569, secret.

us, overthrowing the Andrassy regime and giving place to such a one as would readily lend itself to an anti-German coalition, which could be strengthened every day by the adhesion of France."[1] The identity of language of the French and the Russian press, the intrigues of the Russian Ambassador in Vienna, the intimate relations between Ignatyev and the French delegate at the Conference, the knowledge of Gortchakov's anti-German intrigue with Duc Decazes, the concentration of the Russian troops on the North—all these were symptoms of a forthcoming danger, which, Bismarck considered, demanded special measures on his part.[2] To meet this danger he intended to strengthen his relations with Austria and England, to create an organic alliance with Austria to which England would be won as a party, or at least as a benevolent friend. In order to induce his Emperor to take this step he asked Schweinitz to send him such reports as would influence him in that direction.[3]

The idea of an alliance between Germany and Austria had already been suggested by Andrassy on the occasion of Baron Münch's visit to Bismarck. At that time Bismarck refused it, saying that it could be only the result of more critical times, and that it must be an organic one, i.e. sanctioned by Parliaments. There are no traces of an overture being made to Vienna in January 1877, probably because he was sure of Austria's consent. But there are traces of an attempt to realise an offensive and defensive alliance with Britain. Gortchakov's circular to the Great Powers gave Bismarck the opportunity of approaching England and assuring her of his desire to work in concert with her. He told the British Ambassador that the recent rapprochement between Russia and France might induce the latter to invade Alsace-Lorraine, and that in order to preclude this danger he was obliged to advise his Emperor to concentrate troops at Metz and Strassburg. As this might provoke a war with France, he would like to know what the attitude of England would be in that event. A few days later he said to Russell that the concentration of the French troops on the frontier had compelled him to ask for explanations in Paris, and charged him to sound

[1] G.P. No. 273.
[2] Schweinitz, I, pp. 382–3; Andrassy, II, p. 381.
[3] *Briefwechsel des Botschafters General von Schweinitz*, pp. 125–6; R.D., Shouvalov to Gortchakov, 30 Jan. and 20 Feb. 1877; Schweinitz, I, p. 383.

his Government with a view to an offensive and defensive alliance against France. Shouvalov learned at once of this overture from sources which leave no doubt as to its authenticity, and communicated it to the Tsar.[1] Salisbury wrote to his wife that "Berlin has made new proposals for an offensive and defensive alliance".[2]

The differences among the three Northern Powers disclosed at the Conference and the strained relations between Germany and Russia which followed it, made an impression in London that the Dreikaiserbund was broken. Shouvalov's insistence upon the existence of an intimate understanding among the three Powers found no credence, although it was confirmed by both Salisbury and Russell.[3] Andrassy denied the existence of an understanding, and Derby believed that the story was put forward in order to induce Britain to press upon the Porte the acceptance of the proposals from fear of the Dreikaiserbund otherwise acting together.[4] Disraeli, always eager to take advantage of dissensions in the Dreikaiserbund, tried to approach Austria and also instructed Salisbury to come nearer to Calice, who enjoyed Andrassy's confidence.[5]

Meanwhile Bismarck's warlike threat and his overture of alliance produced great alarm in London. It was believed that Bismarck was inciting Russia to war in order to be able to fall upon France and perhaps take possession of Holland. This fear was shared alike by Disraeli, Derby and Salisbury. "The position of affairs is most critical, and requires decision", wrote Disraeli to Derby. "I believe that, at no moment, was Russia more anxious for peace, than at present. She is perfectly conscious of the intrigues of Bismarck to involve her in a struggle, which, whatever the ultimate result, must be materially disastrous to her; but she must have a golden bridge."[6] "The object most of all desirable is, if possible to keep Russia out of war for the present", wrote Salisbury to Lord Lytton. "If it can be done for twelve months more, France's preparations will be sufficiently

[1] R.D., Shouvalov to Gortchakov, 20 Feb. 1877; Schweinitz, I, p. 383.
[2] Salisbury, p. 127.
[3] B.A., Russell to Derby, 11 Jan. 1877, No. 23, most conf.
[4] B.A., Derby to Salisbury, 15 Jan. 1877.
[5] R.D., Shouvalov to Gortchakov, Jan. 1877.
[6] Disraeli, p. 126.

complete to make a *coup de main* from Berlin impossible. Till that time the danger is serious. Nothing but the counterweight of Russia prevented it in 1875, and if that counterweight is removed, the policy of terrors of Bismarck may again become uncontrollable."[1] To counteract Bismarck's designs they all endeavoured now to deter Russia from war by providing her with "a bridge over which to retreat".

After the failure of the Conference Gortchakov directed a circular to the Great Powers stating that the proposals rejected by the Porte were the work of all the Powers and that their rejection affected the honour and dignity of the whole of Europe. The Eastern Question was not a Russian or a Slav affair, it was the concern of all the Powers. "It is necessary for us to know what the Cabinets with which we have hitherto acted in common, propose to do with a view to meeting the refusal and securing the execution of their wishes", wrote Gortchakov to Shouvalov.[2] This circular was timed to reach London simultaneously with Salisbury's return. Gortchakov was informed by Ignatyev that Salisbury favoured an "intimate alliance" with Russia respecting Eastern affairs, and that he was prepared "to work for the adoption of that line of conduct even at the risk of quarrelling with Lord Beaconsfield and bringing out a new political grouping".[3] Gortchakov knew naturally that there was no hope of the Powers joining Russia in imposing their will upon Turkey. His circular was a bid for time, as Russia was unable to undertake military operations before the spring. But it was also the consequence of the lost confidence in his allies, which made him fear unforeseen complications and anxious to accept any honourable peaceful solution.

The British Government was now disposed to facilitate Russia's retreat. Disraeli considered that the matter could be settled if Russia and Turkey could be brought to agree upon the following three points: "(1) That the Vali should be appointed for a fixed term, removable only on recommendation of some Turkish authority.... (2) That the Provincial Assembly should have the control over the raising and spending of some considerable

---

[1] Salisbury, p. 129.
[2] P.P., Gortchakov's circular to the Great Powers, 19 Jan. 1877.
[3] R.D., Ignatyev to Gortchakov, 22 Jan. 1877.

portion of the direct taxes. (3) That there should be a police and a militia containing Christians in proportion to the population."[1] Salisbury proposed this programme to Shouvalov suggesting that, if Russia agreed with it, the Powers should take note of it and declare on their part that if Turkey failed to carry it out within six months, the guarantees of the Treaty of Paris would cease to exist. Shouvalov declined to sound his Government on this proposal. Gortchakov, who learned of it having been communicated to the Porte, informed him that Russia would not be a party to a "comedy of that nature", but that she would take into consideration the real results which Turkey might show on the field of reforms.

This plan having failed, Disraeli tried to dissuade Russia from war by pointing out the danger of its provoking a general European conflagration, and assuring her of his friendship and his readiness to help her get out of the present difficulties. To the Russian Ambassador he expressed his fear of a rupture between Germany and France, telling him that England and Russia were equally interested in preventing the further weakening of France.

"Let us begin by eliminating an error", he said. "I know that bellicose sentiments towards Russia are attributed to me...and you believe them. Well, I assure you it is a pure calumny propagated by my enemies: I am not only pacific, but I am your friend and want to work together with you. Last summer we were on the point of agreeing, and this would have forestalled many things. You know as well as I who it was who prevented our Entente. I told you at the same time what I thought of the Ottoman Empire, whose days are numbered: one must not precipitate its fall, but consider seriously what will happen after and prepare ourselves for it. I also told you that we are not prepared, and that its collapse at that moment would provoke a war, soon involving all Europe and England in her turn. As the Tsar desires peace, I shall second his intentions, but there is no other pacific solution than to grant the Porte a lapse of time necessary to execute its reforms....I shall use all my influence to make the reply to your Circular satisfying to Prince Gortchakov and I should like it to be not only that golden bridge of which so much has recently been said, but a bridge of diamonds and rubies."[2]

Disraeli's pacific assurances encouraged Russia to take one more step towards a peaceful solution, which she herself desired

[1] Disraeli, p. 126.
[2] R.D., Shouvalov to Gortchakov, 21 Feb. 1877.

now more than ever. At the beginning of February Midhat
Pasha was dismissed, and his successor, Edhem Pasha, announced
a wide programme of reforms which embodied most of the
demands of the Powers. Russia consented to give Turkey a
period of time for the execution of reforms, but required that
the Powers should engage in a protocol to concert upon further
measures to be taken if she failed to carry them out. At the end
of February General Ignatyev was sent to Europe to explain to
the Great Powers the real intentions of the Tsar and win them
over for signing such a protocol. Bismarck accepted the Russian
proposal under the condition that it should be accepted by all
the other Powers, but he believed that England would refuse it
and that Russia herself did not expect a favourable issue to this
step.[1] In London indeed many objections were raised both as to
the contents and the purpose of the protocol. Derby refused to
sign it unless Russia engaged to demobilise her army simultaneously with Turkey. He endeavoured also to modify it so as
to avoid any precise engagement on the part of either Turkey or
England, the non-fulfilment of which might serve Russia as a
pretext for demanding coercive measures against Turkey. Derby
was supported by Disraeli and the Queen, but there was a strong
party in the Cabinet urging a change of policy and co-operation
with the Great Powers. Salisbury warned Disraeli that if the
protocol were rejected, Russia would go to war backed by Austria
and Germany, and would seek compensations in Asia to the
detriment of England.

This then would be the result of the policy of isolation which we
should have to present to Parliament. We should have restored the
alliance of the three Empires; established Russia on the Armenian
hills; lost all hold on Turkey—and got nothing whatever in compensation.
For these reasons it seems to me vital to the ministry if we can
manage it, to accept this protocol. Even if it involves some difficulties
in the future, they are trivial compared to those which surround us
now.[2]

After long deliberation and owing chiefly to Russia's yielding
to the last limit and to British fear of isolation the protocol was
signed on 31 March. The six Powers restated their "common

[1] G.P. Nos. 276, 279.   [2] Salisbury, pp. 131–2.

interest in the amelioration of the lot of the Christians" and in the introduction of reforms accepted by the Porte. They took note of the conclusion of peace with Serbia, and recommended the rectification of frontier in favour of Montenegro. They invited the Porte to reorganise its armies on a peace footing and to introduce within the shortest time possible the reforms necessary for the tranquillity and the welfare of the provinces, and which were unanimously considered as indispensable for the peace of Europe. The Powers proposed to watch the fulfil-ment of these promises through their representatives. If their hopes were once more disappointed and the position of the Christians were not improved in a way which would prevent periodical unrest, they reserved to themselves the right to con-sider in common as to the means which they might deem best fitted to secure the well-being of the Christian populations, and the interests of general peace. The question of disarmament was regulated by two declarations on the part of Derby and Shouvalov. Shouvalov declared that if peace with Montenegro were con-cluded, and the Porte accepted the advice of Europe, and showed itself ready to replace its forces on a peace footing and seriously undertake the reforms mentioned in the protocol, she should send to St Petersburg a special envoy for a discussion of dis-armament to which Russia was ready to consent. Derby declared that in the event of "reciprocal disarmament on the part of Russia and Turkey, and peace between them" not being attained, this protocol "should be regarded as null and void".[1]

In proposing this protocol Russia desired to unite the Powers once more on a common programme, hoping that this united action would induce the Porte to accept it; but if it failed she wished to have a direct pretext for declaring war, a pretext of a European character. Her constant wish was to act as a European mandatory. She therefore yielded more than it became a Great Power and more than was in accordance with her policy of serious reforms. She had already reduced her "irreducible minimum" to the limit which was in fact a virtual abandonment of the Christians. She abandoned now even that little guarantee and asked Turkey to introduce those reforms only which she had accepted. The protocol hardly offered any guarantee against

[1] G.P. No. 282.

Turkish misrule. Yet the Turks remained obstinate. On 9 April they rejected the protocol on the ground that it was "annulling the Treaty of Paris" and encroaching upon their independence.

Serbia and Montenegro desired to send their representatives to the Constantinople Conference to give the necessary explanations to their questions, but the Conference refused to receive them. Nevertheless the Belgrade Government forwarded two memoranda to the Conference in which they refused the Turkish accusation of having provoked the war and asked for radical reforms for the revolted provinces.[1] Greece also endeavoured to interest the Great Powers in her kinsmen in Turkey, demanding for them the same privileges as those to be accorded to the Slavs.[2] England and Austria defended her cause, seeing in it a counterpoise to the Slavs, but failed to achieve anything for her as the Conference confined itself to the revolted provinces only.

When the Conference broke up the Porte offered direct negotiations to Serbia and Montenegro for the conclusion of peace. This overture was accepted and on 16 February peace was concluded with Serbia on the basis of the *status quo*. Negotiations with Montenegro were protracted owing to her insistence upon obtaining territorial rectifications recommended by the Conference, which the Porte refused. When Russia entered upon war Montenegro broke up the negotiations and resumed hostilities.

---

[1] J. Ristić, *Diplomatska istorija Srbije*, I, pp. 214–30.
[2] M. Lhéritier, *op. cit.* III, p. 404.

CHAPTER VII

*

THE RUSSO-TURKISH WAR

AFTER nearly two years of futile efforts to bring the crisis to an end in a peaceful way, Russia found herself compelled to have recourse to arms. She was from the outset confronted with the dilemma: to content herself with palliative reforms which Austria was ready to accept, or to impose her demands upon both Turkey and Austria by force. Neither of these solutions suited her. She could not abandon the revolted Christians to further oppression by the Turks without losing the influence she enjoyed with them and throwing them into the hands of Austria. This influence, earned by great and continual efforts and sacrifices for the improvement of their position, represented a strong political weapon for the realisation of her own aims in the Balkans, and she could not afford to be deprived of it. Yet still less could she think of entering into a war, as it was sure to provoke a European coalition against her, as in 1854, and end in disaster. Put between these two impossibilities Russia avoided taking any decision, and endeavoured to achieve her purpose by diplomatic means. Gortchakov adopted Andrassy's reforms in the hope that their failure would persuade the Powers of the necessity of more efficacious measures; to vanquish Andrassy's resistance, he endeavoured to bring the other Powers into negotiations of the measures for appeasement; having failed with it, he tried to win over England and afterwards Germany for his programme of autonomy. But all his efforts to circumvent Austria and compel her into accepting what she was opposed to, proved to be unavailing. They had only prolonged the crisis and encouraged the other provinces to revolt, which made the Russian position still more difficult, and forced her to take up arms.

At the beginning of November negotiations were opened between Andrassy and Novikov with the view of formulating the conditions of Austria's neutrality and defining the consequences of the war. The results of these negotiations were embodied in two conventions, the military and the political one, which bore the date of 15 January 1877. By the military convention Austria engaged to maintain benevolent neutrality towards Russia and to paralyse by her diplomatic action all attempts at intervention or collective mediation on the part of the other Powers. She engaged further not to co-operate in the execution of the treaty of 15 April 1856 nor lend her assistance to an effective action on the basis of Article VIII of the treaty of 30 March 1856. She promised also not to oppose a temporary closure of the Danube and to allow the purchase and transport of war material on her territory so far as this was compatible with her international obligations. She was free to choose the moment and manner of the occupation of Bosnia and Herzegovina, without giving this measure the character either of hostility or solidarity with Russia. Russia engaged not to extend her military action to Serbia, Montenegro, Bosnia and Herzegovina; and Austria agreed not to extend hers to Roumania, Bulgaria, Serbia and Montenegro. Serbia, Montenegro and the Sandjak of Novipazar were to form a neutral zone destined to prevent the contact of the two armies. But Austria promised not to oppose their combined action with Russia beyond their frontiers.[1]

The idea of creating a neutral zone proceeded from Gortchakov, but he wished that Serbia and Montenegro should be free to join Russia. Andrassy was strongly opposed to their co-operation with Russia, and asked that they should be forbidden to enter the war again. He argued that this co-operation would give the war a Slav character and transform it into a revolution. If Russia made the aspirations of these provinces her own this would have a bad effect on the Austrian Slavs. If she adopted all the hitherto isolated Slav tendencies, public opinion in the Monarchy would consider its existence endangered.[2] But Gortchakov insisted upon the impossibility of Russia depriving herself of Serbia and Montenegro as bases of operations and as efficacious diversions, and refused to consent to their neutrality. Finally, Austria agreed to their co-operation

---

[1] G.P. No. 265.
[2] A.A., Andrassy to Langenau, 26 Dec. 1876, geheim.

beyond their frontiers; she admitted also the possibility of Russian troops entering Serbia in the event of her existence being threatened by the Turks, but this was not embodied in the convention.[1]

From the correspondence exchanged between the two Emperors Gortchakov concluded that Austria, although refusing common action, consented to "an action independent in appearance and concerted in reality so as to tend to a common purpose by ways appropriate to the particular position and Parliamentary necessities of Austria-Hungary". The convention had therefore to bind the two Governments by precise engagements "destined to supplement what that action, combined but independent, contained of vague, by establishing clearly their complete solidarity in view of common purpose".[2] Andrassy repudiated the idea that there existed a positive common purpose between Austria and Russia, calling it a self-delusion. A common purpose could exist if they were to act jointly. Since this was not the case, their only common purpose was a negative one: to avoid collision. Austria could not take an attitude which might be interpreted as co-operation or solidarity with Russia. She would give her action the character of an unavoidable defensive protection of her interests in the south.[3]

The consequences of the war were to be regulated by a special convention which would state clearly the reciprocal interests of the two parties on the basis of the Reichstadt Agreement. Gortchakov desired that it should stipulate expressly the perfect solidarity of the two parties with respect to their interests, and that they should engage to maintain it on the diplomatic field, should the territorial changes resulting from the war give place to a collective deliberation of the Powers.[4] Andrassy refused the idea of solidarity, but consented to mutual diplomatic support, which he interpreted as excluding all claims for compensation on the part of the other Powers. He wished therefore that an agreement about the definite results of the war should be reached simultaneously. Without it he considered the military convention invalid.[5]

[1] A.A., Gortchakov to Novikov, 15 Dec. 1876.   [2] *Ibid.* 2 Nov.
[3] A.A., Andrassy to Langenau, 26 Dec. 1876, geheim.
[4] A.A., Gortchakov to Novikov, 2 Nov. 1876.
[5] A.A., Andrassy to Langenau, 26 Dec. 1876, geheim.

Gortchakov was not in haste to conclude the convention. He wrote to Novikov on 5 December that the Reichstadt Agreement was of a contingent nature and presupposed the dissolution of Turkey as a condition of its execution. In so far it was not actual. Andrassy had himself proposed Bessarabia and Batum for Russia as compensation for Austria's annexations. Should the crisis end peacefully and Turkey remained, Russia would take nothing of her territory nor claim an exclusive influence.[1] Gortchakov wished that the political convention should be put into operation only in the event of the dissolution of Turkey, like the Reichstadt Agreement, on the basis of which it was to be concluded. He demanded therefore that the word "war" should be omitted from Andrassy's project of convention, which stated in its preamble that the purpose of the convention was to regulate territorial changes which the war or dissolution of Turkey might have as a result. In his opinion the convention ought to regulate the changes which a dissolution of Turkey and not war alone would have as a result. The war might but need not necessarily lead to dissolution.[2]

Andrassy explained to Gortchakov that so long as Turkey existed he had no interest in annexation, but that "every alteration of the *status quo*" would affect the equipoise and security of the Monarchy and would force it to protect itself by annexing Bosnia and Herzegovina. Austria could not abandon them after occupation, for she would thus pave the way to the creation of a great Slav state, and admit its legitimacy as the only possible solution. The war itself was not sufficient for the realisation of the Reichstadt Agreement, but its execution could not depend upon the dissolution of Turkey, the beginning and the end of which could not be determined. Andrassy demanded therefore that the convention should be put into operation in case of territorial changes which the war or dissolution might have as a result.[3]

This view was not in accordance with the provisions of the Reichstadt Agreement, but it secured Austria against all eventualities. Gortchakov was not satisfied with it and delayed

[1] A.A., Gortchakov to Novikov, 5 Dec. 1876.
[2] A.A., Gortchakov to Novikov, 25 Jan. 1877; Andrassy to Langenau, 28 Feb. 1877, No. 27, secret.
[3] A.A., Andrassy to Langenau, 28 Feb. 1877.

concluding the convention as long as he could. Finally an arrangement was reached, which gave satisfaction to Andrassy. It was stated in the preamble of the convention that it was "destined to regulate in advance territorial rearrangements which the war or dissolution of the Ottoman Empire might have as a result".

Among the consequences of the war the convention provided for the annexation of Bessarabia, ceded in 1856, to Russia, and of Bosnia and Herzegovina, excluding the portion between Serbia and Montenegro, about which an accord was to be reached when the moment for the disposing of it came, to Austria. The question of the limits of Austrian acquisitions provoked long discussion. At Reichstadt it was agreed that parts of both Bosnia and Herzegovina should fall to Serbia and Montenegro; now Austria required the whole of both provinces for herself, and in addition free communication through the Sandjak for her trade in the East.

Gortchakov made no objection to Andrassy's claims in Bosnia, but protested against the inclusion of Herzegovina, which according to his own and the Tsar's memory was not ceded to Austria at Reichstadt.[1] Andrassy referred him to an *aide mémoire* which Novikov had written at his dictation after the interview at Reichstadt, and in which both provinces were clearly designated, with the exception of the part of Herzegovina which was allotted to Montenegro. He had asked Novikov to send this memorandum to his Government and had hitherto received no objection to it.[2] To appease Gortchakov's anxiety about Montenegro, for which he asked him to have special regard, Andrassy worked out a map of her future acquisitions which doubled her territory. But Gortchakov was not satisfied with it, for Montenegro did not obtain sufficient arable land. He demanded an increase of territory in the north and in the south up to Antivari, and proposed at the same time that the frontiers of Austria's acquisitions should run along the River Drina up to Piva and Tara, following from that point the line between Lipik and Ravno so as to embrace Sutorina and Zupci.[3] As to the Sandjak of Novipazar,

[1] A.A., Gortchakov to Novikov, 5 Dec. 1876.
[2] A.A., Andrassy to Novikov, 19 Dec. 1876.
[3] A.A., Novikov to Andrassy, 28 Feb. 1877. Aide mémoire confidentiel.

Gortchakov insisted upon its being divided between Serbia and Montenegro, as was agreed at Reichstadt.[1] He admitted the justice of Austria's claims for the security of her trade communications through the Sandjak, but excluded every military servitude. He proposed, however, that an agreement about it should be reached later on, to which Andrassy consented.[2]

The second article engaged the two Powers to mutual diplomatic assistance in the event of "territorial rearrangements resulting from a war or dissolution of the Ottoman Empire" giving place to collective deliberations of the Powers. Gortchakov's idea of solidarity was abandoned, but mutual assistance was extended to all territorial changes, and not only to the reciprocal interests of the two parties.

The third article stated that the two Powers had agreed in principle at Reichstadt to the following points: "in case of territorial rearrangements or dissolution of the Ottoman Empire, the establishment of a great compact Slav state, or other, is excluded; in return Bulgaria, Albania, and the rest of Roumelia might be constituted as independent states; Thessaly, a part of Epirus and the island of Crete might be annexed to Greece; Constantinople with suburbs, the boundaries of which remain to be determined, might become a free city."[3] They stated further that they had nothing to change in these views and that they would maintain them "as bases" of their subsequent policy. This text was identical neither with Andrassy's nor with Gortchakov's text of the Reichstadt Agreement, though it was nearer to that of Gortchakov. Beside several minor differences, the most interesting is the omission to provide for any territorial aggrandisement for Serbia and Montenegro, though this question was discussed during the negotiation.

After having secured Austrian neutrality, Russia might fairly regard it as very improbable that any combination could be made against her. Public opinion in England had been so roused against Turkey as to render active support on her part impossible; and it was certain that a Russian war would be accepted without

---

[1] A.A., Novikov to Andrassy, 28 Feb. 1877. Aide mémoire confidentiel.
[2] A.A., Andrassy to Langenau, 28 Feb. 1877, No. 27, secret.
[3] G.P. No. 266.

opposition, so long at least as Russia desisted from all conquest. "Never", wrote Schweinitz, "had Russia begun a Turkish war in such favourable circumstances,...never had the diplomatic field been so well prepared."[1]

War was declared on 24 April and the Russian army, already massed on the Roumanian frontier to guard the bridges on the Sereth, crossed it at Yassy and Galatz. The Russians took a rather long time to reach the Danube and concentrate for action. It was only at the end of June that they succeeded in crossing the river, and not without strong resistance on the part of the Turkish troops. The Russians soon occupied Tchernavoda, Nikopol and Tirnova, and continued to advance to the south. The vanguard of General Gurko reached the Balkans and crossed it at Kazanlik, forcing the Turks to abandon the Shipka Pass, thus opening the way to Southern Bulgaria. But on the extreme right they met with unexpected resistance. On 20 July they attacked Plevna with insufficient forces, hastening to chase the Turks from that place before Osman Pasha from Vidin came to their help, but were repulsed with heavy losses. The attack was renewed on 30 July in much greater force, but was repulsed again, causing still greater losses. In August the Turks took the offensive and drove the Russians from Roushtchuk, even threatening their communications with the centre. They delivered a series of attacks on Shipka, and compelled General Gurko to retreat, but failed to dislodge him from the Balkan ridges.

In Asia the Russians immediately took the offensive, occupied Bayazid and surrounded Kars. Soon afterwards they took Ardahan and continued to advance towards Erzerum. By the end of June their offensive was stopped by Muktar Pasha, who during July forced them to abandon all their conquests, except Ardahan, and to retreat to their frontier. In August the Turks made an attempt to reconquer Georgia, where an insurrection had broken out among the Moslems, but were repulsed.

In going to war Russia discouraged any attempt of Serbia, Greece and Roumania to join her against Turkey. Although defeated and exhausted in the first war, Serbia desired to continue the struggle, and already in November sent a special envoy to St Petersburg to express this wish and to ask for financial help.

---

[1] Schweinitz, I, p. 421.

The Tsar wrote to Prince Milan that he expected an energetic co-operation on his part in the event of war.[1] But when the war began he asked him to refrain from action before his army crossed the Danube. In June Milan visited him at his head-quarters in Ploeste, but received the same advice: the Tsar told him that after the crossing of the Danube he might join Russia if he wished.[2] It was evident that the Tsar did not wish nor count much upon Serbia's assistance.

Greece had also begun military preparations and offered an alliance to Russia. In April Gortchakov informed his Ambassador at Athens that "every diversion in favour of our troops would be desirable at present", but he refused to give the formal engage-ment which the Greek Government desired.[3] In June and July negotiations were renewed, Greece again offered her co-opera-tion, but insisted upon a treaty of alliance and guarantees for her future acquisitions. Russia refused these conditions and advised her to act on her own hand.[4]

Roumania had already on 13 May proclaimed independence and declared war on Turkey. She offered to join Russia as her ally, but was refused. Nelidov, who acted as director of the Grand Duke's diplomatic office, informed Prince Charles on 25 May that the Russian army was strong enough and had no need of Roumania's support.[5] Yet the Russians desired to use the Roumanian army for secondary services. After crossing the Danube they asked them to occupy Nikopol and take charge of the Turkish prisoners in order to relieve their troops for action. But the Prince did not wish to play a secondary rôle, and insisted upon the conclusion of a formal alliance.

There were various reasons for which Russia refused to accept the Balkan States as her allies. She believed the war would be a short one, that the forces she had mobilised would suffice to overcome Turkey. She did not wish to have Roumania, from whom she intended to wrench Bessarabia, as an ally, nor to have her hands bound by engagements to the Balkan States. Above all she hoped that Turkey would submit to her demands after the first defeat, and did not wish to give her action the character

---

[1] J. Ristić, *op. cit.* I, p. 232.   [2] *Ibid.* II, p. 39.
[3] M. Lhéritier, *op. cit.* III, p. 415.   [4] *Ibid.* p. 422 *passim.*
[5] P. Lindenberg, *König Karl von Rumänien,* I, p. 376.

of a general Balkan movement, as it might lead to the disruption of Turkey and provoke complications with the other Powers. But the unexpected resistance of Osman Pasha and the failure to win England over for a "small peace" changed the situation completely. Heavily pressed by the Turks the Russians wanted an immediate diversion, and therefore invited the Balkan States to join them at once. The Tsar sent a personal appeal to Prince Milan to begin hostilities within twelve days, adding that he would consider it as a "considerable personal service" for which he would pay the account. At the same time he ordered a million roubles to be given to Serbia for war expenses.[1] But Serbia was unprepared for an immediate action, and, discouraged by Russia's defeat, recoiled from war. Colonel Bobrikov, who was sent in August to examine her military conditions, did not think her capable of entering the struggle for some time. She was asked, therefore, to send her regular troops only to the south-eastern frontier to keep a portion of the Turkish troops engaged.[2]

At the same time the Grand Duke asked Greece to make an immediate diversion on her frontier, and invited Roumania to start at once with military demonstrations on the Danube and to cross it as soon as possible. But the Greek Government insisted upon their demands being previously accepted. Gortchakov promised them Thessaly and Epirus in the event of Turkey breaking up, and instructed Saburov to suggest a treaty of alliance as his own proposal. The negotiations dragged on, as Russia shrank from giving more than a promise, whereas Greece insisted on a formal agreement. Russia hoped that Greece would be forced into action by her own public opinion. But the Greek Government was irresolute and discouraged by Russia's defeat. On the other hand England pressed them to keep quiet, and even demanded a declaration that they would preserve neutrality. Austria also advised them not to start a war too soon, as this might induce Turkey to conclude peace with Russia, which would have been a Russian peace. Thus Greece wavered, but remained quiet.[3]

Roumania was ready to come to the help of Russia, but she did not mean to recede from her demands. Having failed to

---

[1] *Zapisi Jevrema Grujića*, III, p. 295.
[2] G. T. Bobrikov, *U Srbiji*, p. 36. [3] M. Lhéritier, *op. cit.* III, p. 423.

draw Serbia and Greece into the war, the Russians found themselves compelled to yield to Roumania. An arrangement was reached by the end of August and Prince Charles was given the command over the troops at Plevna.

A new attack on Plevna was prepared for 11 September, the date of the Tsar's Name Day. The battle, which was opened with a field mass, attended by the Tsar and Prince Charles, lasted two days and inflicted heavy casualties on both sides. The Russians and the Roumanians lost 30,000 dead and wounded, without considerably improving their position. It was realised then that Plevna could be conquered only by a regular siege, and during September and October this was the chief aim of the operations.

The outbreak of war gave a fresh impetus to the agitation of the Slavophils, who considered this war as their own work and believed that it was undertaken for the Slav Idea. Popular excitement stimulated by the press and at meetings was now general. Alexander II was hailed as the Tsar of all the Slavs, whereas Europe was fiercely attacked.[1] "The Russian flag is already waving beyond Russian limits", declared Aksakov at the meeting of the Slav Committee—"and this flag has been raised for the recovery of the liberty and human rights of the oppressed, humiliated and despised by civilised Europe. The slumbering East is awakening, and not only the Slavs of the Balkan peninsula, but also the whole Slav world awaits its resurrection. A new era is approaching; the dawn of the great Slav day is on the point of breaking."[2] "Let us endeavour to reach Constantinople", wrote *Novoe Vremja*, "and we shall find there the honourable peace desired by all, without sacrificing our convictions."[3] The choice of the Grand Duke Nicholas—whose Slavophil sympathies were notorious—as commander of the Balkan army, gave a still more Slavophil character to the war. He took as his councillor General Ignatyev and appointed as the Chief of his political department Nelidov, the creator of the famous memorandum of 1875.[4]

Under the impulse of the enthusiasm by which the war was hailed, the Liberals and the Revolutionaries remained calm, but

---

[1] Schweinitz, 1, pp. 422–32.   [2] *Moscow Gazette*, 11–23 May 1877.
[3] *Novoe Vremja*, 5 July 1877.
[4] Nelidov was the secretary of the Russian Embassy in Constantinople. In the autumn of 1875 he wrote a memorandum urging the Tsar to wage a war against Turkey.

the defeat at Plevna encouraged them to raise their heads again. In Liberal circles the war was indeed considered as a means for attaining political freedom. They hoped that defeat would demonstrate the impossibility of the absolutist regime and lead to reforms, as it had done after the Crimean War. Their criticism became now more open and sharper. Under the title "Whom we must fight, our one real foe", *Golos* wrote that the real enemy of Russia was the internal corruption, and general ignorance of Russian society. The Revolutionaries profited also by this situation for their propaganda. This agitation represented no serious danger, but it was a clear illustration of the internal conditions of Russia: the hatred of the autocratic regime led the Russians to desire the disaster of their own country.

In entering upon war Russia issued a Circular Note explaining that she had exhausted all the means in her power to arrive at a lasting peace by a common action with the Great Powers. The Turks had rejected all their proposals, and it was no longer in the interest of Europe to allow the prolongation of such a state of things. Russia had therefore undertaken the execution of the work, in which she had hitherto co-operated with the Great Powers.[1] This note was left unanswered by all the Powers except England, who declined to see an interest of her own in the Russian war. "In taking action against Turkey on his own part and having recourse to arms without further consultation with his allies", replied Lord Derby, "the Emperor of Russia has separated himself from the European concert hitherto maintained, and has at the same time departed from the rule to which he himself had solemnly recorded his consent".[2]

Disraeli did not confine himself to refuting the ideas of the Russian circular. He desired "to occupy the Dardanelles as a material guarantee against Russia seizing on Constantinople",[3] and endeavoured to persuade his colleagues that the Russians would reach Constantinople in nine weeks after crossing the Pruth, "and that it would take nearly that time for us to reach and entrench ourselves in the Dardanelles".[4] The Cabinet strongly opposed this measure, fearing lest it should lead to an

[1] P.P., Gortchakov to Shouvalov, 19 April 1877.
[2] P.P., Derby to Loftus, 1 May 1877.
[3] Queen Victoria, p. 530.   [4] Salisbury, p. 139.

alliance with Turkey. "This, of course, is his real intention", wrote Salisbury to Carnarvon, communicating to him his conversation with Disraeli. He tried to deter Disraeli from this step, advising him to wait for the conclusion of peace and then interfere if British interests were injured by it. "But he was not at all satisfied with this idea—and used some phrases indicating an intention to assist the Sultan to maintain his position in Bulgaria."[1]

The maintenance of the Ottoman Empire had been regarded in England ever since the Crimean War as identical with the interests which she had in keeping Russia far from the Mediterranean and preventing her from becoming preponderant in Asia. The rapid advance of Russia in Asia and the ever-increasing importance of India for the British Empire gave still greater value to the maintenance of Turkey. But the massacres in Bulgaria alienated public opinion from Turkey and "produced in the Cabinet as in the country a strong indisposition again to be allied in arms with so barbarous and purblind a State".[2] Faithful to the traditional policy, Disraeli had to overcome enormous difficulties both in the Cabinet and in Parliament in order to make them adopt the measures which would facilitate eventual action. But in spite of all his tact and ability the Cabinet only moved forward very cautiously, and retreated as soon as they felt that some step might lead to the consequences which they did not want. "We never came to an actual division", wrote Northcote in his memorandum, "...but the ultimate views of some of us differed from those of others, and we more than once, after adopting a particular measure one day, found ourselves on the next adopting another wholly inconsistent with the intentions, at all events, of the day before."[3] This situation induced Disraeli to work behind the back of the Cabinet, in agreement with the Queen, and thus to make up, by secret ways, so far as it was possible, for what the Cabinet refused to do.

By this time the Queen came to share completely Disraeli's feelings and views about Russia. She was quite convinced that the realisation of Russia's aims would humiliate England and force her to abdicate her position as a Great Power. She wrote a letter to be read in the Cabinet stressing the necessity of

[1] Salisbury, p. 140. [2] Disraeli, p. 138. [3] Ibid. p. 139.

complete unanimity and "of showing a bold and united front to the enemy in the country as well as outside....It is not the question of upholding Turkey," she wrote, "it is the question of Russian or British supremacy in the world!"[1] In a private letter to Disraeli she said that "if England is to kiss Russia's feet, she will not be a party to the humiliation of England and would lay down her crown...". "To let it be thought that we shall never fight", she wrote again, "and that England will submit to Egypt being under Russia would be to abdicate the position of Great Britain as one of the Great Powers—to which she never will submit, and another must wear the crown if this is intended."[2]

Having failed to win the Cabinet for an occupation of Gallipoli, Disraeli proposed that Russia should be informed of the interests which Great Britain was resolved to defend in the East, and asked to give an engagement that she should respect them. This measure was intended, on the one hand, to restrain Russia from going beyond the limits thus set up, on the other, to bind the Cabinet to defend these interests in the event of their being injured. At the same time he proposed to reach an agreement with Austria as to a joint action for the defence of Constantinople. Both these proposals were adopted by the Cabinet. On 6 May Derby directed a note to the Russian Ambassador telling him that the British Government had warned the Porte from the outset

"that it must not look to them for assistance and they are determined to carry into effect the policy thus announced, so long as Turkish interests alone are involved....Should the war now in progress unfortunately spread, interests may be imperilled which they are equally bound and determined to defend....Foremost among them is the necessity of keeping open, uninjured and uninterrupted, the communication between Europe and the East by the Suez Canal. An attempt to blockade or otherwise to interfere with the Canal or its approaches would be regarded by them as a menace to India and a grave injury to the commerce of the world. On both these grounds, any such step...would be inconsistent with the maintenance by them of an attitude of passive neutrality.

An attack on Egypt or its occupation could not be "regarded with unconcern" by England. She is "not prepared to witness with

[1] *Ibid.* p. 133.   [2] *Ibid.*

indifference the passing into other hands than those of its present possessors" of Constantinople.

"The existing arrangements made under European sanction which regulate the navigation of the Bosphorus and Dardanelles appear to them wise and salutary, and there would be in their judgment serious objection to their alteration in any material particular.... The course of events might show that there were still other interests, as for instance on the Persian Gulf which it would be their duty to protect: but they do not doubt that they will have sufficiently pointed out to Your Excellency the limits within which they hope that the war may be confined, or at all events those within which they themselves would be prepared, so far as present circumstances allow of an opinion being formed, to maintain a policy of abstention and neutrality."

Derby pointed out further that in defining their interests the British Government desired "to respond to the assurances given" by the Tsar at Livadia "that he had no intention of acquiring Constantinople and that if necessity should oblige him to occupy a portion of Bulgaria, it would only be provisional...".[1]

Count Shouvalov, who was well informed of the disposition of the British Government, and the intentions of Disraeli and the Queen, realised that despite England's isolation and internal dissensions, they would not allow the solution of any question in the East without their participation. Had they succeeded in finding an ally they would have joined Turkey at once. But if this had hitherto restrained them from action, the first decisive success of the Russian army would unite the Cabinet and lead them to decisions that might bring about a war with Russia. He proposed therefore to Prince Gortchakov to acquaint England at the favourable moment with the eventual conditions of peace and the limitations he would be ready to accept if she remained neutral. This seemed to him to be "an efficacious means, perhaps the only one, of maintaining the neutrality of England".[2]

By the end of May Shouvalov was summoned to St Petersburg to report on the situation in England. He found his fears shared by some responsible men in the capital, who with Gortchakov constituted the group of the so-called "small peace". These men desired to see the war ended as soon as possible. They were

[1] R.D., Derby to Shouvalov, 6 May 1877.
[2] R.D., Shouvalov to Gortchakov, 20 April 1877.

afraid of revolutionary demonstrations if it were prolonged. They understood also that Europe was not prepared for a definite solution of the Eastern Question and that Russia could not go beyond the limits of general European interests without risking a conflict. They were willing therefore to put an end to the hostilities before Turkey was crushed if there were any possibility of an honourable peace.[1]

Gortchakov answered Derby's note by repudiating any intention on the part of Russia to blockade the Suez Canal or occupy Egypt. She had neither an interest in it nor the means of executing it. He assured Derby that Russia would not take possession of nor permanently occupy Constantinople, but refused to bind himself as to a temporary occupation, although he did not intend it, for this might make the Turks obstinate and provoke a contrary effect. As to the Straits he asked that their status should be revised in the spirit of equity so as to remove the present inconveniences to Russia. He refused the idea that Russia desired or had an interest in disturbing England's possessions in India or her communications. "But we may be forced to seek measures of defence against her hostility", he wrote. "Our attitude depends entirely upon hers.... We are quite disposed to come to terms frankly and loyally on all these questions."[2]

At the same time Gortchakov proposed to Britain that the war should be stopped if the Great Powers remained neutral and Turkey sued for peace before Russia crossed the Balkans. In that event peace would be concluded on the following terms: Bulgaria as far as the Balkans should be constituted as an autonomous vassal state under European guarantee, with the national militia and without Turkish garrisons; Bulgaria south of the Balkans and the other Christian provinces would have the best guarantees for a regular administration; Montenegro and Serbia would receive an augmentation of territory to be agreed upon in common; Bosnia and Herzegovina "would be endowed with institutions judged by common accord as compatible with their internal state and apt to assure to them a good native administration"; Serbia and Roumania were to remain under the Sultan's

---

[1] "La Guerre Russo-Turcque", *La Nouvelle Revue*, 1880, vi, pp. 734, 736. A.A., Langenau to Andrassy, 18–30 June 1877, No. 39.
[2] R.D., Gortchakov to Shouvalov, 30 May 1877.

suzerainty. As to Roumania, this question would be solved by a common agreement. If the Turks accepted these conditions Russia would be entitled to demand the restitution of the part of Bessarabia ceded in 1856 and the cession of Batum with an adjacent territory as a compensation for war expenses. In that event Roumania could be compensated in the Dobrudja. "If Austria-Hungary on her part claimed compensation whether for the acquisitions made by Russia, or as a gage of security against the territorial changes mentioned above in favour of the Christian principalities of the Balkan Peninsula, Russia would not oppose her seeking such compensations in Bosnia and in part in Herzegovina." If the Powers agreed with these conditions they could bring their collective pressure to bear on the Porte in order to make it accept them. Should it reject these counsels, Russia would continue the war and peace would depend on war events and the military situation. Nevertheless, if the Powers remained neutral peace would be concluded with their assent. This neutrality excluded, however, even temporary occupation of Constantinople and the Straits by England.[1]

In communicating Gortchakov's proposal to Derby, Shouvalov told him that it "offered the means of localising the war and preventing a dissolution of the Ottoman Empire. But the Tsar must know whether, within the limits indicated, he can be sure of the neutrality of England."[2] But as soon as he acquitted himself of his mission, Gortchakov wired him not to communicate the proposal, or if he had already done so, to inform the British Government that experience on the spot had shown the impossibility of dividing Bulgaria, "as such an arrangement would exclude from autonomous institutions the most industrious and intelligent part of the province and that which had most suffered from the Turkish misrule".[3] The reason of this change was the opposition of the Russian headquarters, who were not consulted, to the programme set up by Gortchakov. They found it contrary to Russian interests and to their military plans. This change had only impaired the already bad impression London had of the Russian answer and of her proposal. The refusal to give precise

[1] R.D., Gortchakov to Shouvalov, 30 May 1877.
[2] R.D., VI, p. 427.
[3] "Les Russes devant Constantinople", *La Revue de Paris*, 1897, IV, pp. 406–7.

engagements as to Constantinople and the proposed peace terms only tended to increase British suspicions. Derby informed Andrassy of them, and asked for the opinion of Sir Henry Layard, who in April had succeeded Elliot at Constantinople. Andrassy advised him not to reject the proposal, but to take it as a basis for further discussion.[1] Layard disapproved strongly of it, arguing that its adoption would amount to the disruption of Turkey. "I cannot but suspect", wrote Derby to him, "that these conditions have only been put forward in the conviction that they would be rejected."[2] He left the Russian proposal without an answer. The attempt of St Petersburg to come to an agreement with London as to the conditions of peace, and thus avert an eventual conflict in the future, was frustrated.

Meanwhile Disraeli and the Queen continued to press a forward policy on the Cabinet, and were greatly distressed at the difficulties they encountered. Disraeli feared particularly the Opposition taking advantage of the embarrassed position of the Government and making an appeal to the country against them. Gladstone was convinced that "it was only by an un-remitted action that we can keep Dizzi's hands from mischief".[3] He stood once more against the policy of supporting Turkey, and asked the Government to use their influence and work in concert with the Great Powers in order to ensure self-government for the Christians. "There were other days," said Gladstone, "when England was the hope of freedom. Whenever in the world a high aspiration was entertained, or a noble blow was struck, it was to England that the eyes of the oppressed were turned."[4] "The tactics of the Opposition are clear", wrote Disraeli to Derby. "...Having successfully acted on a nervous and divided Cabinet, and prevented anything being done, they will now turn round and say, 'This is the way you protect British interests!' They will probably turn us out in this Parliament, or they will force us to a dissolution under the influence of a disastrous defeat abroad."[5] A few days later he communicated to him a letter of the Lord Chancellor, who complained of the Government doing nothing to protect the

---

[1] B.A., Derby to Buchanan, 22 Dec. 1877, No. 494, most conf.
[2] Layard, v, 51.   [3] R. W. Seton-Watson, *op. cit.* p. 192.
[4] J. Morley, *op. cit.* pp. 174–5.   [5] Disraeli, p. 140.

interests they had defined and pointed out the danger of Russia bridging over the few weeks, "which will make her safe against any action of ours...". "I must say that all this expresses very much my own views," wrote Disraeli, "and indeed I often ask myself, if you had resolved to do nothing, why not have accepted Bismarck's offer? Nothing can justify isolation on the part of England but a determination to act."[1]

Fearing disastrous consequences both for his party and British interests, Disraeli resolved to force the Cabinet into action even at the price of breaking it up. On 6 June he wrote a secret letter to Layard asking him to induce the Porte to demand the presence of the British fleet at Constantinople and the occupation of Gallipoli by it. This measure would "maintain generally the *status quo*, and, at the same time, place England in a commanding position when the conditions of peace are discussed...". "If such a proposal came from the Porte, I would recommend its adoption by the Cabinet, but the proposal must come from Constantinople."[2] At the same time he intended to ask for a vote of credit for the military expedition. "My colleagues are bound to no particular course of action by the vote", he wrote to Derby, "...All I want now is, to reassure the country, that is alarmed and perplexed; to show that we are in a state not of puzzled inertness, but of preparedness for action; so to assist the negotiations which will be constantly cropping up, and place ourselves in a position, if there be eventually a crash, to assume a tone, which will be respected."[3]

But Disraeli found out that his difficulties lay not solely in the Cabinet. He managed to win over Salisbury and Derby for the vote of credit, but the obstacles were not thereby overcome.

"It is impossible to obtain a vote of money and men", he wrote to the Queen, "until the war estimates are passed, that is to say, so long as we may remain in a state of neutrality. If we had men and money, we could not despatch them to any part of the Turkish Empire without the permission of the Porte, and the Porte will not grant that permission, unless we occupy the Dardanelles, or otherwise, as their avowed allies. All these difficulties would be removed if we declared war against Russia: but there are not three men in the Cabinet, who are prepared to advise that step."[4]

[1] Disraeli, p. 141.　　[2] *Ibid.* pp. 142-3.　　[3] *Ibid.* p. 146.　　[4] *Ibid.* p. 149.

Disraeli tried also to induce Bismarck to support at Constantinople his proposal for occupation, and "in some way, to co-operate with that step".[1] Already at the end of May he took steps to sound his views with regard to the Eastern crisis. Bismarck "dwelt at length on the debt of gratitude which Germany owed to Russia...and concluded by saying that he would give his last effort to bring about a cordial and intimate understanding between England and Russia, to which Germany would become a party".[2] Indeed, Bismarck remained convinced that the partition of Turkey was the only means of settling the Eastern Question definitely, and at that time occupied himself with an outline of mutual compensations, which would satisfy all the Great Powers at the cost of Turkey and strengthen the position of Germany. On 6 July Russell, acting upon verbal instructions from Disraeli, communicated to Bismarck that Disraeli was prepared to advise the Queen to send the fleet to Gallipoli and that he "reckoned on the support of Germany in maintaining the Sovereignty of the Sultan at Constantinople and the principles which regulated the navigation of the Bosphorus and Dardanelles".[3] Bismarck dissuaded him from sending the fleet, and from intervening in the struggle before it was ended. He suggested that England should inform Russia of the proposals she would consent to, and make known the changes she was not prepared to sanction, "so that a clear basis could be established on which to negotiate a lasting European agreement". In his opinion the decision must be left to Russia and Turkey, and the Powers would do well "to force the question and settle it once for all...". "Russia and Austria will", he said, "take care of European Turkey; England had better secure the road to India—and if France would help herself to something in the East and leave Germany alone—he [Bismarck] would be heartily glad."[4]

Bismarck's attitude increased the distrust towards him and provoked great discontent in London. "Germany is strictly Russian," wrote Derby to Layard, "though Bismarck would be willing, for the sake of his own future plans, to embroil us in a

[1] *Ibid.* p. 149.
[2] B.A., Russell to Derby, 27 May 1877, No. 221, secret.
[2] B.A., *ibid.* 6 July 1877, No. 280, secret.
[4] *Ibid.* 9 July, No. 283, secret.

war with Russia."[1] Disraeli instructed Colonel Wellesley to tell
the Tsar that his true enemy was not he, but Bismarck—"the
Chancellor that has done all in his Power to urge Russia to
undertake this disastrous war."[2] Even in Serbia's intention to
resume hostilities he saw Bismarck's fingers. "No, there must
be an end to this", he said to Beust. "...I find Bismarck every-
where in my way.... I have much less against Russia than
against Bismarck and I am determined to oppose him."[3]

Disraeli did not confine his efforts to taking material guarantees
for the protection of British interests: he endeavoured at the
same time to find an ally, who would help him to resist Russia.
The Cabinet, while opposing the occupation, were prepared to
come to an agreement with Austria for a common defence of
their interests. On 19 May Derby invited the Vienna Government "to consider and discuss a plan of joint action in the event
...of a Russian march on Constantinople...". "The acquisition of Constantinople had notoriously been for generations past
an object of Russian ambition", he wrote to Beust. "Her
Majesty's Government cannot doubt that the independence of
Constantinople and the freedom of the Straits are objects not
less important to Austria than to England, and which Austria
like England will not be prepared to forego without an effort.
If such be the case, it ought not to be difficult to come to an
understanding according to which common interests shall be
defended by previously concerted action."[4]

Meanwhile, before this step was discussed and approved by
the Cabinet, Disraeli approached the Austrian Ambassador and
told him that the declaration of neutrality was a mere "formality"
and that it was necessary to come into the open as to the possibility of a common action. "What would you require from us?"
he asked of Count Beust.[5] At the same time, his private secretary,
Corry, used his secret channels with the Austrian Embassy,
established already in October 1876 through Count Montgelas,
to discuss the question more fully. "How much money do you
want?" he asked of Montgelas without any introduction. Montgelas answered that an agreement must be first reached as to the

[1] Layard, v, p. 51.   [2] Disraeli, p. 175.
[3] Andrassy, III, p. 50.   [4] Derby to Beust, 19 May 1877, conf.
[5] A.A., Beust to Andrassy, 1 May 1877, No. 36A-D, vertraulich.

purpose of common action. Corry replied that England could make far-reaching proposals to Austria if she were sure that they would not be communicated to Russia via Berlin. He believed that Russia and Germany would come to an understanding in the shortest time, for otherwise Russia's action could not be explained. "Why then, if this is not so," he said, "do the Germans for two years do nothing else but exhort us to annex Egypt and Crete?"[1] These secret conversations took place a fortnight before the British note was officially communicated to Andrassy. On 6 May Andrassy telegraphed to Beust that in his opinion it would be desirable that the two Cabinets should be in intimate contact during the present crisis, but that the question of the Blue Book must be regulated first. Up till then he should keep to his instructions: "neither provoke nor refuse the confidences."[2] On 9 May Disraeli and Derby suggested to Beust an *entente* between the two countries.[3] Francis Joseph instantly wired to Andrassy that these conversations had already gone too far and were compromising, and asked him to recommend more moderation to Beust.[4] Andrassy informed the latter that the British conditions of neutrality gave him the impression that the British Government were convinced in advance that Russia did not think of refusing them, and that they asked for Austria's co-operation solely with a view of showing their success to the Opposition. He bade him keep to former instructions, and breathe nothing to the German Ambassador about the rapprochement, which he did not seek for.[5]

This exchange of telegrams shows clearly that Austria did not welcome the British proposals. But when the overture was made officially she could not avoid an answer, though she gave it ten days later. Andrassy had to deal with an unpleasant situation, namely: to avoid compromising himself with Russia by an *entente* with England, and to avoid losing England's support by refusing her overture. Rejected by Austria, England would undoubtedly come to the conclusion that she was bound up with Russia, and would endeavour to safeguard her interests herself through an

---

[1] A.A., Montgelas, Montgelas to Beust, 1 May 1877.
[2] A.A., Andrassy to Beust, 6 May 1877. Tel. No. 59.
[3] A.A., Beust to Andrassy, 9 May 1877. Tel. No. 40B.
[4] A.A., Orczy to Andrassy, 10 May 1877. Tel. No. 943.
[5] A.A., Andrassy to Beust, 11 and 29 May 1877.

understanding with Russia—an understanding which might be reached to the detriment of Austria and which would undoubtedly weaken her position towards Russia. Andrassy solved this dilemma by applying his old principle of concerted but independent action, the one which he used in his negotiations with Russia, thus succeeding in preserving England's support without estranging Russia from himself.

On 29 May he answered Derby that he consented to an *entente* with England, but that its purpose could not be to oppose Russia's military operations.

"Had it been thought fit to stop Russia in the war she had undertaken, England, like us, was in possession of the means" for it in the Treaty of 1856. "The basis of an understanding lies rather in the answer to the question: What are the consequences of the present war which we can accept, and what are those which we cannot allow?

"Although we consider the Treaty of Paris as capable of modification, and would not insist upon its full maintenance, yet we adhere to the fundamental ideas of that Treaty. Consequently we could not accept:

"(1) That the exclusive protectorate over the Christian populations of the Balkan Peninsula should be conceded to any one Christian Power.

"(2) That the definite settlement of the results of the war should take place without the participation of the Guaranteeing Powers, and that the creation into a State ('Constituirung') of the Christian populations of the Balkan Peninsula should be granted ('octroyirt') through the action of a single Power.

"(3) An acquisition of territory by Russia on the right bank of the Danube.

"(4) The incorporation of Roumania with Russia, or the dependence of that Principality on the Russian Empire.

"(5) The erection in the above-named countries of a *secundogenitur*, whether Russian or Austro-Hungarian.

"(6) The occupation by Russia of Constantinople.

"(7) Finally, no large Slav State should be established at the expense of the non-Slav elements of the Balkan Peninsula, and in any case the reconstitution should be limited at most to the autonomy of the present provinces under a native Chief....This is the position we have taken up. It was our view before the war and will unchangeably remain so.

"We have not, on the other hand, avoided pointing out to the

Russian Government the essence of the points in which our interests might be affected." Already at the time of the Sumarakov mission, "we have rejected the idea of a Russian occupation of Bulgaria", and "have likewise declared that an invasion of Serbia...would be incompatible with our interests....In both these cases we have received from the Russian Government assurances in substance satisfactory, and we have also observed nothing in the attitude of Russia to give us reason to suspect that the Cabinet of St Petersburg contemplates acting without regard to our interests."

But if Russia breaks these promises Austria will oppose her with all her power.

As to the English reserves to Russia, Andrassy considered that the question of Constantinople and the Straits was closely connected with the interests he had defined above for

"the power in possession of Constantinople must, in the natural course of events, command Bulgaria and other districts of the Balkans, just as the State which holds Bulgaria and the districts beyond must inevitably obtain possession of Constantinople. We accordingly consider all the interests which require protection in the East as bound up together, and are of the opinion that no one of them can be given up without sacrificing the other." If Lord Derby shared this view "the natural solidarity of our interests stands out prominently of itself, and there remains for a further exchange of ideas the question of coming to an understanding as to the means by which these interests can be most surely protected, if possible without endangering the peace of Europe."[1]

In a confidential telegram to Beust, Andrassy threw the responsibility for the war on England, who had refused to support those Powers who desired to maintain the *status quo*, and had demanded reforms which Turkey must have rejected. He refused to "hold the same language" to Russia as England proposed. Since she has informed Russia of the points of her interest, every further demand would be considered in St Petersburg as coming from Austria.[2]

Andrassy's answer increased the suspicion in London "that between the three military empires of Eastern Europe there is an understanding as to what shall be done."..."Our *entente* with Austria-Hungary is for me the question which comes before all others," said Disraeli to Beust, "but every time I broach it in

[1] A.A., Andrassy to Beust, 29 May 1877.   [2] *Ibid.*

the Cabinet I run against the doubts of the existence of a perfect liberty of action on your part...."[1] "The Russians as well as the Germans are constantly telling us", said Derby to Beust, "that Austria-Hungary is engaged with Russia, and that the latter has not to fear serious difficulties from your side...."[2] "I fear that we shall not go beyond phrases", continued Disraeli, "whereas the question is whether we can and ought to act together.... I am not talking of a war against Russia, nor of a common language in St Petersburg. But we must agree that Russia shall not be permitted to cross the Balkans. When she crosses the Danube and satisfies her military honour with one victory then we must press together for the conclusion of peace, which naturally must not be concluded without our assistance. Should Russia refuse the peace and cross the Balkans, then we must ourselves take material guarantees for the maintenance of the Treaties." England would then occupy Gallipoli and Austria should enter Serbia and Roumania.[3]

On 13 June Derby asked of Beust whether the Austrian Government were "willing to accept the fact of the Russian occupation of Constantinople, or would they in case of need join with that of England to prevent" it. Did they think it safe that Russia should go there "relying on her assurance that she will not stay?" He proposed at the same time an active alliance for the defence of Constantinople.[4] But now as before he was forestalled by Disraeli who told Montgelas a week before Derby made his proposal, and in fact before it was sanctioned by the Cabinet, that England's aim was to conclude an offensive and defensive alliance with Austria. She was ready to consider Andrassy's seven points as a *casus belli*. An agreement between the two countries would be useful to both of them as much for the preservation of the *status quo* as for the partition of Turkey. "What I want to know", said Disraeli, "is this: is Austria ready in certain eventualities, when we occupy a point in Gallipoli and send our fleet to Constantinople, to concentrate her army on the Roumanian frontier (Siebenbürgen)?"[5]

[1] A.A., Beust to Andrassy, 11 June 1877, Tel.
[2] *Ibid.* 13 June 1877.
[3] *Ibid.* 11 June.
[4] B.A., Derby to Buchanan, 13 June 1877, No. 204, most conf.
[5] A.A., Montgelas, Montgelas to Hübner, 18 June 1877, letter.

Since Andrassy's answer was not forthcoming, Derby reminded Beust on the 19th that the Russian scheme was to create a semi-independent Bulgaria which would leave open the road to Constantinople "whenever a Russian army was ordered to march there.... It was impossible, I said, that such a proposal could be favourably viewed by Austria", he wrote to Buchanan. "It might be that Count Andrassy relied on the opposition of the other Powers, but I did not hesitate to express it as my personal opinion that England would be reluctant to enter into a second Crimean War without an ally. An Austrian refusal to co-operate might therefore lead to, and justify inaction on our part: whereas if the two countries acted together, there was not only no doubt of success, but no danger of war, since Russia would not provoke hostility of two leading Powers while already engaged in hostilities."[1] The Queen was discontented with this language of Lord Derby, but he defended it to Disraeli saying that "the great object of Austria was to see England accomplish what was necessary—unaided: and that if Austria suspected that England would not act alone, there might be an increased inducement to join us".[2]

Andrassy answered that his confidence in Russia was not absolute, but Austria and England united had it always in their power to prevent any consequences injurious to their interests. The geographical position of Austria and the British fleet were sufficient guarantees against any accomplished fact. Russia was conscious that her position would become more difficult with every step she took in the Balkans. She knew also that she could not stay in Constantinople against the will of England and Austria. Her retreat from it would be a fiasco before the whole of the Slav world, which she could not risk, and which she was trying to avoid by an agreement with England and Austria. There was no reason therefore to oppose her action. If Britain thought it necessary to take measures for the protection of her interests, Austria would raise no objection. For her part, she relied on her geographical position and the promises of Russia, and would not prevent her crossing the Balkans. But Austria might be also compelled to take material guarantees. In that event she would

[1] B.A., Derby to Buchanan, 19 June 1877, most conf.
[2] Disraeli, p. 147.

not occupy Serbia, which was protected by the Treaty, nor Roumania, which was occupied by Russia.[1] Andrassy did not add, but it was evident, that it was in Bosnia and Herzegovina that he intended to seek for guarantees. He laid once more "the greatest stress on the principle that peace shall not be concluded without our participation", and that "the results of the war must be subject to European approval".[2]

In a confidential letter of the same date he explained to Beust that his purpose from the outset was to protect his interests without having recourse to arms. He had therefore opportunely explained himself to Russia and had obtained satisfactory assurances from her. So long as she kept her promises, Austria could not oppose her action. But as the unforeseen might happen, he had entered into an exchange of views with England to meet it. Since England accepted his seven points, he was ready to accept those which she had communicated to Russia. Thus a solidarity in principle would be established between them. "To give it at present the solemn sanction of an alliance, seems to us to be superfluous.... Under the impression of a too intense distrust towards the Russian projects, I fear Lord Beaconsfield might avail himself of an eventual convention with us to threaten Russia with it, or to force a conflict on an accessory incident."[3] Andrassy concluded by saying that he could not allow anybody to choose the moment of action which would fall on his shoulders.

Derby expressed his fears to Andrassy that public opinion in England might be "so aroused at the sight of the Russian army in possession of Constantinople and the Straits as to lead to war". He proposed at the same time "that a protocol should be signed placing on record the understanding arrived at between the two Governments".[4] But Andrassy refused to sign the protocol, as it would represent an act of hostility towards Russia. He was ready to add to his seven points the English reservations about the Straits, and declare that he would defend them together with England. He would be equally satisfied with a simple declaration on the part of England stating the points which she was resolved not to cede.[5]

[1] A.A., Andrassy to Beust, 22 June 1877.   [2] Ibid.
[3] Ibid. Lettre particulière.
[4] B.A., Derby to Buchanan, 30 June 1877.
[5] A.A., Andrassy to Beust, 7 July 1877, Nos. 83, 84, Tel.

This answer greatly disappointed the British Government. Already on 30 June Disraeli had asked a pledge from Beust that Austria had free hands towards Russia.[1] On 12 July Derby said to Beust: "If only you would tell us whether you had any binding engagement with Russia?"[2] To these questions Andrassy replied that "no engagement exists between Austria and Russia other than that which results from the despatches and telegrams already communicated" to England.[3] On Derby's question what was meant by this phrase, Beust said "that the Austrian Government have accepted certain assurances given by Russia, and consider themselves pledged to treat those assurances as sincere unless evidence should appear to the contrary".[4]

Buchanan declared to Baron Orczy, Andrassy's intimate collaborator, that "the reason why the English Government was anxious to fix the solidarity of the interests of the two countries in a protocol or by some other form in writing, was because Parliament would only vote the supplies necessary for any action if the co-operation of a Great Power could be counted upon as certain. On the other hand, the British Government were convinced that a joint warning addressed to Russia by England and Austria-Hungary would always suffice to check Russia without there arising any necessity for resorting to war." He added also that the British Government "in case their wish were not acceded to—or only acceded to in vague phrases—would have to waive the idea of an eventual appeal to arms and would then confine themselves to the taking of precautionary measures".[5] Andrassy protested against any reference to an engagement hostile to Russia being made in Parliament or to other Powers. "We certainly would prefer England confining herself to measures of precaution than that we should risk to be used as a scare against Russia before she has given us any serious reason for hostile action."[6]

Derby denied that Buchanan was "instructed to use this language". In fact it represented the real view of the British Government. Before accepting Andrassy's formula, Derby

[1] A.A., Beust to Andrassy, 30 June 1877, No. 49A–D, Tel.
[2] *Ibid.* 12 July, Tel. No. 142.
[3] B.A., Derby to Buchanan, 16 July 1877.   [4] *Ibid.*
[5] A.A., Andrassy to Beust, 11 July 1877, No. 89.   [6] *Ibid.*

wished to clarify some further points. He asked him whether the Russian scheme of an autonomous Bulgaria extending south of the Balkans was compatible with his conception of a great Slav state, and in what manner he proposed to distinguish between a permanent occupation of Constantinople and a temporary one, "which nevertheless might be prolonged for an indefinite time".[1] Andrassy replied that "some sort of autonomy must be conceded to Bulgaria...although it would be difficult to concede it in the way foreshadowed in the Russian proposals". He was opposed to a "large Slavonic realm" including non-Slav elements, but he could not consider every extension of Bulgaria beyond the Balkans as a *casus belli*. The important question was not whether Bulgaria should receive some districts on the Balkan range, but whether Russia should evacuate her and refrain from every special protection. "When the wishes of the Bulgarians shall be satisfied, especially if the frontiers of their country are not measured with too much stint, it can be foreseen that aspirations towards independence would get the upper hand. The peoples' ingratitude has numerous examples in history."[2] He said nothing, however, about the occupation of Constantinople.

Having failed to induce Andrassy to sign the protocol, Derby consented to give the declaration proposed by Andrassy. On 26 July Andrassy sent his declaration to London in which he recapitulated his seven points, adding to them the English reservations about the Straits. He took the view "that the ancient rule as to the closing of the Straits should be maintained, and that if there should be an occasion to make in it any modification of detail, such modification could only be effected by means of a general agreement among the Guaranteeing Powers". In his opinion "the best method of guaranteeing the interests above defined would consist in parallel but independent action by each of the two Powers on its own part, and without reference to the other, as necessity may arise". He had reason to believe that Russia would respect these interests; should she, however, injure them, he would be ready to join with England "in considering the further measures which might be necessary for the defence

---

[1] B.A., Derby to Buchanan, 11 and 21 July 1877.
[2] A.A., Andrassy to Beust, 14 and 26 July 1877.

and material preservation of such of our reciprocal interests as might be menaced". He asked Lord Derby to send him a corresponding declaration and to promise again absolute secrecy and not to mention it in Parliament or to the other Powers.[1]

Derby sent his declaration on 14 August only. Similarly to Andrassy, he recapitulated the points expounded in the note addressed to Russia on 6 May and the answer received from her. With regard to modifications in detail of the status of the Straits, Derby did not reject it, but considered it undesirable, "and that, in any case, it would be necessary to guard carefully against proposals calculated to leave Constantinople at the mercy of the Russian fleet, or to allow unrestricted egress to the Russian naval forces for aggressive purposes from the Black Sea into the Mediterranean". As to the mode of proceedings, he understood Andrassy's objections to joint action, though he was of opinion that the proposed one was not "perhaps, calculated to secure the same attention to the representations of the two Powers as might be effected by a more openly concerted action in the first instance".[2]

The exchange of these declarations closed the Austro-British negotiations for a common action against Russia. England desired to co-operate with Austria in defence of Constantinople and the Straits, starting with the supposition that she was equally interested in it, whereas in fact the interests of Austria lay in the West. England desired to interfere during the war in order to prevent the downfall of Turkey and reduce as much as possible the changes it might bring about. The interests of Austria demanded, if not dissolution, at least territorial rearrangements which would enable her to annex Bosnia and Herzegovina. She could not therefore interfere to stop the war before this was accomplished. Besides, she was bound by her engagement to Russia not only not to interfere in the war, but to prevent any intervention on the part of the other Powers. This divergence in interests and positions between the two countries was not realised by the British Government, who, though suspecting, were never convinced that Austria was engaged to Russia.

Although Andrassy insisted on absolute secrecy being pre-

[1] *Ibid.* 26 July 1877.
[2] B.A., Derby to Buchanan, 14 Aug. 1877.

served about these negotiations, Shouvalov was able to inform the Tsar of its substance.[1] The Tsar thought it necessary to reassure Vienna as to his further intentions and instructed Novikov on 26 July to communicate to the Austrian Government that he would remain faithful to the letter and spirit of his engagement: "We have no intention of creating for ourselves a definite order of things", read the document. "We reserve to the interests of other Powers *de se faire valoir à la fin de lutte*."[2]

Meanwhile Disraeli did not abandon the idea of occupation. He proposed in the Cabinet to send the fleet to Constantinople and consider its occupation by Russia as a *casus belli*. He was prepared " to accept the resignations of Lord Salisbury and Lord Derby, had they alone been the obstacles", but he discovered that except for two members he was opposed by the whole Cabinet.[3] He therefore abstained from forcing the issue, and satisfied himself with making "something like an ultimatum notice to Russia", believing it to be "still a step in advance, and which may lead to all that is required".[4] Derby communicated to Shouvalov on 18 July that an occupation of Constantinople, even if temporary and dictated by military necessity, would threaten the good relations of the two countries and that in that event England would be free "to take such measures as British interests should require".[5] Shouvalov answered that Russia preferred to achieve her purpose without occupying Constantinople, but that she could not give an engagement not to march on the enemy's capital.[6]

The Queen was not satisfied with this evasion. She was distressed at nothing material being done, and reminded Disraeli of his earlier promise to declare war on Russia if she entered Constantinople and did not quit it "at a given day". Her insistence and the negative answer of the Russian Government induced the Cabinet to decide to declare war on Russia if she "occupies Constantinople and does not arrange for her immediate retirement from it".[7] At the same time orders were given "for

[1] R.D., Shouvalov to Gortchakov, 3 July 1877.
[2] A.A., Novikov's communication, 26 July 1877.
[3] Disraeli, p. 152.   [4] *Ibid.*
[5] R.D., Shouvalov to Gortchakov, 6–18 July 1877.
[6] *Ibid.* 19 July 1877.
[7] Disraeli, p. 154.

strengthening the Malta garrison by 3000 men.... It is Lord
Beaconsfield's present opinion", wrote Disraeli to the Queen on
that occasion, "that in such a case Russia must be attacked from
Asia, that troops should be sent to the Persian Gulf, and that
the Empress of India should order her armies to clear Central
Asia of the Moscovites, and drive them into the Caspian."[1]

But the rapid advance of the Russians in July and the crossing
of the Balkans by General Gurko made these decisions insufficient. Fearing an imminent invasion of Gallipoli, Layard
appealed for its immediate occupation. The Queen was also
alarmed by the situation and insisted upon this measure being
taken at once.[2] Derby wrote to the Queen "that it would be too
late to occupy Gallipoli, even if that step were desirable..."
and that "the great bulk of the nation desires nothing so much...
as the maintenance of peace".[3] Nevertheless the Cabinet agreed,
and instructed Layard to ask the Sultan's permission for the
dispatch of the fleet to Constantinople.[4] At the same time
Disraeli sent him a secret telegram telling him that the one sent
by the Cabinet "opens a prospect of recurring to the wise and
ancient policy of England. The British fleet in Turkish waters
...may be the first step in the virtual preservation of his
Empire."[5] But the Sultan refused his consent unless England
came out openly on his side. He suspected her of wishing to
defend her own interests only and leave Turkey to her fate.
"Their feelings against us are such", wrote Layard to Disraeli,
"that they might go over to the Russians 'bag and baggage', if
the Russians made it worth their while. If the fleet is sent up to
Constantinople, it must be in the interests of the Turkish Empire,
and the Turks must understand that it is done for their protection
against the designs and ambitions of Russia. We cannot tell
them that it is entirely and exclusively in our own interests."[6]
Disraeli admitted these suspicions to be "reasonable"... "but
they are not true", he wrote in a secret letter to Layard,

at least so far as I am concerned, being resolved to maintain if possible
the integrity and independence of the Ottoman Empire.... If there
is a second campaign I have the greatest hopes this country will

[1] *Ibid.* p. 155.   [2] *Ibid.* p. 157.
[3] *Ibid.* p. 158.   [4] *Ibid.* pp 158–61.
[5] *Ibid.* pp. 160–1.   [6] Layard, Layard to Disraeli, 1 Aug. 1877.

interfere....As we have command of the sea, why should not a British *corps d'armée* (via Batum) march into Armenia and even occupy Tiflis? We might send another to Varna and act on the Russian flank....

The thing is to secure another campaign, or rather the necessity for one, for if Russia is told by England that another campaign will be a *casus belli*, she may be inclined to make what Prince Gortchakov calls *une paix boiteuse*.

The danger is, if the Russians rally, again successfully advance and reach Adrianople this autumn. What then is to be done? With her suspicions of England, Turkey would be ruined. That is why I should like to see our fleet in her immediate waters, and Gallipoli in our possession as a material guarantee, and with her full sanction. We should then be able to save Turkey.[1]

The opposition of the Cabinet to a military expedition and the refusal of Austria to join in an action against Russia, compelled Disraeli to seek for other means for the defence of British interests. The defeat of the Russians relieved, for the time being, his fears of an immediate threat to Constantinople, but he was resolved not to let England come again to such a position. Had the Russians continued their advance, British interests, he believed, would have been endangered without her being able to defend them effectively. Having failed to find an ally, he decided to defend Turkey alone. He already considered himself "virtually" an ally of Turkey and was looking for an occasion to come to her help. "If they [i.e. the three Northern Powers] continue their dark game of partition", he wrote to Derby, "they must come in collision with England, who will not permit the breaking up of the Ottoman Empire."[2]

Believing that Russia was no longer able to obtain a decisive victory before the winter, and that she contemplated suspending hostilities during the season and renewing them in the spring, he resolved to prevent the second campaign by force. He was prepared to consider it as a *casus belli* irrespective of whether British interests were threatened by it or not. The question of an occupation of Constantinople by Russia and of a possible second campaign was discussed in the Cabinet on 15 August. Seeing that his colleagues were still averse to an alliance with

---

[1] Layard, Disraeli to Layard, 6 Aug. 1877.
[2] Disraeli, p. 178.

Turkey, Disraeli separated the question of occupation from that of the means of preventing it, and induced them to agree "that, if the tide of affairs changed and that the occupation by the Russians of Constantinople this year appeared to be on the cards..." they should "take such steps as the exigency required and of a similar character as previously contemplated".[1] In this way he avoided dissensions which a discussion of the means of action would have provoked. He proposed also that "when it was apparent, and avowed, that the first campaign could not be decisive, the Cabinet should meet, and consider the course to be adopted to prevent a recurrence to arms in the spring". After much discussion there was "a general, if not universal, opinion, that the British policy, under such circumstances, would be to prevent a second campaign".[2] On Derby's observation that England "had no allies", Disraeli replied that "no other ally than Turkey was required; that...it was not for us to reconquer Bulgaria; that we were masters of the sea, and could send a British force to Batoum, march without difficulty through Armenia, and menace the Asiatic possessions of Russia".[3]

The Tsar was well informed of the real disposition and intentions of the British Government. Fearing that the question of Constantinople might lead them to abandon their neutrality, he thought it necessary to explain to them confidentially his real motives and intentions and dissipate their suspicions. At the beginning of August he invited Colonel Wellesley, British military attaché, to an audience and told him that he had no intention of injuring British interests, that his sole purpose was to improve the lot of the Christians, and that he would not go beyond the programme already communicated to England. He desired therefore to see the war ended as soon as possible, and prayed the Queen and her Government to use their influence with the Turks and induce them to accept his terms of peace.[4]

Colonel Wellesley concluded from this declaration that the position of the Tsar was very difficult, that whereas a defeat would provoke an internal revolution, a victory might bring him into conflict with England. He went to England and brought the Tsar's message to the Queen, advising her to inform him of

[1] *Ibid.* pp. 171–2.   [2] *Ibid.* p. 172.
[3] *Ibid.*   [4] *Ibid.* p. 173.

the limits beyond which she would not let him go. He believed that if the Tsar knew them, he would respect British interests and would stop the war before injuring them. The Queen told him that she "could not submit to Russia preponderating in the East".[1] She insisted to Disraeli "that the Emperor should be told distinctly though confidentially that we will not allow him to go to Constantinople, and that that would be a *casus belli*."[2] But Disraeli insisted for his part on not permitting the second campaign. Wellesley was therefore ordered to tell the Tsar that "the Queen and H.M. Government have a sincere desire to see the speedy re-establishment of peace on terms honourable to Russia and would be glad to contribute to such a result; should, however, the war be prolonged and a second campaign undertaken, the neutrality of England could not be maintained and she would take her part as a belligerent".[3] In informing the Queen of the way in which he had discharged his mission, Wellesley expressed his belief that it "has already had much effect, and that every effort will be made to bring the war to a speedy termination".[4]

It is not clear, however, what Disraeli really intended by his idea of the second campaign: to prevent it, or to provoke it? Judging from his instructions to Wellesley, it seems that he wished to prevent it, or better, to induce Russia to end the war in the first one by threatening to intervene in the second. This conclusion is confirmed by what he said to the Queen in November, explaining why he had abandoned the idea of the second campaign. He told her that that plan was put forward in order to deter Russia from it. But this explanation does not fit in with his instructions to Layard of 6 August, cited above, telling him that the important thing was "to secure another campaign" and that if Russia knew it she might be induced to come to terms with Turkey.[5] Moreover, though wishing to keep it secret, he told the Russians that another campaign would be a *casus belli*, and thus deceived both the Turks and the Queen, who believed that he really intended to prevent the second campaign and insisted on the measures being taken for that.

[1] Queen Victoria, pp. 560–1.   [2] *Ibid.* p. 562.
[3] Disraeli, p. 174.   [4] Queen Victoria, pp. 565–7.
[5] Layard, Disraeli to Layard, 6 Aug. 1877.

For Disraeli, who besides a vague desire to preserve the Ottoman Empire had no clear line of policy, and was in character essentially an opportunist, the idea of the second campaign was a tactical manœuvre only. He feared lest the indifference of the British Government should discourage the Turks and induce them to submit to Russian demands; he feared also the anger of the Queen whom he had led to believe that British interests would be preserved. The idea of the second campaign was put forward in order to persuade the Turks that England would help them if they persisted in the struggle and forced the Russians to another campaign; it was also intended to appease the Queen by showing her that the Government was prepared to withstand Russia under certain circumstances.

Disraeli now came to the idea of sounding the Porte "as to the terms of peace it is prepared to offer. If they include the settlement of Bulgaria on the basis of the protocol of London, and the restoration to Russia of the portion of Bessarabia...it would seem that the honour of Russia would be sufficiently vindicated." He believed that the Porte "would agree to these, or any other reasonable terms", if England assured her that in case of their being rejected by Russia, she would afford her material assistance to prevent the seizure of Constantinople, if it were menaced.[1] On 5 October he proposed this plan to the Cabinet, but found that they "seemed indisposed to mix up the question of mediation with anything like a threat", and that "it was generally felt...that it was impossible to take any active step in the prosecution of the proposal while the campaign was not concluded".[2] Nevertheless Disraeli wrote to Layard to sound the Porte as to its terms and promised to consider them and recommend them to Russia. "If Russia refused," he wrote, "she would put herself much more in the wrong, and if the terms were publicly acknowledged by England as just and satisfactory, it would be very difficult for us to adhere to our present neutrality. Opinion at home would force us to action."[3]

Throughout this time Disraeli was in constant secret communication with his Ambassador at Constantinople, who com-

[1] Disraeli, p. 182.
[2] *Ibid.* pp. 183-4.
[3] Layard, Disraeli to Layard, 11 Oct. 1877.

pletely shared his views. Layard was convinced that the purpose of Russia was to break up the Ottoman Empire, and that she was supported by Germany and Austria. The proposed autonomy for Bulgaria would be enough, in his opinion, to attain that purpose. It was vital for Britain to decide whether she would be prepared to accept such a result of the war or not. If not, then the occupation of Gallipoli would serve as a preventive measure. He proposed at the same time that England should "assist the Turks actively by money and officers and by troops"; that she should "incite the Hungarian Poles to take part against Russia"; that she should use the Sultan's influence in Central Asia and raise the Mohammedan states against Russia; that she should prevent Greece from entering the war or promoting an insurrection. When in August Serbia intended to join Russia he wrote that "the only thing to be done is to get up a revolution in the Principality and to put Karageorge against Milan".[1]

How much of this programme was adopted by Disraeli is not known, but his action concurred singularly with the views of his Ambassador. The British Government made strong remonstrances in Belgrade against the renewal of hostilities, and asked Austria to restrain Serbia even by means of force.[2] They also exercised pressure upon Greece to stop her war preparations and restrict her from every action.[3] The anti-Russian agitation in Hungary was supported by the Porte and Disraeli's secret agents. A deputation of Turkish students was sent to Budapest to return the visit made by Hungarian students to Constantinople after the defeat of Serbia. "It was understood", wrote Layard in his Memoirs, "that Mr Butler Johnston had paid the expenses of this mission."[4] This Butler Johnston was the same person who during the Constantinople Conference came to Constantinople representing himself as Disraeli's secret agent and encouraged the Turks to reject the proposals of the Powers.[5] He was also mixed up in an attempt to provoke an insurrection among the Austrian Poles, as can be seen from a report of Elliot to Salisbury.

[1] Layard, v, p. 34.
[2] Andrassy, III, p. 48.
[3] M. Lhéritier, op. cit. III, p. 429.
[4] Layard, v, p. 79.
[5] Salisbury, p. 111.

"Count Goluchowski", wrote Elliot, "a Polish gentleman, asked to see me this morning on behalf of a number of his countrymen. He said that last year while the war between Russia and Turkey was going on Mr Butler Johnston had put himself in connection with himself and other Poles with the view to getting up an insurrectionary movement, saying that he would promise them the support of England, but they declined to fall in with his designs. Things would have a different aspect if war broke out between England and Russia. If England intended to reduce the power of Russia, Poland would be prepared to play her part."[1]

Already in April the Khedive had sent his former Foreign Secretary, Nubar Pasha, to London to offer Britain the protectorate of Egypt.[2] The idea found little response at the moment with the British Government, who did not wish to embroil themselves with France. Nubar came again in June with the same proposal, but failed to win over the British Cabinet for it.[3] At the same time the Grand Vizier opened unofficial negotiations through Colonel Gordon, a subordinate of the War Office, with a view of selling to Great Britain the suzerainty of Egypt, or Crete and Cyprus.[4] The British Government were informed of this offer, but took no step upon it. Meanwhile Disraeli endeavoured to furnish the Porte with the money necessary to enable it to continue the war. Owing to the suspension of payments on its part he was unable to guarantee the loan which the Porte demanded, but he hoped "that some substantial assistance might be afforded to the Porte, if we could contrive to purchase some territorial station conducive to British interests". He wrote about it to Layard on 22 November and asked for his advice. "If a sum could be secured to the Porte", he added, "which would render it possible to enter into a second campaign, the result, as to after negotiations, might be great. If we could combine with it the presence of the English fleet in the Bosphorus, and a British army corps at Gallipoli and Derkos, and all this without a declaration of war against Russia, I think the Ottoman Empire, though it may have lost a province or two,...might yet survive, and though not a

---

[1] B.A., Elliot to Salisbury, 25 May 1878, No. 418, conf.
[2] G.P. Nos. 289, 290.   [3] G.P. No. 295.
[4] Disraeli, p. 257.

G

first-rate Power, an independent and vigorous one...."[1] When after the fall of Plevna the Turks appealed again for financial assistance, Disraeli promised to help them but asked for some "material guarantee".[2] The question was discussed between Layard and the Porte, but without result.

Meanwhile the Cabinet postponed asking an engagement from Russia about Constantinople. The Queen continued protesting and urging "in the very strongest manner that the necessary steps should not be delayed". It was only on 4 December that the matter was brought again before the Cabinet, when it was found out that some misunderstanding existed as to the contents of the note to be addressed to Russia. It was agreed then to warn Russia "that if her armies appeared to menace Constantinople or the Dardanelles, Great Britain would reserve her liberty of action", intimating at the same time her readiness to "tender its good offices for pacification".[3] Derby, however, was not prepared "to make the occupation of Constantinople, or rather the menaced occupation of that city, a *casus belli*". Disraeli expressed his regret at this and wrote to him that in his opinion "both this event, if impending, as well as the simultaneous opening of the Straits to Russia and their closing to other Powers, should decidedly be *casus belli* for this country with or without allies".[4]

Throughout the war Disraeli made efforts to induce his colleagues to take the measures necessary for the protection of Constantinople, or at least to agree upon their being taken in case of its being threatened. He endeavoured at the same time to win Austria over to co-operate in this design. He tried to persuade the Cabinet that, having defined British interests, they were bound to provide for the means of defending them. In fact both the measures he proposed and his intentions went far beyond a mere defence of the interests as they were defined in the note of 6 May. Disraeli desired not only to prevent an occupation of Constantinople, but to intervene in the war and compel Russia to stop it and accept conditions convenient to England. This comes out clearly from his declaration to Beust to the effect that when Russia crossed the Danube England and

[1] Disraeli, pp. 251-2.   [2] R. W. Seton-Watson, *op. cit.* p. 243.
[3] Disraeli, p. 198.   [4] *Ibid.* p. 199.

Austria must press together for the conclusion of peace, and if Russia refused it England should occupy Gallipoli, and Austria should enter Serbia and Roumania. It is still more evident from his later plan to offer Russia, in agreement with Turkey, some conditions of peace, which, if refused by her, would be considered by England as a *casus belli*. In short, Disraeli sought for an occasion and for means to ally himself with Turkey, and hoped at first to accomplish it in co-operation with Austria, and having failed in this he was ready to act alone. Small wonder that his colleagues saw through his real intentions, and that they resolutely refused to be drawn into a war for the maintenance of Turkey.

By the end of October Plevna was surrounded on all sides. The Turks began to mass troops in Sofia in order to come to the help of Osman Pasha, but the Russians forestalled them by a rapid advance to the south, thus cutting off all communications with Plevna. Osman resisted for another month in the hope of getting assistance, but as it was not forthcoming, he decided to try to force his way through the Russian lines. On 10 December he went out with all his troops and attacked the Russian and the Roumanian positions, but failed to break through them. Exhausted and completely defeated, he surrendered on the next day.

With the fall of Plevna the Turkish resistance was practically broken. In spite of the wintry season the Russians continued their advance, and a month later forced the Shipka Pass and occupied Sofia. On 20 January Adrianople was seized. When the armistice was signed the Russian troops stood before the walls of Constantinople.

CHAPTER VIII

✻

THE ARMISTICE OF ADRIANOPLE

AFTER the fall of Plevna the Turks realised that they could no longer offer serious resistance to the Russians and appealed to the Great Powers for mediation, hoping that they would prevent Russia from imposing humiliating conditions upon them. Already by the end of November they had asked the German Government to use their good offices with Russia to cease hostilities. But Bismarck refused every mediation for the sake of Turkey, considering that such a step would have been understood in St Petersburg as pressure on his part.[1] For the same reason the Powers refused the Porte's appeal for mediation. England alone desired to intervene with the belligerents in order to stop the further disintegration of Turkey and prevent Russia from imposing terms of peace which might injure her own interests.

The defeat of Turkey created great alarm in London. It seemed that the road to Constantinople lay open to the Russian armies and that nothing could restrain them from occupying it. Fearing the bad effect this would have on public opinion and its reaction upon the Government, Derby at once presented his long delayed warning note to the Russian Government, asking them to avoid even a temporary occupation of Constantinople. He pointed out to the Russian Ambassador that in that event Great Britain would be compelled to take measures for the protection of her own interests.[2]

Disraeli was resolved not to let Russia dictate her conditions and advised the Porte to address itself directly to England for mediation. He told the Turkish Ambassador on that occasion that "if Russia refused the offer and persisted in continuing the war, England would then proceed to take other measures to

[1] G.P. No. 298.
[2] R.D., Shouvalov to Gortchakov, 11 Dec. 1877.

bring it to an end".[1] To strengthen his position for future negotiations he proposed to the Cabinet to call Parliament together and ask for an increase of armaments. He explained to his colleagues that he wished "the country to be placed in a position which would give her authority in arranging and settling the terms of that peace".[2] The Cabinet was united in the wish to prevent "arrangements hurtful to England", but they were also afraid "of sliding insensibly into an alliance with the Turk". An increase of armaments would inevitably encourage the Turks to further resistance; if England were to defend Constantinople she must send her army there and co-operate with the Turks. The suspicion "that a call to arm, hasty and urgent, may have the effect, and probably proceeds from the wish, of involving us in war to uphold Turkey",[3] united the pacifists in opposition to Disraeli's proposals. The first sitting ended without any decision being taken; at the second he found "half his Cabinet ...arrayed against him. It was only at the third sitting, and after Disraeli had threatened his resignation, that his demands were adopted."[4] Parliament was to meet on 17 January.

When the Porte appealed to the British Government, Derby prepared a note for the Russian Government explaining that events had created the situation contemplated by the Tsar in June, that the Porte had by its circular signified the intention to ask for peace, and that Great Britain was now prepared to communicate Russian proposals of 8 June to it "without either criticising them or advocating their acceptance, in order to facilitate the negotiations for peace".[5] Before sending this note he communicated it to Andrassy, and asked for his opinion.

Andrassy was decidedly opposed to this step, and endeavoured to dissuade Derby from it. He feared lest England's separate mediation should lead to an arrangement between her and Russia, which would leave Austria isolated and would compel her "to sound Russia and to draw nearer to her...".

"Russia would in that case easily have turned our mutual isolation to her profit", he wrote to Beust, "in order to exact her most sweeping conditions....All along we have refused to take the initiative of

[1] Layard, v, p. 308.   [2] Disraeli, p. 202.
[3] Salisbury, pp. 164–7.   [4] Disraeli, pp. 204–7.
[5] B.A., Derby to Loftus, 19 Dec. 1877.

mediation and we still refuse to do so. The following were and are the reasons for our refusal:

"(1) We cannot imagine any conditions of peace to which it would be possible to make the neutral Powers agree.

"(2) We cannot either imagine any propositions emanating from Powers that have not taken part in the war, which the belligerents would not necessarily reject.

"(3) We do not feel ourselves called upon to take the responsibility for insoluble problems, that have been put forward by others: such for instance as the Russian idea of a Bulgarian vassal state, in which Christians and Mussulmans are to live peaceably together."[1]

Andrassy was "equally determined that peace shall not be made without our participation and that of England". But he wished that Turkey should be left to address herself

first of all to Russia directly in order to induce the latter to state her conditions....The Porte will hardly assent to the Russian conditions without at least making an attempt to get them softened by an appeal to Europe. It will surely be easy to convince Turkey that it must serve her interests better to make such an appeal to Europe, only when she is able to point to tangible signs of the injustice and oppressiveness of the propositions actually put forward by Russia.[1]

In that case every guaranteeing Power would be obliged to take up a position in view of those specific conditions.

Austria and Germany had hoped that the Russo-Turkish War would bring about the complete dissolution of Turkey and thus compel the Great Powers to proceed to a definite solution of the Eastern Question. Austria had already secured her share of the spoil by the Budapest convention and agreed with Russia as to the future organisation of the Balkan peninsula. In June Bismarck worked out a plan of partition of Turkey and set up the aims he wished to achieve thereby. He was confident that the solution of this question would give Germany added guarantees for the maintenance of the present *status quo*, and secure her a preponderant influence in Europe.[2] But the unexpected resistance of the Turks Russia met with in Bulgaria, England's refusal of the idea of partition and her intention to prevent the break-up of Turkey, had frustrated these hopes. Though it was beyond doubt that

---

[1] B.A., Buchanan to Derby, 22 Dec. 1877, No. 901, secret. Also Beust's communication to Derby from 23 Dec., secret.
[2] G.P. No. 294.

Russia would be victorious in the end, it was evident that this victory would not be complete, and that it would at best lead to a partial solution of the question. Such a solution had great inconveniences for both Austria and Germany. Were the map of Turkey clear, the three Powers could have proposed a definite arrangement of Eastern affairs on the basis of territorial compensations for the Great Powers and the creation of independent Christian states in the Balkans. Since Turkey was only defeated, and not dissolved, the Powers could not dispose of her territory. As a belligerent party Russia could undoubtedly claim some aggrandisement for herself, but Austria, as a neutral Power, had no pretext to demand Bosnia and Herzegovina. Her public opinion, already dissatisfied with the subordinate rôle Austria had played during the crisis, and particularly the Hungarians, who were against an increase of the Slav element, would have opposed such a demand. Turkey could hardly be expected to cede her territories willingly, and it could be foreseen that the other Powers would also oppose it. In face of such obstacles it mattered little that Russia and Germany agreed thàt Austria should take these provinces. It is true that she could fairly hope to crush Turkish resistance with her army, and with the support of her allies, accomplish her aim without provoking a European war. But this would have forced the other three Powers, Italy, France and England to a more close co-operation against the Dreikaiserbund—a consequence which neither Andrassy nor Bismarck desired. Besides, it would have placed Austria in complete dependency upon Russia. She could not prevent Russia from creating a large Bulgaria, which would give her a commanding position in the Balkans, nor could she deprive her of the influence she had won among the Christians by her sacrifices for their liberation. While Russia stood as their protector, Austria would have come into Bosnia as the conqueror of their lands, thus forcing the Balkan Christians to seek protection in Russia against Austrian aggression. By putting herself at the head of the nationalist aspirations of the Balkan peoples, Russia would represent a much greater danger to Austria than the great Slav state, which she tried to prevent by the occupation of Bosnia and Herzegovina. Instead of protecting herself against the consequences of the dissolution of Turkey, Austria would have lost her influence in the East and opened the door to Slav agitation in her own provinces.

The only way out of this situation lay in refusing the validity of the Budapest convention and forcing Russia to submit the question of peace to a conference of the Great Powers. The Powers would endeavour and no doubt would have succeeded in driving Russia out of the Balkans and in reducing her influence there to the smallest measure. It would not be difficult for Austria to convince them that she alone could check the further advance of Russia, and that for that purpose she should be given a mandate to occupy Bosnia and Herzegovina. She would thus have achieved all her aims without incurring any inconvenience.

The idea of the participation of all the Powers in the conclusion of peace was put forward by Andrassy for the first time in the course of negotiations with England in June and July of the previous year. It constituted one of the seven points which Andrassy declared himself prepared to defend.

In a conversation with Count Montgelas, in July, Andrassy told him that if Russia won the war she would find herself faced with the alternative of retreating without any gains in Europe except autonomies—which would make her a laughing-stock and reduce her to bankruptcy—or if she refused "to make herself ridiculous" she would be attacked by England and Austria. "The Russians, with all respect be it said, are in a cul-de-sac", said the Count, "and we must take care that they do not get out of it.... We must let the Russians rush in, till they are completely enmeshed." In order that this plan might succeed it was necessary to avoid every pressure upon Turkey. Austria therefore would not occupy Bosnia and Herzegovina for the moment. "If such an occupation should take place, it will be as an offensive movement against Russia, as a strategic thrust, before we fling them out of Bulgaria..., if this should ever prove necessary."[1]

In September Bismarck and Andrassy met at Salzburg. What they told each other on that occasion is not exactly known. Wertheimer states that Andrassy disclosed to Bismarck his agreement with Great Britain, which the latter received with great satisfaction, and that he assured him that he would never have to regret the weakening of Russia, as he could count on

[1] A.A., Montgelas, Montgelas to Beust, 18 July 1877.

Austria for every eventuality. Bismarck, according to Wertheimer, suggested that Austria should come to the help of Russia, to which Andrassy turned a deaf ear.[1] Rachfahl states that Bismarck proposed to him either to help Russia or to take the first opportunity of attacking her in the rear.[2] These statements are contradictory in themselves and with each other, but it is noteworthy that both Wertheimer and Rachfahl talk of hostile intentions against Russia as a subject of conversations at Salzburg.

Bismarck shared Andrassy's opinion that the conditions of peace should be defined in concert with all the Powers. Moreover he suggested himself the mode of introducing them into the negotiations. He informed Andrassy on 25 November that the Porte had solicited his mediation with Russia for the conclusion of peace and that he had refused it, since it would necessarily have the character of pressure on Russia. The mediation of any Power would have the same character. "The fear", he added, "that in direct negotiations between Russia and Turkey a peace could perhaps be concluded which would touch the interests of Austria more nearly, will hardly prove true in practice: first of all, the views of both belligerents differed very much from each other, and the Porte, before submitting to the far-reaching Russian demands, will in any case have time to communicate them to the other Powers and bring them into negotiation. Should the Russian demands be so moderate that Turkey would be ready to accept them at once, then it would be very sure that they would not encroach on Austrian interests."[3] Andrassy adopted this view and acted upon it. In his answer to Derby he used Bismarck's arguments to deter him from mediation.

Andrassy failed to impress Derby with his arguments. His attitude only revived the distrust which he entertained towards Andrassy. Derby could not understand why Andrassy was opposed to the Russian conditions being communicated to Turkey, when in June he had himself asked England not to reject them, but to take them as a basis for further discussion. Already suspicious of Andrassy, he seems to have been convinced now that he was bound to Russia by an agreement, and

[1] Andrassy, III, pp. 42–3.
[2] F. Rachfahl, *Deutschlands Weltpolitik*, p. 182.
[3] G.P. No. 298.

that he was playing a double game. "I have no doubt that such an understanding does exist," he wrote to Layard, "and that upon it the Andrassy note and the Berlin Memorandum were founded. To anyone who watched events at the beginning of 1876 it was probable then, and it is to my mind certain now that the diplomatic move which began with the Andrassy note was not consequent on the petty disturbance on the Bosnian borders, but that the opportunity of that disturbance was seized and utilised to execute a policy which had been already determined on."[1] In a private conversation with Beust he told him that "it was taken for granted in every European capital that the three Emperors had acted in concert from the first and intended to do so to the end". He considered that "we had much less chance of arriving at an amicable arrangement" with Russia if she remained under the impression that she could "rely absolutely and unconditionally on Austrian support..." and that "it would be more fair" to the Russian Government if they were acquainted with the real state of things.[2] Andrassy emphatically denied that the three Emperors' alliance ever "had the Eastern complications specially in view", and asked Derby to get rid of the idea "of some mysterious understanding between Russia and Austria".[3]

The attitude of Austria did not deter the British Government from intervention. Lord Derby only modified his note and communicated to Russia that Turkey desired peace and that England was prepared to mediate. Gortchakov answered that Russia was also desirous of peace, but that the Porte should apply to the Russian Commanders-in-Chief, who were in possession of the conditions of armistice.

Having failed in his attempt to interfere between the belligerent parties, Disraeli advised the Porte to address itself directly to Russia. But when the Turks appealed to the Grand Duke, he answered that the armistice could be negotiated with him, but only after the acceptance of the bases of peace. The Sultan implored the Tsar to cease hostilities during the negotiations, but the Tsar refused this. He ordered the Grand Duke

---

[1] Layard, v, p. 286.
[2] B.A., Derby to Buchanan, 28 Dec. 1877, No. 422, secret.
[3] *Ibid.* 3 Jan 1878, No. 10, most conf.

to advance further and to postpone the communication of the conditions. "God help us to achieve the holy work which we have started", he wrote to Nicholas.[1]

The aim of Russia was to crush Turkey completely and occupy as much territory as possible. The Turks would then be obliged to accept unconditionally the Russian demands, while the strategic position of the Russian army would give her a virtual command over the Straits, and prevent intervention on the part of England. Gortchakov endeavoured to postpone the beginning of negotiations as long as possible and gain time to come to an arrangement with Austria. He desired also to deprive Disraeli of any pretext for asking an increase of armaments in Parliament. At first he left Nicholas without instructions; then he asked him not to communicate the conditions but to ask the Turks to bring forward their own and to send them to St Petersburg.[2] When on 19 January the negotiations were opened at Kazanlik, he threatened the Turks with breaking them off if they disclosed the Russian terms.[3]

Russia was willing to concert with the Powers about questions of European interest, but she could not let them participate in the solution of those questions which, in her opinion, concerned belligerent parties only. This would mean submitting to the demands of the Powers whose interests were opposed to her own, and abandoning the gains bought by so great and expensive sacrifices. Gortchakov considered that the conclusion of peace in concert with other Powers would be impossible, for their conflicting interests and jealousy would prevent any agreement among them. He believed that Disraeli aimed at depriving Russia of all the fruits of her victory and of every remuneration for her sacrifices, and that he had offered his mediation with the view of inducing her to disclose her terms and getting a pretext "to put before Parliament the question of England's participation in the negotiations".[4]

Russia's intention to impose the bases of peace together with the conditions of armistice provoked a protest on the part of England and Austria. They declared to the Porte that they must

---

[1] S. S. Tatiščev, op. cit. II, p. 430. [2] Ibid. p. 432.
[3] B.A., Layard to Derby, 26 Jan. 1878, No. 127.
[4] R.D., Gortchakov to Shouvalov, 31 Dec. 1877.

be consulted in any arrangement to be concluded with Russia, and requested that its plenipotentiaries should not be empowered to accept terms contrary to the Treaty of Paris.[1] The British Government declared also in St Petersburg that no treaty contrary to the Treaty of Paris would be considered as valid without their assent.[2] Andrassy made a similar protest, but in a somewhat milder form. He asked Gortchakov not to create an accomplished fact beyond the limits they had agreed upon. He had several times reserved the right of participation in the definite settlement of the conditions of peace. If Russia alone were to impose them upon Turkey, he would be obliged to protest against every possible damage to his interests or to ask for his share of influence in the conditions of peace. Such a step would create in Turkey and England an impression contrary to the interests and mutual feelings of Austria and Russia. All this could be avoided if the armistice were concluded without the conditions of peace, or with their being confined to a basis of principles, which would not prejudice Austria's influence upon the definite settlement.[3] Gortchakov replied that the interests of Austria would in no way be affected by the conclusion of an armistice. To England he answered that Turkey was asked to accept the bases of peace only, and that the points of general interest would be discussed by all the Powers.

Such an answer appeased neither London nor Vienna; it was considered as an attempt to exclude the Powers from the conclusion of peace. The Queen was already alarmed by the rapid advance of the Russians and "distressed at the low tone" of the country. She wrote to Disraeli that she was "utterly ashamed of the Cabinet", and that she could not "remain the Sovereign of a country that is letting itself down to kiss the feet of the great barbarians...".[4] After the fall of the Shipka Pass she wrote a memorandum to the Cabinet asking them "to determine at once what means should instantly be taken to prevent Constantinople from being attacked". She reminded them of their declaration "that any advance on Constantinople would free us from our position of neutrality" and insisted upon their acting on it.[5]

[1] B.A., Layard to Derby, 15 Jan. 1878, No. 66, conf.
[2] A. d'Avril, *op. cit.* p. 276.
[3] A.A., Andrassy to Langenau, 17 Jan. 1878, No. 6, secret.
[4] Disraeli, p. 217.   [5] *Ibid.* p. 218.

Disraeli read this Memorandum in the Cabinet on January 12 and proposed "to send the fleet to the Dardanelles and forces to Boulair, if the Sultan permitted".[1] This proposal was strongly criticised by both Derby and Salisbury, who threatened to resign, but it was decided to send the fleet to Beshika Bay and previously to ask the Sultan's consent for free passage through the Straits. In order to secure the retreat of the fleet, Russia was requested to give a clear promise that she would not occupy Gallipoli. But before the answer from St Petersburg and Constantinople arrived, Disraeli pressed again on the 15th for dispatch of the fleet, and taking advantage of Derby's absence, induced his colleagues to adopt it and to invite Austria to join in it. Carnarvon opposed this step and tendered his resignation in the event of its being taken. Derby strongly objected to it "as contrary to the Treaty, as increasing the risk of collision with Russia". Meanwhile the Sultan refused his permission and Austria refused her co-operation. On the other hand Russia gave an assurance that she did not intend to march on Gallipoli unless the Turks concentrated their troops there. All this induced the Cabinet to countermand the decision on the next day.

Although failing to mix themselves up in the negotiations, England and Austria were resolved to oppose a separate arrangement between Russia and Turkey. On 15 January Francis Joseph summoned a conference of the leading military men to discuss the alterations in the war plan, which the present position of Russia imposed. Opinion was divided as to whether the main attack should be directed to Galicia or to Roumania, but Andrassy spoke with confidence of the prospects of Austria in the event of war with Russia. He believed that Austria was in a very favourable position, and that she could force Russia at any moment to evacuate Bulgaria and Roumania. He was convinced that Germany would rejoice in a Russian defeat, and that Italy, if she moved, would be blockaded by England.[2]

On the same day the British Government decided "to draw closer" to Austria for further action. But the Cabinet was still divided as to the policy to be pursued. Disraeli's draft of the opening address was criticised by Derby "as a menace to Russia",

---

[1] *Ibid.* p. 219.
[2] A.A., Ministerrath Protokol, 15 Jan. 1878. Also Andrassy, III, pp. 60–1.

and he was compelled to alter it. When on the 17th Parliament was opened, he was unable to propose any clear course of policy. Russia had not yet begun negotiations with Turkey, and he had no pretext to ask for an increase of armaments. He expressed only his confidence that the Government would not hesitate to take the measures necessary for defence of the honour and interests of the Empire. Northcote confessed in the House of Commons that "until we know what the Russian conditions are, we have no proposals to make".[1] The Queen stated in her address that the conditions upon which Britain's neutrality rested were not hitherto infringed, and hinted only at the possibility of adopting the measures of precaution if "some unexpected occurrence" rendered them necessary.[2] This was all that Disraeli was allowed by his colleagues to tell Parliament. All his efforts at asserting his determination for action afforded only new proofs of the weakness and irresolution of the British Government.

The hesitating attitude of the British Government gave Andrassy a pretext to refuse her invitation for co-operation. He replied to the British Ambassador that should the moment for action come, he would endeavour to come into the open in a more binding way as to its modus. He expressed his surprise at England's abandoning all idea of occupying Gallipoli or sending her fleet to the Dardanelles, and declared that he "certainly was not prepared for nothing being done...".[3] Andrassy had reason to join England against Russia, as his plan of bringing all the Powers into the peace negotiations had been frustrated by Russia. But an open co-operation with England would have broken up the Dreikaiserbund and probably deprived him of Germany's support. He therefore insisted upon England's acting alone and showing her "capacity for action".

Disraeli did not perceive these hidden motives of Austria's attitude, and pressed her to side openly with England. He told Beust on the 17th that the moment for action had come and passed, and that something must be done within forty-eight hours to save the situation. "We want to act together with Austria," he said, "and not separately. Will Count Andrassy play the *grand coup*, i.e. mobilise, then I propose at once to my

---

[1] R. W. Seton-Watson, *op. cit.* p. 291.   [2] Disraeli, p. 224.
[3] B.A., Buchanan to Derby, 22 Jan. 1878, No. 38, very conf. Tel.

colleagues to give an equivalent."[1] Andrassy refused this overture under the plea that the British Government had not "given a visible sign of their determination to protect at least their maritime interests..." nor "created confidence in their being able to act...". "The position taken up by the British Government in the speech from the Throne," he said to Buchanan, "without at the same time asking Parliament for a money vote, has made not only in Austria but throughout Europe an impression detrimental to the weight of England.... Under these circumstances we could not make an ostensible political alliance acceptable to our public opinion...."[2]

In order to convince Andrassy that he was prepared for action Disraeli decided to offer him a defensive alliance and joint diplomatic and military pressure on Russia. On 21 January he proposed in the Cabinet "that we should offer to Austria a defensive alliance with this country; if necessary, a pecuniary aid, provided she would mobilise a sufficient force upon her frontier, and join us in an identic note to Russia. Our fleet, of course, to go up to Constantinople."[3] Expecting the opposition of his colleagues to these measures, he wrote to the Queen that "he foresees disruption of the Cabinet, inevitable war with Russia, though not without allies, and many other trials".[4] She encouraged him not to "give way an inch.... War with Russia is, the Queen believes, inevitable now or later", she wrote. "Let Lord Derby and Lord Carnarvon go, and *be very firm*. A divided Cabinet is of *no use*."[5] Disraeli informed the Queen that his proposals were "warmly adopted" by ten members, but that Derby "fiercely" opposed them and consented only to the identic note. The main question was therefore left to be decided the next day, after obtaining the reply of Austria on the identic note. Nevertheless Disraeli saw Beust the same evening and offered him an alliance. "The identic note is for me only a starting point for action", he said to Beust. "I understand that you cannot accept it, from fear of losing your old allies without getting new ones. In such a situation there is only one thing to do: to conclude a defensive alliance, and then the English fleet

[1] Andrassy, III, p. 61.
[2] B.A., Beust's communication to Derby, 21 Jan. 1878, private and strictly conf.
[3] Disraeli, p. 227.
[4] Queen Victoria, p. 597.
[5] *Ibid.*

and money will be at your disposal. If I have a treaty of alliance I can obtain ten million pounds from Parliament."[1]

The Vienna Government was officially invited to join in a note to Russia declaring that a prolonged occupation of Bulgaria or other Turkish provinces, the opening of the Dardanelles and other changes in the Straits should be considered as invalid without the consent of Austria and England.[2] Andrassy suspected that the British Government had invented the note in order to forego every real action and to threaten Russia by the aid of Austria. He told Buchanan that English statesmen

appear unwilling to take any responsibility on themselves and that the action of England may depend on an adverse vote of the House of Commons: and therefore until Her Majesty's Government have taken some active and material measure proving that the country will support them in protecting English interests against the pretensions of Russia he cannot commit himself before his country to the adoption of any course in concert with England...."He repeated, on my endeavouring to ascertain what he expected England to do," wrote Buchanan, "that she should, for the protection of her own interests in Constantinople, send her fleet there, and she should ask the credit for the expenses of the measures she may have to adopt to cause her voice to be heard by Russia....If she does this, he said, it will be seen that she is in earnest, and those who are disposed to act with her will know that they will find in her an ally to be depended on."[3]

Andrassy's insistence on England's being "one length forward", on showing her capacity for action, induced Disraeli to force the Cabinet into action even at the price of breaking it up. On the 23rd, having obtained the Queen's permission to accept the possible resignations, he pressed the proposal to send the fleet immediately to Constantinople and to ask for a vote of credit. The majority of the members consented to these measures, and orders were given to the fleet to proceed to Constantinople. Not knowing the Russian terms they feared "a private arrangement would be made about the Straits between the Turks and Russians, to the exclusion and detriment of other Powers".[4]

[1] A.A., Beust to Andrassy, 21 Jan. 1878, No. 24, Tel.
[2] A.A., Andrassy to Beust, 22 Jan. 1878, No. 23, Tel.
[3] B.A., Buchanan to Derby, 22 Jan. 1878, No. 42, secret.
[4] Disraeli, p. 230.

But Derby and Carnarvon disapproved of this step and resigned at once.

Meanwhile the Sultan protested against the violation of the Treaties, fearing Russia might take it as a pretext to occupy his capital, and asked the British Government to inform Russia that they were acting on their own authority. At the same time Layard wired that the Porte had accepted the bases of peace, and that they provided among other things for the regulation of the question of the Straits between "the Congress and the Emperor of Russia". Shouvalov also assured Derby that this question would be settled by all the Powers. The fleet was therefore recalled, though it had already entered the Dardanelles without any resistance on the part of the Porte. But as soon as this was done it was discovered that Layard's cyphers were altered in transmission, and that it was not between the Congress and the Tsar, but between the Sultan and the Tsar that this question was to be regulated.[1] This provoked new alarm. Shouvalov, seeing the storm approaching, communicated to Derby the exact text of the Russian conditions, according to which a "subsequent agreement to safeguard Russian rights and interests in the Straits" was to be reached later on. On Derby's question as to what was meant by this phrase, Gortchakov admitted that it was vague, and offered to suppress it altogether.[2] He declared, however, most emphatically that Russia considered this question as a European one, and that it would be regulated by common agreement among the Powers.

The withdrawal of the fleet removed the reason of Derby's resignation. His retirement provoked great discontent in the Conservative ranks and threatened to break up the party itself. "A general disintegration is taking place", wrote Disraeli to the Queen. "The vote of Monday next, which would have originally been carried by a large majority, and on which I depended as exercising a great influence on Austria and Russia, is, with this disruption of the Cabinet, not only endangered but even problematical."[3] He therefore implored the Queen to let Derby resume his post, to which she consented, though with reluctance. Derby returned, as he wrote, "rather in the hope of preventing mischief

---

[1] Disraeli, p. 231.   [2] A. d'Avril, *op. cit.* p. 289.
[3] Disraeli, p. 234.

as long as I can, than from sympathising with the views of my colleagues".[1]

The communication of the Russian terms brought about some appeasement in London. But though their substance did not seem to be so hurtful to England as it was expected, the British Government could not consent to their being imposed on Turkey without their participation. On the 28th they addressed a circular note to the Guaranteeing Powers stating that in so far as the Russian conditions tended to modify the existing treaties and affected general European and British interests, they would be considered invalid without formal sanction on their part.[2] To this Gortchakov answered that the terms accepted by the Porte and affecting European interests were not definite without the sanction of the Powers. He said nothing however about those terms which affected British interests.

Andrassy insisted upon England showing her determination in a practical way to oppose a one-sided settlement in order to be able to press Russia, but he did not mean to side openly with her against Russia. He refused even a "public intimation of the negotiations, or of the understanding existing between the two Governments", which Elliot asked him to allow in order to facilitate the vote of credit in Parliament. In a telegram to Beust on the 28th he said that he wished "one might count also upon the other signatory Powers and not anticipate them by an identic step. The latter would develop (*entpuppen*) an Anglo-Austrian alliance which could induce the other Powers to remain reserved. If we act separately but concordantly then our stand-point appears as a European one, and the other signatories could not very well refuse it."[3]

Andrassy wished to co-operate with England on the same basis upon which he had co-operated with Russia during the war: "separately but concordantly". By giving his own interests the form of European ones, he hoped to mobilise all the Powers against Russia and to realise his aims without personally coming into opposition to her. This was essential for winning over Russia and the Powers for a European conference.

Throughout the war the Turks were in hopes that warlike

---

[1] Disraeli, p. 237.   [2] A. d'Avril, *op. cit.* p. 277.
[3] A.A., Andrassy to Beust, 28 Jan. 1878, No. 32, geheim, Tel. Sir Henry Elliot was appointed as Ambassador in Vienna at the end of January 1878.

feelings would finally prevail in England and bring her to their help. Though England declared neutrality and defined the points of her interests in order to avoid collision with Russia, Disraeli constantly encouraged them to resistance and assured them of his determination to preserve their Empire. His efforts to send the fleet to Constantinople and an army corps to Gallipoli, to prevent a second campaign and to secure a loan which would enable them to continue the struggle, left no doubt of his intentions. Even after the fall of Plevna he assured them that England would take "other measures" to obtain the armistice if Russia refused her mediation, and that the calling of Parliament would have a most favourable effect upon their affairs. He advised them to mass 100,000 men at Adrianople and defend it for two months or at least six weeks more. If they were capable of defending it, he told them to refuse to discuss the bases of peace together with the conditions of armistice.[1]

The attitude of Lord Derby was quite the opposite. He avoided all that might inspire the Porte with hopes of British assistance, and endeavoured to remove every misconception on their part. He explained that "the unusually early meeting of Parliament did not imply any intention on the part of Her Majesty's Government to depart from the policy of conditional neutrality".[2] He advised them to conclude the armistice as soon as they could. When the negotiations were opened, he wrote to his Ambassador in Constantinople that "Her Majesty's Government do not think that the Porte should be encouraged to break off negotiations and allow the Russian armies to advance under the expectation that Austria and England would afford military aid to preserve the integrity and independence of the Ottoman Empire...".[3]

This contradictory advice made the position of Turkey still more difficult. She was inclined to listen to Disraeli, but she did not know whether he would be able to fulfil his promises. The rapid advance of Russia began to shatter her hopes and provoked feelings of irritation and resentment. The idea of a separate and direct arrangement with Russia found more and more partisans in Government circles. The Sultan asked for Layard's "personal opinion and advice as a friend" as to whether England would

[1] Layard, VI, p. 23.
[2] Ibid. V, p. 310.
[3] B.A., Buchanan to Derby, 18 Jan. 1878, No. 31, secret.

defend him in case he were obliged to reject the Russian demands. He told Layard that "he was pressed by a powerful party supported by foreign influence, to separate himself altogether from England, to come to a direct understanding with Russia and to ally himself for the future with that country as the only means of saving his Empire. This course was repugnant to him..." but "he would have to bear an immense responsibility if he were to continue the war relying upon the aid of England, and Russia were to end by dismembering his Empire."[1] The Grand Vizier was more open in his utterances. He told Layard that England "has abandoned her old and faithful friend, and leaves her to be crushed by her and our implacable enemy. Why should we listen any more to her? Let us accept the best terms we can get from Russia and endeavour to make a friend of her...."[2] "It must be honestly confessed", wrote Layard in his Memoirs, "that the Sultan and his advisers had reason for their mistrust of England and for their complaints against her. Two languages were held in London. The Prime Minister and Lord Derby differed widely in their opinion, and the Porte was inclined to attach more value and importance to the views of the Premier than to Lord Derby."[3] In such circumstances it was impossible for Layard to give them any clear advice, though he was personally in favour of allying England to their side.

Feeling themselves abandoned the Turks hastened to conclude the armistice and save what was still left of their Empire. But the Russians devised all sorts of means to protract the negotiations. They moved from Kazanlik to Adrianople and suspended the negotiations for four days. When on the 24th they were resumed, Nicholas asked for further instructions from St Petersburg, since the situation had changed in the meantime.[4] On the same day the Tsar telegraphed to him not to conclude the armistice, but wait for the arrival of General Ignatyev, who was entrusted with further negotiations.[5] But this telegram did not reach the Duke until five days later, when the Porte had already accepted all his demands. He felt it impossible to prevaricate any longer and signed the armistice on 31 January. The

[1] B.A., Layard to Derby, 7 Jan. 1878, No. 26, secret.
[2] Ibid. No. 30, 8 Jan. 1878.   [3] Layard, VI, p. 22.
[4] Revue de Paris, 1897, IV, p. 419.   [5] A. Onou, op. cit. II, p. 635.

bases of peace accepted by the Porte provided for an autonomous Bulgaria "within the limits of the Bulgarian nationality", an autonomy for Bosnia and Herzegovina and a subsequent agreement to safeguard the rights and interests of Russia in the Straits. Serbia, Montenegro and Roumania were to obtain an increase of territory and to be proclaimed independent. Russia was to obtain an indemnity the form and the amount of which should be determined later.

Gortchakov believed that England, although dissatisfied with the rejection of her mediation, would not go further than demonstrations if she remained alone. The important thing was to prevent co-operation between her and Austria. With Austria Russia had already agreed upon the organisation of the Balkan peninsula and upon common defence of that programme against the other Powers. So long as they remained faithful to that agreement, it was hardly likely that England would oppose them by force.

But Gortchakov had lost his influence on affairs as soon as the war began. He spent the war period in Bucarest "like a station master", as he complained to Schweinitz.[1] The Tsar no longer listened solely to his advice, but drew other persons into consultation, and discussed the most important matters in committee. Headquarters assumed the direction of both political and military matters, and Gortchakov was left to carry out its decisions. Elated by their victory, the soldiers desired to take full advantage of it. They intended to create a great Bulgaria, which would secure for Russia exclusive domination in the Balkans, and to prevent Austria from annexing Bosnia and Herzegovina, which had been ceded to her by the Budapest Convention. In this policy they were supported by Ignatyev and Nelidov, who trusted they would be able to play off both Austria and England. When by the end of November a conference was summoned at Poradim, the Tsar's headquarters, to draw up the bases of peace, Gortchakov was not invited to take part in it[2]. Yet he approved these bases and undertook the ungrateful task of defending them towards Austria, whose co-operation he needed now more than ever.

[1] Schweinitz, I, pp. 442–3. Also Disraeli, p. 185.
[2] A. Onou, *op. cit.* II, pp. 632–3.

The bases of peace drawn up at Poradim provided for an autonomous and tributary Bulgaria, roughly in the limits agreed upon in the Constantinople Conference, to be occupied by a Russian army corps for two years in order to ensure its organisation. Bosnia and Herzegovina were to be organised in conformity with the proposals of the Constantinople Conference. Austria was only allowed "to assume a participation and a control analogous to those to be exercised by Russia in Bulgaria, in order to insure the introduction and regular functioning of the institutions to be given to them". But Russia reserved the liberty for herself of exchanging the Dobrudja and the Delta for Bessarabia, and to dispose of her conquests in Asia. The points of general interest were to be settled in agreement with all the Powers, but the treaty of peace was to be concluded directly between Russia and Turkey.

On 9 December the Tsar communicated these conditions to Austria and Germany. In an accompanying letter to Francis Joseph he pointed out that these views were the bases only, "the development of which would depend on the events of war and the necessities and rights created thereby. I believe them to be in the spirit if not in the letter of our arrangement", said the Tsar, "to which I will remain faithful. A co-operation on your part would have rendered them as complete as I would desire." He asked his ally to tell him frankly his views, promising to take them into just consideration.[1]

Russia's intention to play off her treaty obligation only rendered a service to Austria. She had already had reasons of her own to separate from Russia and side with the other Powers against her. By refusing to fulfil her obligations Russia only gave a pretext to Austria to reject on her part also the validity of their arrangement and avoid any responsibility for it.

Andrassy agreed with Gortchakov in considering that the moment of dissolution of Turkey had not yet arrived and that consequently the organisation of the Balkan peninsula could not this time take a definite form such as had been foreseen at Reichstadt. But he concluded from it that the conditions of peace must be conformed to the resolutions of the Constantinople Conference. That Conference did not provide for the creation

[1] R.D., The Tsar to Francis Joseph, 9 Dec. 1877.

of a great autonomous Bulgaria, but for two Turkish *Vilaets* with
a Christian governor and an internal autonomy. Bulgaria, he
argued, can be either completely independent or remain under
Turkish rule. Both these solutions were acceptable to Austria.
But the first one could be realised only in the event of the dissolution of Turkey. Since that was not the case, Austria could
not admit of a great autonomous Bulgaria, which represented a
great Slav state, nor of her being occupied by the Russian army,
which would mean a truce only.

Serbia and Montenegro likewise could not obtain territorial
increase beyond the limits set up by the Constantinople Conference. Even the independence of Serbia must be proclaimed
by all the Powers, and not by Russia alone. Andrassy intended
to make it conditional upon some economic and commercial
concessions on her part.

An exception from that principle Andrassy made only with
regard to territorial compensations for Russia and Austria. He
refused the idea of a temporary occupation of Bosnia and Herzegovina and reminded the Tsar that according to their arrangement
these provinces were to be annexed by Austria in the event of
territorial rearrangements or retrocession of Bessarabia. Strictly
speaking, neither Russia nor Austria had a right to annexations,
since Turkey was not dissolved, but he consented to it under
the condition that Austria should obtain an equivalent.

Finally, Austria could not allow Russia to conclude peace
directly with Turkey. Turkey, in her opinion, was under the
protection of the Guaranteeing Powers, and no change could be
introduced there without their consent. Austria had from the
outset reserved for herself the right to participate in the conclusion of peace together with the other Powers.

This was the substance of the answer which Francis Joseph
sent to the Tsar on 8 January. He observed in an accompanying
letter that in entering the war the Tsar had declared that he had
no desire of conquest, but wished only to secure reforms for the
Christians. In the limits he had proposed to himself the result
of the war gave him full satisfaction. He could also continue the
struggle, but it was unlikely to create a more favourable situation
for Russia, or a more reassuring one for European peace, since
it had little chance of achieving a definite solution. "It is quite

possible", he wrote, "to finish with Turkey by force of arms, but not to create conviction in the public opinion of Europe that she died a natural death, from lack of vitality. This point of view, which is decisive for public opinion of my states, has directed me in examining the proposals contained in the notices annexed to your letter."[1]

Russia and Austria agreed in considering that the results of the war did not allow complete realisation of their agreement, but they drew from this conclusions which were contrary both to the letter and the spirit of the Budapest Convention. That Convention did not foresee the dissolution of Turkey as the condition of its fulfilment. Its purpose was "to regulate in advance territorial rearrangements which the war or dissolution of the Ottoman Empire might have as a result". Consequently, Russia and Austria had the right to territorial compensations both in the case of the dissolution of Turkey and of a mere victory of Russia. This comes out also from the fact that compensations for Austria were provided for both in the political and the military part of the Convention. It was Andrassy himself who during the negotiations which led to the conclusion of that Convention rejected Gortchakov's proposal to limit its application to dissolution only. He argued that every change in the *status quo* of Turkey affected the interests of Austria, and that therefore the realisation of their agreement could not depend upon dissolution only, but upon territorial arangements which the war or dissolution might have as a result. It is natural that the application of the clauses relating to the organisation of the Balkan peninsula depended also upon the results of the war. It was for Austria and Russia to decide how much of them could be realised. Instead of that they recognised the validity of the Convention in so far only as it suited their interests.

Francis Joseph's answer provoked great surprise and discontent in Russia. The Tsar refused to believe that he wished to put him "before impossibilities", but he found it difficult to understand his demands. On 16 January he replied pointing out the difficulties of his own position. Public opinion in Russia could never consent to the war being stopped before its purpose, the

[1] A.A., Francis Joseph to the Tsar, 8 Jan. 1878.

liberation of the Christians, was achieved. The reforms proposed by the Constantinople Conference, which the Austrian Government itself considered insufficient and inefficient, could not be applied in Bulgaria after so much blood had been shed for her liberation. The only real solution was a tributary autonomy. Every other transaction would be "bastard, lying, illusory", and he would in no way consent to it. Russia would consider it irreconcilable with her task and the sacrifices she had sustained. It was equally impossible to leave Bulgaria to stand alone after the conclusion of peace, for this would throw the country into anarchy. Her occupation for some time was therefore inevitable. The difficulties which Austria raises to it "rest mainly upon suspicion and prejudices". The Tsar explained also that he had never refused a collective examination of the questions of European interests, but that this examination would lack a practical basis if it were not preceded by a preliminary peace between the belligerent parties. For this reason he must insist upon the conclusion of a preliminary treaty directly with Turkey.

"I have expounded to you not only my views", said the Tsar, "but also the absolute necessities of my position. I reject the idea that you wish to put me before impossibilities.... The acquisitions reserved for her [Austria] in principle under certain circumstances remain intact despite the turn which events have taken. In offering you latitude to occupy Bosnia and Herzegovina temporarily, as I have Bulgaria, I had in view to leave you the option of transforming this temporary occupation into an annexation later on, if you found it necessary for your security—even if my troops had evacuated Bulgaria.... But if you renounce the advantages reserved to you by our arrangements and adhered to by me, you will, I hope, understand that I could not subordinate what is for me a necessity to what is for you only a matter of convenience. In any case, any scheme or compensation which you may think likely to conciliate your interests with mine will be examined by me in the same spirit which has hitherto presided over our *entente*."[1]

The Tsar communicated this letter and the Austrian answer of 8 January to the German Emperor, complaining of the attitude taken up by Austria and asking him to use his influence in Vienna for moderation. William readily accepted the Tsar's invitation and expressed his conviction that there was "no essential diver-

[1] A.A., The Tsar to Francis Joseph, 16 Jan. 1878.

gence which could not be smoothed over".[1] Bismarck informed
Andrassy that the *entente* between Russia and Austria remained
still the purpose of his policy, and proposed that the points of
divergence should be examined at a conference between Andrassy,
Novikov and Stolberg.[2]

Bismarck feared lest William, in his desire to help the Tsar,
should make some promises contrary to Germany's interests,
and insisted upon being consulted in the correspondence which
was being exchanged between them. He succeeded in preventing
the delivery of a letter already sent by his Emperor, and in
replacing it by another one. The content of his letter may be
judged by the Tsar's commentary on it, who told Werder that
it was dictated by a Minister and that there was not a friendly
word in it.[3]

The attitude of Germany was not without its influence on the
conduct of Austria. Throughout the crisis Andrassy was attentive
to Bismarck's advice and endeavoured to conform his action to
his wishes and possibilities. As his son put it, he "played his
cards in suchwise that it should be to the interests of Germany
to stand by Austria-Hungary at the critical moment".[4] He
answered Bismarck that he would endeavour as much as possible
not to compel him to choose between Austria and Russia prematurely and before he wanted it himself.[5] On the 26th Francis
Joseph answered the Tsar that he agreed with his taking Bessarabia, but that he could not consent to the occupation of Bulgaria.
He expressed the hope, however, that all the controversial points
would be regulated by common agreement.

But although Russia consented to Austria taking Bosnia and
Herzegovina, Austria's position was by no means facilitated.
Russia could not give her a mandate for occupation, and an
understanding with her was therefore without practical value.
The main problem for Austria was a European conference.
Russia had frustrated her attempt to realise it at the demand of
Turkey. The only way open to it was to win over Russia, and
it seemed that her consent could be secured if the Conference

---

[1] R.D., William I to the Tsar, 23 Jan. 1878.
[2] A.A., Karolyi to Andrassy, 25 Jan. 1878, No. 15, Tel.
[3] Schweinitz, II, pp. 5–6.
[4] J. Andrassy, *Bismarck, Andrassy and their Successors*, p. 20.
[5] Andrassy, III, p. 72.

were proposed to her as a condition of Austria's further co-operation. On 28 January Andrassy addressed a note to Gortchakov declaring that the terms accepted by the Porte represented a "whole political programme", and that they prejudiced Austria's legitimate influence on the peace settlement. He could not defend such a policy in Parliament, and would be obliged either to resign or to declare that the arrangement of Kazanlik, in so far as it modified the existing treaties, would be invalid without the sanction of the Guaranteeing Powers. If he resigned, he might be replaced by a Cabinet who far from working in the sense of the arrangements with Russia, could work but in the opposite direction and make it impossible for his Emperor to keep to his engagements. If he made the above declaration, he would preserve his post, but this would not be sufficient to make Parliament accept the results of his policy. To achieve that purpose there existed one means only—the meeting of a European Conference, which alone could justify the attitude he had maintained during the war and allow him "to bear longer the responsibility for the line of conduct concerted with Russia".[1]

In a dispatch to Karolyi on the same date Andrassy stated that the only way out of the situation created by Russia was conflict with her or a conference.

"The Russian preliminaries", he wrote, "make us appear as passed by and duped. A conference is necessary in order to repair the damage of our authority before public opinion. It would be a satisfaction that Russia gives us, a real recognition of our rights. Were this reconciliation accomplished, then the gap might be bridged over, and, with the exception of the occupation of Bulgaria after the peace, as well as her extension offending our arrangement at the cost of the Greek and other elements, the programme set up by Russia might be carried out entire and complete....In this way only the programme which we have agreed upon with Russia might be carried out, our influence on the order of things made visible, and the crisis ended with the appearance at least of the preservation of the *entente* of the three Emperors."[2]

Andrassy proposed the Conference on the 28th; at once on the 29th he received Gortchakov's consent to it. This prompt decision in a matter of such importance gives the impression

[1] A.A., Andrassy to Langenau, 28 Jan. 1878, Tel. No. 8.
[2] G.P., No. 303.

that the question was arranged beforehand. Indeed Russell had reported already on 20 January that he had been informed that Andrassy and Bismarck had consented to Gortchakov's desire to have the question settled in a conference after the conclusion of preliminaries, should an agreement not be reached otherwise.

"Being at peace", wrote Russell, "Austria has no excuse for wresting any portion of territory from Turkey. At the same time a rectification of frontier may become desirable for the greater safety of Austrian interests according to the nature and extent of the Russian peace conditions. If Austria attempted to obtain that rectification of frontier by force, it is not impossible that Italy might follow her example and equally claim some increase of territory, whilst by submitting the question to a conference, as suggested by Prince Gortchakov, the sanction of Europe may possibly be obtained to a new state of things in Turkey without further bloodshed. Count Andrassy has undertaken to promote the idea of a conference later on."[1]

Schweinitz says that on 29 January he saw Giers who had just returned from Holland, where he had attended the wedding of his son. Giers told him that he had passed through Berlin on his way home and had spoken to the Emperor William about the "congress" without encountering any decided resistance on his part.[2] This information confirms the view that the matter was arranged before Andrassy sent his note of 28 January, and explains Russia's prompt acceptance of the Conference. On 2 February Andrassy invited the Great Powers to meet in a conference at Vienna in order to decide upon the modifications which it would be necessary to make in the treaties regulating the political system in the East.

[1] B.A., Russell to Derby, 20 Jan. 1878, No. 42, secret.
[2] Schweinitz, II, pp. 6–7.

CHAPTER IX

✻

THE TREATY OF SAN STEFANO

THE consent of Russia to the Conference softened for a while the tension between Russia and England and Austria. It seemed that it offered a suitable form to satisfy the pretensions of both parties. Russia was left to conclude the peace directly with Turkey, and the other Powers were admitted to take part in the final settlement of Eastern affairs. Meanwhile an incident soon provoked a new and much more serious crisis, bringing even European peace into jeopardy.

By the protocol of armistice the Turks engaged to withdraw their troops within three days beyond the line of demarcation, which runs from Derkos to Grand Tchekmedje on the east, and from Ourcha to Charkeui on the south. But the Turkish delegates failed somehow to inform the Porte of this,[1] and, as it appeared, the Russian Government was also left in ignorance of the precise lines of demarcation.[2] Thus when the Russian troops proceeded to occupy the abandoned positions Layard telegraphed to London that they were advancing on all sides in spite of the armistice. On the same day, 4 February, the Queen wired to Lord Derby: "I have just heard from Berlin that the Russians are pushing on Constantinople as fast as they can wishing to imitate Germans at Paris, that Russians are only trifling with the Turks about armistice—and that it is well known at Berlin that they only want to gain time to reach Constantinople."[3] On 5 February Layard telegraphed again: "Telegraph from Europe cut off, except through Bombay. State of affairs very grave. Russians in force close to Constantinople. Protocol of the bases of peace not yet received."[4]

This news provoked consternation in London. It seemed that

---

[1] B.A., Layard to Derby, 17 Feb. 1878, No. 240.
[2] B.A., Loftus to Derby, 9 Feb. 1878, Tel. No. 22.
[3] B.A., The Queen to Derby, 4 Feb. 1878, Tel.
[4] B.A., Layard to Derby, 5 Feb. 1878, No. 167.

Russia was determined to get hold of Constantinople and place herself in the position which would enable her to defy all the British demands. Derby asked Layard if he could ascertain "whether the occupation of Tchataldja lines by Russia was included in the protocol of armistice".[1] On the 7th Layard sent a summary of the terms regulating the line of demarcation, without stating precisely the line itself. They spoke only of Russia's right to occupy Bourgas and Midia, and of Turkey's obligation to withdraw her troops within three days. He pointed out that these terms were "placing almost the whole of Bulgaria, Roumelia and Thrace up to the line of Constantinople and Gallipoli in Russian hands".[2] On the 8th he sent the text of the conditions of armistice copied from the original, giving exact lines of demarcation.[3]

Meanwhile the excitement in England was growing rapidly and a war with Russia seemed to be unavoidable. The Queen urged Disraeli to fulfil his former promise to prevent by force the occupation of Constantinople. "She cannot speak strongly enough, for Great Britain's safety and honour are at stake...", she wrote. "She cannot rest day or night till she hears that strong measures are taken to carry out these principles."[4] Under the pressure of these events the Opposition in Parliament gave way, after successfully fighting for nine days against the increase of armaments, and the vote of credit was carried out by an overwhelming majority. On the 8th the fleet was ordered to proceed to Constantinople to protect British life and property, and the other Powers were invited to associate themselves with this step.

It appears that Gortchakov himself was not acquainted with the details of the armistice. On the 7th he asked Shouvalov to inform Derby that the troops had been ordered to stop any further advance both in Europe and Asia. But on the 9th he declared that the line of demarcation had been fixed up in agreement with Turkey and that it concerned the belligerent parties only.[5] The Grand Duke Nicholas warned the Turks that "if danger was to

[1] B.A., Derby to Layard, 7 Feb. 1878, Tel.
[2] B.A., Layard to Derby, 7 Feb. 1878, No. 173, Tel.
[3] *Ibid.* 8 Feb. No. 195.
[4] Disraeli, p. 243.
[5] A. d'Avril, *op. cit.* p. 303.

be feared to the Christian and Russian subjects of the Capital, he should be compelled to have recourse to similar measures".[1] Fearing that the entry of the British fleet might serve as a pretext to Russia to occupy Constantinople, the Sultan implored the Queen to withhold the fleet, and the Porte protested formally against the violation of the Treaties. "Were we going to war with Russia or with Turkey", wrote Layard in his Diary, "or with both, or against Turkey as the ally of Russia? It was impossible for me to say."[2] "What do you want me to do?" he asked of Lord Derby. "There is no reason to apprehend any danger to English subjects or property here."[3]

By this time the British Government was in possession of the protocol of armistice and knew that the Russians were not marching on Constantinople but simply occupying the line of demarcation, but they found it impossible to recall the fleet for the third time. The order was reiterated to Admiral Hornby on the 11th to enter the Straits with or without the Porte's permission and to stop at Prince's Island. Layard succeeded in persuading the Turks to confine themselves to a formal protest, and soon afterwards removed the fleet to Mudania.

On the news of the entry of the British fleet into Turkish waters, the Russian Government protested against the violation of the Treaties and declared that in that event they also would be compelled to occupy Constantinople, but that they would afford protection to the whole population. Gortchakov considered that this work "pacific in its nature" should not "assume the character of hostility".[4] Derby refused "to acknowledge that the circumstances are in any way parallel", and to admit that the dispatch of the fleet "has any bearing on entry of Russian troops".[5] He insisted upon Russia refraining from going to Gallipoli or in any way endangering the communications of the British fleet, and warned Shouvalov that upon it depended peace and war between the two countries. Gortchakov promised not to go to Gallipoli on the condition that England should not land troops on either side of the Straits, but treated the entry into Constantinople as

[1] B.A., Layard to Derby, 11 Feb. 1878, No. 204.
[2] Layard, VI, p. 138.
[3] B.A., Layard to Derby, 10 Feb. 1878, No. 187.
[4] R.D., Gortchakov to Shouvalov, 12 Feb. 1878.
[5] B.A., Derby to Loftus, 13 Feb. 1878.

unavoidable.[1] The Grand Duke was indeed ordered to occupy Constantinople "with or without the agreement of the Turks" if the British fleet entered the Bosphorus, but not to go to Gallipoli.[2] But he considered the occupation dangerous without a previous possession of Gallipoli, and since the fleet did not enter the Bosphorus, he started negotiations with the Porte with a view of arranging a peaceful occupation.

Meanwhile the Sultan, whom the Tsar informed that a temporary occupation of his capital was inevitable, though imploring England to withdraw her fleet, offered her at the same time to resist the Russian occupation "if England would come to his help with men, money, or in any other way".[3] Derby replied that he could not advise armed resistance under present circumstances. England would make all efforts to restrain Russia from occupation, but in case this could not be prevented, the chief interest of Turkey would be to defend Gallipoli. Should this prove to be impossible it would be of the greatest importance to protect the ports on the Asiatic shore, and he asked therefore the Sultan's permission to occupy them with the British army.[4]

Fearing a sudden seizure of the Turkish fleet by Russia, the British Government instructed Layard to purchase secretly from the Porte four of its best ships of war.[5] Gortchakov learned somehow of this attempt and asked Shouvalov for information. Derby denied the fact, but asked Layard how the matter had leaked out. Layard suspected the Turkish Ministers of in-discretion and wrote on that occasion: "There is no State secret in Turkey which cannot be bought, and scarcely a single employee who is not ready to sell one. One lives here in an atmosphere of intrigue, corruption and rascality that only those who have personal experience of the place can appreciate. It is Byzantium over again. The threatened fall of the Turkish Empire can be sufficiently accounted for by this state of things."[6] This opinion from one who was the champion of Turkish integrity against "Slav barbarism" is very interesting and instructive.

---

[1] R.D., Gortchakov to Shouvalov, 15 Feb. 1878.
[2] A. Onou, *op. cit.* III, p. 113.
[3] B.A., Layard to Derby, 15 Feb. 1878, No. 238, most secret.
[4] *Ibid.* 20 Feb., No. 257, secret.
[5] Layard, VI, p. 182. Also B.A., Layard to Derby, 20 Feb. 1878, No. 257, secret.   [6] B.A., Layard to Derby, 20 Feb. 1878, No. 261, secret.

To prevent the selling of the Turkish fleet the Grand Duke requested its immediate surrender to Russia and announced that he would occupy Constantinople with 30,000 troops.[1] The Sultan refused to deliver the ships, threatening to sink them if a forceful seizure were attempted. Layard wired to London that the Russians were pushing on to Constantinople. Alarmed by this news Derby at once sent an ultimatum to Russia threatening to recall his Ambassador if she entered the city without the Sultan's permission.[2] To avoid the invasion of his capital the Sultan finally consented to the Russians occupying San Stefano, eight miles south of Constantinople, where the Grand Duke entered on 23 February with 10,000 troops.

Throughout February the relations between England and Russia remained very strained. Peace hung on an incident which might have happened at any moment; and it was due chiefly to the efforts and determination of Derby and Shouvalov that it was preserved. "My sole occupation for the last three days", wrote Shouvalov on 17 February, "is to postpone an explosion on the part of the British Ministers. To gain a day, an hour, is perhaps to avert rupture between the two countries."[3]

The presence of the Russian and the English forces in the neighbourhood of Constantinople and their determination to prevent each other from occupying that city created an atmosphere of war fever and confusion. Public opinion in both countries was daily growing more and more warlike and incited their Governments to resistance. The Governments themselves took the possibility of war into consideration and began to prepare themselves for it. Russia placed large orders for guns and ammunition in Germany. Disraeli started preparations for the mobilisation of the reserves and ordered a great increase of arms. "There is no time to be lost," he wrote to his War Minister, "much depends upon the power to act, when we do act, with promptness."[4]

Besides military preparations both Russia and England endeavoured to obtain support from abroad. Disraeli made one more effort to win over Austria for open co-operation. Secret negotiations had been conducted for some time between his

---

[1] *Ibid.* 22 Feb., No. 265.
[2] R.D., Shouvalov to Gortchakov, 21 Feb. 1878.
[3] *Ibid.* 17 Feb.   [4] Disraeli, p. 251.

private secretary, Corry, and Graf Montgelas of the Austrian Embassy as to a pecuniary aid for Austria if she consented to mobilise and join England in an identic note to Russia. The illness of his secretary compelled Disraeli to take the negotiations into his own hands. By the beginning of February they had advanced so far that the Vienna Government took into discussion the question of financial means for the event of mobilisation. For that purpose the Cabinet was summoned on 7 February, which was attended by military experts and presided over by Francis Joseph. The War Minister stated that it was necessary to mobilise the whole army, and that the expenses for the first three months amounted to 310 million gulden. Von Hofmann, the joint Minister of Finance, explained that this sum could not be obtained from the Treasury, that a loan required the sanction of Parliament and presented many other difficulties, and that there therefore remained two ways only to get it: the issuing of treasury notes or subsidy. He reminded his colleagues that "at present too there existed the conditions nearly similar [the last two words struck out]; we have got the troops, England the money". Should it be impossible now to come to a similar agreement, then a larger credit could be hardly obtained in time from Parliament, or not at all. "But if we succeed in covering the necessities of the first three months to the amount of 300 million by way of subsidies", then Parliament could be asked for the vote of credit after the declaration of war. He wished to know first of all whether a subsidy could be obtained from England. If Parliament were told that the first necessities would be covered by England, they could be counted upon for the vote of the rest of the sum.

Andrassy answered that he had just seen the British Ambassador and believed that England would be ready to give money. But he refused to take subsidies in the old sense of the word, namely that Austria should fight so long as England paid. In his opinion England should be told how many troops must be mobilised to begin the struggle. She might find it more convenient to help Austria than to send out her own army.

Andrassy considered the sum of 310 million to be too high for immediate necessities. The Monarchy was not threatened from all sides, not for instance from Italy, who would rather join England. A mere announcement of mobilisation would suffice to prevent war. It would be easier to obtain the vote of credit for defensive purposes. England was also asking for a small sum only. A large sum would alarm Russia and induce her to begin preparations at once, whereas Austria would have to wait for the vote of credit, which would mean giving Russia a start. It might also induce her to make up her differences with England and Turkey and leave Austria isolated. Besides, the matter did not seem to be so pressing, since there were some previous questions which had to be cleared up before the Conference. "Our duty is to give events the direction which lies in our interests", said Andrassy. Russia feels that she must go home at the moment Austria acts, and the main thing is to catch her on her retreat. He proposed that the sum for the first expenses should be reduced as much as possible, so that it could be obtained without appealing to Parliament.

Von Hofmann, General Beck and Francis Joseph considered that the sum could not be reduced if the mobilisation were to attain its purpose. The latter argued that every day of delay was an advantage for Russia and that every day of conference deliberations strengthened her position. Andrassy replied that the position of Russia was weak, that she would be obliged to evacuate Bulgaria when Austria attacked her, and that even if she had the time to do that, Austria would be equal to her. The task of the Conference was to prevent Russia from again becoming the master of the East. Austria must be clear whether she could wage a war even without England. Francis Joseph considered that the position of the Mónarchy was more favourable while Russia remained in Turkey and that she must endeavour to keep her there. A speedy dissolution of Turkey was no agreeable thing for Austria, but she must be careful not to wage a war for Turkey's sake only. In his opinion it would be difficult to enter the war without English subsidies. He advised caution, since Austria, even if she were on Russian soil, would not be in such a favourable position as was Germany in France. He would consider Russia's position endangered only if England cut off her retreat in the Black Sea.[1]

On 10 February, when the British fleet was dispatched to

[1] A.A., Ministerrath Protokol, 7 Feb. 1878.

Constantinople, Andrassy asked Disraeli whether he remained
faithful to his declaration in the event of Russia occupying
Constantinople, and whether in case of Austria being obliged
to mobilise he could guarantee her a certain sum at once.[1]
Disraeli answered that he had already secured the credit, but
Austria had not followed and the matter had dropped in London.
He was sure he could obtain a loan. England was going to act
and expected Austria to do the same.[2] On 12 February he
declared to Beust that his colleagues had left him free hands
under the condition of Austria mobilising immediately. They
were resolved to go forward and must be certain whether Austria
would co-operate with them or not. If England remained alone
she would confine her action to two points: Egypt and the
Dardanelles; should Austria act in common, she would fight for
her interests and for the seven points. They must agree among
themselves and request Russia not to occupy Constantinople
before the meeting of the Conference, and to let a neutral Power,
Italy or Austria, occupy the Dardanelles and the fortresses.[3]

Baron Nopcsa, who accompanied the Crown Prince and the
Empress Elisabeth on their visit to England, sent the following
telegram to Andrassy on the 13th:

Just spoke with the Prime Minister. He stressed that he was prepared now (but not later) to make great financial sacrifices in order
to come instantly to an agreement with Austria. If no satisfactory
answer came till to-morrow, he must act, but then for English
interests only. His financial proposal has been laid before the whole
Cabinet and he is empowered to conclude it. In my opinion considerable subsidies could now still be obtained, later no longer. But
even now only under the condition, as...[cipher lacking] the Prime
Minister said himself, that England's position towards Austria was
clear, what it now is not, that is to say the acting together openly
begun and mobilisation ordered.

Nopcsa added further that he had informed the Empress
Elisabeth of this, since she entirely shared Andrassy's views,
and that Beust need not be informed about money.[4]

Andrassy communicated this telegram to Beust and sent him
the following instructions for Disraeli:

[1] A.A., Andrassy to Beust, 10 Feb. 1878, Tel. No. 46.
[2] A.A., Beust to Andrassy, 11 Feb. 1878, Tel. No. 54.
[3] A.A., *ibid.* 12 Feb. 1878, No. 55, geheim.
[4] A.A., Baron Nopcsa to Andrassy, 13 Feb. 1878, Tel. No. 867/630.

"It is certainly clear to Lord Beaconsfield", he wrote, "that it would be for us as easy to save all the points of our interest in the *entente* of the three Emperors as it would be for England with Russia separately. We prefer a safer basis. I am convinced Lord Beaconsfield does the same. As to ourselves, our standpoint is the following: we remain solidly with all the points agreed upon and are determined to step in that none of them should be injured. We will engage ourselves that the English fleet should not be molested by the Russian army, that the Russians should not occupy and remain in Constantinople, if they entered it at all, which would provoke a protest on our part, at least before the Conference met. This is valid for all eventualities and is not dependent on an understanding about mobilisation.

"As to mobilisation the following come into consideration: We cannot set up a part of the army, but only the whole war power of 1,100,000 men. This mobilisation costs 300 million gulden for three months. The question is then: can England take on her account as a subsidy half or at least the third part of this sum and keep it ready for us for the first day of mobilisation? If not, then we must wait for the mobilisation till we secure the means. Both Delegations would have to discuss the proposal, and four Parliamentary Houses the security. My colleagues consent under no condition to a loan without previous permission of the Delegations. All this would rob us of a favourable moment. A discussion of the question in the English Parliament would have the same disadvantage. The question which I pray Lord Beaconsfield to answer is practically this: could England take upon herself and put to our disposal a subsidy of 150 or at least 100 millions?... Is the answer yes, then I can bring formally before the Cabinet the proposal for mobilisation and it can be sanctioned without a public consultation irrespective of whether one of the points were really injured or not. After the mobilisation we will ask our Legislatures for the sanction of the rest, and apply to England for the loan. *But the fact of subsidies must remain secret.*"

Andrassy explained further to Beust that he had not spoken earlier of subsidies because he had wished to avoid them if possible, but the above reasons and Disraeli's intimation of financial sacrifices and subsidies had induced him to formulate the question so as to bring it to the quickest result. He asked him to refer himself to Disraeli's conversation with Baron Nopcsa, but not to leave him anything written.[1]

But when Beust communicated this telegram to Disraeli he denied having ever talked to Nopcsa and even of knowing him,

[1] A.A., Andrassy to Beust, 14 Feb. 1878.

adding that all that he had said was nonsense. He had never spoken about subsidies. Besides, he could not understand why the whole of the army must be mobilised.[1] Disraeli indeed did not speak to Nopcsa, but to Montgelas, who induced Nopcsa (probably in order to keep it secret from Beust) to send this telegram with his own ciphers.[2] The negotiations with Montgelas were secret; that is why Disraeli resented their disclosure and denied them.

But this little misunderstanding did not hamper further conversations. On 16 February Disraeli wrote to the Queen that "he has been obliged to conduct secret and unofficial negotiations with Austria, which he hopes he has now brought to a conclusion, and that she will put into the field immediately at least 300,000 men, and join Great Britain in an identic note to Russia, which will announce, that we cannot consent to go into conference unless Russia retires from Constantinople, or places Gallipoli, and the fortresses of the Straits, in the custody of Great Britain, or of garrisons of the neutral Powers."[3] He informed her at the same time that the Cabinet had "considered the Austrian alliance...and sent instructions to Sir Henry Elliot". Elliot was instructed to declare that the British Government was "prepared to negotiate a convention for securing the immediate mobilisation of the Austrian army with the view of attaining certain purposes, which would be specified in conformity with the understanding existing between the two Governments. They are prepared to propose to Parliament to guarantee an Austrian loan."[4]

Disraeli succeeded in winning over the Cabinet for a loan only, as can be seen from this declaration. Whether he himself favoured a subsidy is not clear. Meanwhile a loan did not at all suit Andrassy. He had stated in his telegram to Beust that his colleagues consented under no conditions to a loan without a previous permission of the Delegations, and that its discussion in the Austrian and the British Parliaments would prolong the matter and "rob us of a favourable moment". He repeated these arguments to the British Ambassador, adding that the

---

[1] A.A., Beust to Andrassy, 15 Feb. 1878, Tel. No. 58, geheim und vertr.
[2] *Ibid.* 20 Feb. Letter.
[3] Disraeli, p. 248.
[4] A.A., Elliot's communication to Andrassy, 16 Feb. 1878.

discussion would alarm Russia and that she might attack Austria before she was prepared for action.[1]

Disraeli wanted the support of the Austrian army in order to make it clear to Russia that she would have to count with the armed resistance of Austria and England if she occupied Constantinople or refused to accept revision of her terms. The purposes to be attained were to be specified "in conformity with the understanding existing between the two Governments", i.e. in conformity with their declarations of July and August. An army of 300,000 men was, in his opinion, sufficient for their realisation. Andrassy offered to mobilise the whole army of 1,100,000 men, and that "irrespective of whether one of the points were really injured or not". The demand for subsidies, and not a loan, he explained by the necessity of keeping the preparations secret and of taking advantage of the favourable moment.

Austria did not mean to co-operate with England for the purpose of mere pressure upon Russia. But she desired to be prepared to back up her claims by force of arms if necessary. Having failed to obtain subsidies, she was compelled to rely on her own resources. It was decided to demand from the Delegations an authorisation to spend the sum of three million florins for preliminary preparations. This sum could not be conceived in Russia as a provocation, and could be represented as intended for occupation of Bosnia and Herzegovina. But in talking the matter over with the Delegates Andrassy found out that none of them was disposed to give an indemnity "in bianco". Some of them were for a mobilisation at once; others for a regular vote of credit. On 24 February Andrassy informed the Cabinet of this and proposed to ask for a vote of credit which would enable the Government to meet requirements. Even the questions which concerned Austria most would be discussed at the Conference in so far as they were European, and she would gain nothing unless she forced the Powers, united in negation only, to take sides in one or other direction. The Delegations should be told that the question was not of a war but of protection of Austrian interests. No one knew how the Powers would be grouped at the Conference. He had hitherto

[1] B.A., Elliot to Derby, 19 Feb. 1878, No. 132, secret.

abstained from doing anything that would increase the financial burden, and if he was asking now for the vote of credit it was to be able to meet events. Even if the sum should appear provocative, it would only help the Conference.

Francis Joseph objected to the idea that the sum of 200–300 million meant provocation.

Pretis, the Austrian Minister of Finance, asked what had happened to justify the demand for such a large sum, when it was decided ten days ago to ask for three millions only. He declared that the Monarchy was not faced with the alternative of war or surrender. Her interests were not directly affected, and she was not in a position to pursue a far-sighted policy. She must wait a more favourable moment for that. Between war and surrender there was a third way: negotiation. Before the Monarchy was confronted with countless dangers, which it was still impossible to foresee, she should choose the lesser evil of occupying Bosnia and Herzegovina.[1]

Andrassy fought against this opinion in principle. He considered that the importance of the moment lay in the fact "that it was the last at which the Monarchy could settle her differences with Slavism in alliance with Europe. If the questions now still open found their solution in the sense of Panslav chauvinists without our raising a resolute voice against it, then a heavy reproach will fall upon us in the future. Should these questions be solved with a defeat of the Monarchy, then after the Turkish, the Austrian question will come to the order of the day slowly but inevitably. What we shall lose then is a hundredfold more than what we should pay now.... An immediate mobilisation would alone be sufficient, for the strategic position of the Russians is just now unfavourable. The Eastern Question does not come every day to solution, now it can and must be resolved." He was not opposed to a smaller sum; the important thing was to take some measures. Andrassy suggested that the Ministers should use their influence on the Delegates for the vote of credit. At the moment peace could still be preserved without war, but the Monarchy might soon be faced with the alternative of war or surrender. The mode must be found then to preserve peace without war and without the sacrifice of her interests.

[1] A.A., Ministerrath Protokol, 24 Feb. 1878.

At the same time while trying to win Austria over for a joint military action, Disraeli endeavoured to learn what attitude Bismarck would take in the event of a war, and "whether he intended to back up England and Austria in trying to modify the Russian plans, or Russia in enforcing them".[1] Bismarck answered that England "can rely with certainty on the neutrality of Germany during a conflict between England and Russia, which he earnestly hopes may be averted by conference.... The Emperor, the Crown Prince, the Government, Parliament—the people of Germany—wished for the friendship of England, and as long as he lived he could promise that Germany would never support any other Power against England...." As to the attitude Austria would take in that event, he thought Andrassy sincerely desired to support England, "but he did not think the Emperor of Austria willing to support Andrassy in a war with Russia.... Much of course must depend upon the conditions England had to offer Austria, who would have to bear the brunt of the war by land.... He thinks Austria less well prepared for war than Russia at present and that the immediate effect of war would be the loss of Galicia and perhaps of the Trentino to Austria, which he would regret." On Russell's question: "whether Germany would not object or interfere?", Bismarck answered that Germany would be neutral, but that he would object to a Russian occupation of Moravia or Bohemia. When Russell observed that his neutrality "was practically more benevolent to Russia than to Austria", Bismarck replied that he was wrong, that

the object of the strictly neutral position he wished to observe was to be able to give his support to a peaceful issue at the first favourable moment. At Gastein he had promised Count Andrassy that he would "befriend" him and that promise was sacred. Besides which the sympathies of the people of Germany were for Austria and in opposition to the Russian sympathies of the reigning families in Germany. The German Parliament if consulted would vote to a man for Austria. But it would be bad policy for Germany to quarrel without cause with so old and safe an ally as Russia, while the alliance of Austria depended in great measure on Count Andrassy's tenure of office. If Count Andrassy were succeeded by a minister less friendly to Germany, the ties between the two countries might slacken.

On the other hand he does not think much will be gained by war,

[1] B.A., Russell to Derby, 17 Feb. 1878, No. 119, secret.

as Russia is in possession of the Danube fortresses and of the seaboard, and that the independence of the Sultan is virtually at an end.[1]

On 18 February Russell was instructed to obtain further information of Bismarck's views on the present situation. Bismarck told him that

the fortunes of war and the neutrality of Europe had enabled her [i.e. Russia] to take possession of Turkey and the reluctance of Europe to contest her conquest by force of arms would enable Russia to remain in possession for the time being.... Elated by their successes the Moscovites and military party, who backed General Ignatyev's policy, thought themselves strong enough, if necessary, to risk a further contest with England and Austria, and it was probably under the influence of that party that Prince Gortchakov sought by various subterfuges to postpone the meeting of the Conference with a secret hope of backing out of it altogether....

Regarding Austria Prince Bismarck said that he did not think Count Andrassy could reckon on the support of his Imperial Master if he proposed war.

He most sincerely and earnestly hoped that notwithstanding his misgiving the Conference would meet and that an agreement among the Powers might be achieved. If it did not he assumed that England would feel bound by the declaration of 6 May to go to war to wrench Constantinople and the Straits from the grasp of Russia.

England had it in her power to do so and to inflict heavy blows and great humiliation on Russia. If England could persuade Austria to fight with her, which he doubted, and if Austria could bring half a million men into the field, Russia might in due course be driven from her present position. But when England and Austria had successfully occupied the positions now held by Russia the independence of the Sultan would not for that be re-established and a redistribution of power in the East would still remain inevitable.

He did not for his part look upon the possession of Constantinople and the Straits as a question of European importance, because the maritime states had it always in their power to shut out the ships of the Government in possession of them and that power was worth more than a treaty in his opinion.

The possession of Egypt and the free passage to India was a question of European interest and he deeply regretted that his wish to see England secure to herself and guarantee to others the road to her Eastern Empire through the Canal had been so strongly and unjustly misinterpreted in England.

For his part he should like to see England, while protesting against Russian aggression and before actually plunging into war, occupy

[1] *Ibid.* Nos. 118 and 119, secret.

Egypt and the islands as a pledge and there concentrate her forces, while Austria acting in concert would simultaneously occupy Bosnia and Herzegovina and even Serbia, and in all probability the effects of those measures would render war unnecessary and the Eastern Question would cease to threaten the peace of Europe.[1]

On 19 February Bismarck made a long speech in the Reichstag about his attitude in this crisis. Like Austria and England he considered that all changes in the Treaty of Paris required the sanction of its signatories. If they failed to agree among themselves about these changes, this must not necessarily lead to a war, but it would inevitably bring about a "waterlogging of the question" (*Versumpfung der Frage*), leaving Russia in possession of her conquest and the Powers retaining their attitude. He believed that a postponement of the solution of the question lay in the interest neither of Russia nor of the other Powers. It was improbable that Russia should impose her conditions by force; should the other Powers try to force her to yield and defeat her in a war, the question of what should be done with the Turkish provinces in Europe would still remain open. He considered it improbable that they could be replaced under Turkish rule. Whatever organisation they were granted, it could not be very different in principle from what was now demanded, and the question of degree could hardly be a reason for a war.

In order to settle these questions the Powers had agreed to summon a conference. The rôle of Germany at the Conference would be to mediate between the contending parties in order to bring about a solution satisfactory to both. Should she define in advance her attitude, she would not be able to play that rôle, for the other Powers would know where she stood and how far she would go. Her relations with her neighbours and England allowed her to mediate between Russia and Austria as well as between England and Russia.[2]

In a conversation with the Austrian Ambassador Bismarck specially drew his attention to the idea of "waterlogging of the question" which he had expounded in his speech in the Reichstag. Karolyi wrote to Andrassy that Bismarck seemed to be of opinion "that this middle course—the recognition of a state in the Balkan Peninsula detrimental to our interests, and the defence of our

[1] B.A., Russell to Derby, 25 Feb. 1878, No. 142, secret.
[2] *Politische Reden Bismarcks*, VII, pp. 85–105.

interests by a warlike policy against Russia—would perhaps recommend itself to us as the most advisable way. From such a situation, namely, from the withdrawal of European sanction, might be developed a very inconvenient situation for Russia and eventually a mighty one for us."[1]

Bismarck told Karolyi further that he assumed Austria would not go to war without England. Had he made in Parliament such speeches as Disraeli, he would have been long ago involved in a war with Russia. England had hitherto retreated step by step from Russia, and he was in the dark as to her future conduct. But he believed that Austria could enter into an alliance with her with complete security. In this connection the question of money came into great importance, "and the English subsidies would be at all events a mighty weapon of war". He had spoken about subsidies to the Prince of Wales on the occasion of his late visit to Berlin, who assured him that they would be found. He was ready to prevent Italy from interfering, if she tried to.[2] Russell wired on 12 February that he had been assured "by a person where information is generally correct that since the vote of credit in England Prince Bismarck has secretly but strongly urged Count Andrassy to offer a firm but determined resistance to the policy Russia is now pursuing if he feels confident that he can secure the support and co-operation of England, but not otherwise".[3] Buckle says also that "there was reason to believe that Bismarck was secretly encouraging Austria to join England in resisting Russia".[4]

It is beyond doubt that Bismarck meant to remain neutral in a conflict between England, Austria and Russia, at least so long as the position of Austria was not endangered. But his efforts to convince England of his absolute neutrality, his assurance that Andrassy was willing to co-operate with her, though his Emperor was not, and that much depended "upon the conditions England had to offer Austria", his endeavour to explain to the Prince of Wales the importance of subsidies for Austria, his assumption that England would be bound to go to war if the Conference did not meet—all these leave the impression that he

[1] A.A., Karolyi to Andrassy, 23 Feb. 1878, No. 12 B, streng vertr.
[2] *Ibid.*
[3] B.A., Russell to Derby, 12 Feb. 1878, Tel. Nos. 98 and 99, secret.
[4] Disraeli, p. 250.

favoured the war. Russell concluded from his conversation with Bismarck that he "would prefer a pacific partition of European Turkey to a prolongation of war, but if that cannot be, that he will do nothing to prevent a war between England and Russia which would leave Germany free to do what she pleased, while it lasted".[1] "My opinion has never varied", said Derby to Shouvalov. "From the beginning of the crisis Bismarck has pushed you constantly into war; now when it seems to be finished, he uses his efforts to make you undertake another one; Russia permanently in war, that is what the German Chancellor wants. He will prevent you from fighting with the Austrians, because it would be inconvenient to him to have a war so near to his frontiers. It is on us that he will fix his choice."[2]

But even if Bismarck favoured war, it was not a war for the maintenance of Turkey. In his opinion the independence of the Sultan could not be re-established, "and a redistribution of power in the East would still remain inevitable". For this reason he advised England and Austria to occupy the provinces they claimed before plunging into war. He believed that this would render war unnecessary.

Bismarck's attitude disappointed all his friends. They all wished him to pronounce himself more openly in their favour, but in spite of all his declarations they remained ignorant as to his real intentions. The leaders of the Austrian Parliament found in his speech a reason for opposing the vote of credit, believing that he would side with Russia in the event of war.[3] Schweinitz says that the Russian higher circles were dissatisfied with Bismarck's speech.[4] The English remained as suspicious of him as ever.

Disraeli failed in winning over Austria for co-operation, but Russia was no more successful in her endeavour to settle her differences with the Dual Monarchy and secure her neutrality. In proposing the Conference Andrassy represented it as the only means which could restore Austria's "legitimate share of influence on the conditions of peace", which would justify her attitude during the war and allow her to continue "the line of conduct

[1] B.A., Russell to Derby, 25 Feb. 1878, No. 142, secret.
[2] R.D., Shouvalov to Gortchakov, 7 March 1878.
[3] Andrassy, III, p. 76.   [4] Schweinitz, II, p. 12.

concerted with Russia". If Russia consented to it, her programme, with the exception of Bulgaria, might be carried through in its main lines. In fact Andrassy did not mean to concert with Russia upon the conditions of peace. An agreement with her might have secured all Austria's interests, but it could not give her the mandate for occupation, nor minimise Russia's influence in the Balkans. England would be the first to refuse a mandate, perhaps even the Conference itself, if it were only to register an arrangement reached beforehand by the three Powers. And without it, all understanding with Russia was useless. The Conference, though demanded to enable further co-operation with Russia, retained therefore its purely anti-Russian character, and only as such had a meaning to Austria.[1] Andrassy had no doubt, as he stated later on, that it would strengthen the position of the Powers desiring revision, and that the "identity of interest between England, ourselves and Europe would only arrive at a clear and practical expression at a congress".[2] The Conference was for him the means to mobilise all the Powers against Russia and drive her out of the Balkans. Only in co-operation with them, and not in keeping solidarity with Russia, as this was foreseen by the Budapest Convention, could he expect to obtain the mandate. That is why he deliberately avoided any discussion of outstanding points with Russia, which Bismarck had proposed in January. As soon as he learned of Russia's acceptance of the Conference he offered to the British Government "to come beforehand to a confidential agreement with them respecting the details of the conditions of peace.... Your Excellency will add," he wired to Beust, "that every step taken by England to evidence her determination to protect her own interests can only tend to strengthen her position at the Conference, a position the strength of which can never be too great for our wishes."[3]

Bismarck saw clearly the real motives which actuated Andrassy's demand for a conference and discarded all his arguments as artificial. "The only explanation for this step of Count Andrassy", he wrote, "lies therein, that it was a *parti pris* in that way—i.e. through a conference—to swing into the English

[1] Andrassy, III, p. 102.
[2] B.A., Andrassy to Beust, 14 April 1878, secret.
[3] *Ibid.* 31 Jan. 1878.

camp."[1] If it were not intended as a bridge for coming nearer to England he had no understanding "for this chess move". At present Austria considered only the extension and the occupation of Bulgaria as inacceptable to herself. This she could have carried through alone by an ultimatum to Russia, or eventually in a Conference of three. "The whole of the other argument of our Vienna friend makes upon me either a nervous or an artificial impression." He believed that Russia would have conceded to all Andrassy's demands had he formulated them "precisely and rattled the sabre" at the time of her defeat at Plevna. Even now an ultimatum and armament would have been more efficacious than a Conference.[2] Nevertheless Bismarck considered it natural that Germany could not refuse a Conference demanded by Austria, so much the less so as Russia accepted it.

It was the promise of Austria's further co-operation that induced Russia to consent to the Conference. Without her support the Conference was not only purposeless for Russia but actually dangerous, as it could only serve to force her to submit to the demands of the neutral Powers. Gortchakov hoped that this concession to Austria would facilitate an arrangement with her, and hastened the meeting of the Conference of three, which was to clear up the remaining points. He asked Bismarck to raise his voice against Austria's demands respecting the occupation of Bulgaria. He reminded the German Ambassador again of the services rendered to Germany in 1870-1 and asked that she should do now something more for Russia. The Tsar also wrote to his uncle, expressing the hope that he would give his full support to Russia at the Conference. Meanwhile Andrassy avoided the Conference of three. He informed Bismarck on 12 February that he was prepared for far-reaching observance of Russia's wishes in all points, but that a great Bulgaria and her occupation after the war were absolutely inacceptable to him. If Germany would support him in these points he could go to the Conference; otherwise he feared that it would lead to far greater and more disagreeable complications. He preferred therefore to deal with them at the Conference of all the Powers, where Germany would not be compelled to abandon her attitude of

---

[1] G.P. No. 305.   [2] *Ibid.*

reserve, and where, with the support of the other Powers, Austria could oppose Russia without thereby coming into opposition with Germany. He told Stolberg on that occasion that he might be soon compelled to mobilise an army corps. Austria must show that she was resolved to defend her position and her vital interests. "The Monarchy finds herself directed, after the changes of 1866," said Andrassy, "to take a dominating position in the East, and can therefore under no circumstances allow of conditions being created there which run counter to her vital interests."[1]

Bismarck refused to abandon his attitude of reserve for the sake of any of his allies. He considered that a greater or smaller Bulgaria was not so important for Austria, since she had recognised the independence of Serbia, Roumania and Montenegro.[2] But he did not wish to put any pressure to bear upon Andrassy, fearing lest this should render his position still more difficult, and bring in his place a man belonging to an anti-German camp. "The insincerity with which Gortchakov has acted towards us for at least three years", wrote Bismarck, "increases our duty to handle our relations with other Powers with caution and restraint."[3] To the Russian demand for support he answered that he did not know her desires, that he was the least informed of her plans, and that he could not judge of the extent to which the Russian terms might be opposed by the other Powers without knowing them. Thereupon Gortchakov communicated to him all his correspondence with Andrassy and promised to keep him constantly informed. He expounded at large his view on the future organisation of the Balkan peninsula, and threw upon Andrassy the whole blame for the present difficulties. He knew that Francis Joseph desired to preserve the Dreikaiserbund for reasons of internal Conservative policy. But Austria had already departed from that alliance and had come nearer to England. Since she began to make opposition, England also took a threatening attitude. It would be Austria's fault if Russia, after a victorious war, came to the danger of suffering a political defeat.[4]

---

[1] G.P. Nos. 318, 319.
[2] A.A., Karolyi to Andrassy, 23 Feb. 1878, No. 12 B, streng vertr.
[3] G.P. No. 310.   [4] G.P. No. 324, also Nos. 315 and 320.

The Conference of three opened on 25 February only. Andrassy probably waited for the results of the entry of the British fleet into the Sea of Marmara, before taking up his attitude towards the Russian proposals. In his instructions to Novikov Gortchakov pointed out that Russia could not consent to the Balkans being organised on the basis of the decisions of the Constantinople Conference. The extension of the frontiers of Bulgaria might be discussed, but she must remain autonomous and tributary, and be occupied by the Russian troops for some time. Russia had nothing against Austria taking Bosnia and Herzegovina, although the condition provided for by the Reichstadt Agreement—dissolution of Turkey—had not arrived. She considered the maintenance of the alliance of the three Emperors as a condition and foundation of peace.[1] Novikov gave a copy of these instructions to Andrassy, who, surprised by his frankness, believed that they were not real, but that there existed other secret ones.[2] At the Conference Andrassy declared that the Russian views were inacceptable to him, and that he could not give counter-proposals before they were modified. He read to Novikov the text of the Budapest Convention in order to show that the proposed Bulgaria was in opposition with its stipulations. There could be no word of modification before Russia recognised the validity of that Convention. Andrassy remained opposed to occupation, and declared that he did not want a tributary, but an independent Bulgaria. The second meeting took place on 2 March, when Novikov brought forward somewhat modified proposals with regard to the period and the number of the troops of occupation. But Andrassy retained his negative attitude. He spoke of an occupation of one month, and asked for guarantees for timely evacuation of the troops. If the western provinces were to remain under the rule of Turkey, as proposed by Russia, then Bulgaria must not stretch so far south as to make the connection with Constantinople impossible.[3] At this stage the negotiations were dropped and were never again resumed. After the ratification of the Treaty of San Stefano Ignatyev came to Vienna trying to reach an agreement and offering large concessions. This time Andrassy no longer dwelt

[1] G.P. No. 320.　　　　　　　　[2] G.P. No. 326.
[3] G.P. Nos. 328–31.

on the execution of the Budapest Convention, but raised his demands to a point which was inacceptable to Russia.

Andrassy's endeavour to avoid the Conference of three, make it evident that he did not desire to come to an agreement with Russia. He could not refuse it, since it was proposed by Bismarck and accepted by Russia, but he did all in his power to render it fruitless. He rejected Russia's proposal about Bulgaria on the ground that it was contrary to the Budapest Convention, which provided for an independent Bulgaria and an independent Roumelia, and not a great autonomous Bulgaria. Here he was right so far as the letter of the Convention was concerned, but he was in contradiction with his former views on that point. In his letter of 8 January Francis Joseph stated that Bulgaria could be either independent or remain under the Sultan's rule, but that she could be independent only in the event of the dissolution of Turkey. Why did he insist now upon an independent Bulgaria despite the fact that Turkey was not dissolved? Andrassy demanded also that Russia should recognise the validity of the Budapest Convention before entering into a discussion of her proposals. Meanwhile on 8 January he had himself rejected the validity of that Convention, stating that the condition of its fulfilment—the dissolution of Turkey—had not been fulfilled.

These changes in his views on the validity of the Convention and the organisation of Bulgaria were in fact tactical moves only, caused by the change of circumstances. In January he rejected the Convention in order to avoid discussing the conditions of peace with Russia, as he hoped that the Porte's appeal would bring all the Powers into the peace negotiations. This plan having failed, he was compelled in February to discuss the conditions of peace with Russia in order to win her over for the Conference. But since Russia's claims were opposed to the Convention he insisted upon its fulfilment in order to avoid an understanding with her. Had he really desired the realisation of that Convention, he would have asked Russia already in January to conform her conditions to its clause. In rejecting it then, and in asking for its recognition now, he pursued in fact the same aim, that of avoiding an agreement with Russia, and allying the other Powers against her.

The impossibility of reaching an agreement with Austria and

of securing her support at the Conference created a very precarious position for Russia. She was left alone to defend her claims against both Austria and England, who, though not co-operating openly, were equally determined to drive her out of the Balkans. In accepting the Conference Russia had only paved the way for their co-operation.

While the February crisis was reaching its climax, threatening to throw Europe into a general war, negotiations were going on between Russia and Turkey for the conclusion of peace. Opinion differed in St Petersburg as to what sort of peace should be aimed at. Fearing possible complications with England and Austria Gortchakov proposed "the conclusion of a preliminary peace and even to limit things to a preliminary protocol with Turkey which would in advance accept a reconsideration of the conditions of peace by a European conference".[1] Ignatyev desired "to conduct final peace negotiations either in Odessa... or in the environs of Constantinople, at Buyukdere, in that case inviting the representatives of the Powers to continue the interrupted sittings of the Conference of 1876". He proposed also a secret defensive alliance with Turkey "to guarantee the inviolability of the Straits".[2] Gortchakov combated vigorously this proposal, and as the Tsar shared his view, the instructions which Ignatyev had worked out for himself were consequently amended. Yet Ignatyev endeavoured and succeeded in extracting from Turkey more than he was authorised by the instructions. The Tsar confessed to the German Ambassador that the peace was better than he had expected.[3]

The negotiations for peace were opened on 11 February at Adrianople. General Ignatyev, who was appointed Russia's chief plenipotentiary, arrived there on 31 January, but the Turks delayed sending their delegates, hoping that a conflict between England and Russia would make it unnecessary. This hope induced them to prolong the negotiations and yield only at the last moment. On 28 February the question of the frontiers of Serbia nearly brought about a rupture. Ignatyev proposed breaking off negotiations and marching on Constantinople. It was his great desire to take possession of the Turkish capital,

---

[1] A. Onou, *op. cit.* II, p. 633.   [2] *Ibid.* p. 637.
[3] Schweinitz, II, pp. 10–11.

and he was eager to profit by this opportunity now. But the Grand Duke, conscious of the grave consequences such a step would bring about, refused this proposal. The negotiations were resumed on the next day, as the Turks accepted all Russia's demands. On 3 March—the day of the Tsar's accession to the throne—peace was signed at San Stefano.

The Treaty of San Stefano proclaimed Serbia, Montenegro and Roumania independent. Serbia was deprived of the districts of Pirot, Trn, and Vranja, which she had occupied with her army, and was given the towns of Nish, Leskovac and a small strip of land in the Sandjak of Novipazar. Montenegro obtained considerable territory in Herzegovina and the Sandjak of Novipazar as well as towards Albania, so that her territory was almost tripled. Roumania was allotted the province of Dobrudja in return for Bessarabia, which she was asked to cede to Russia. Bulgaria was erected into an autonomous, tributary Principality, which extended on the south from the Black Sea to the Aegean, and embraced the whole of Macedonia and a part of Serbia on the west. A prince elected by the people was to rule over this new state with the assistance of a national militia and a national Assembly. The organisation of new institutions was to be conducted under the supervision of a Russian commissioner, and a Russian army corps, not exceeding 50,000 men, was to occupy the country for two years.

Bosnia and Herzegovina were to obtain the reforms proposed at the first session of the Constantinople Conference, with the modifications which should be agreed upon between Russia, Austria and Turkey. The Cretan Organic Statute of 1868 was to be strictly executed, and similar statutes, adapted to local needs, were to be introduced in Epirus, Thessaly, and the other parts of European Turkey. These reglements were to be worked out by provincial commissions including a large number of native elements, and were to be examined by the Porte, who would consult Russia before applying them. In Armenia reforms and ameliorations according to local needs were to be introduced. Russia reserved Bessarabia and a part of Armenia embracing Kars, Ardahan, Bayazid and Batum for herself, and imposed an indemnity of 310 million roubles on Turkey. The Straits were to be open in time of war as in peace time "to merchant vessels of neutral states arriving from or destined to Russian ports". A part of the Russian army might be evacuated through the ports on the Black Sea and the Sea of Marmara.

Such as it was, the Treaty of San Stefano corresponded to two fundamental tendencies of Russian policy: it satisfied the Slavophils, who desired to see as many Slavs as possible liberated; it was in accordance with the traditional policy of Russia, who aimed at establishing her domination over the Straits and expelling Austria from the Balkan peninsula. The eastern frontier of Bulgaria, running from the Black Sea to the Aegean, left Constantinople entirely at the mercy of the Russian fleet and the Bulgarian army, while her western frontier, extending as far as Albania, barred the road to Salonika for Austria-Hungary. Owing to the resistance of the Great Powers Russia was not in a position to solve definitely the Eastern Question to her sole advantage; she desired at least to pave the way to such a solution in the future.

CHAPTER X

*

THE REVISION OF THE TREATY
OF SAN STEFANO

THE Treaty of San Stefano was only a preliminary. With regard to Turkey it retained its full validity, but so far as Europe was concerned, it had to be sanctioned by all the Great Powers. In what exactly consisted this sanction? Was it merely an act of formality, or had the Powers the right to demand its revision? If so, was it the revision of the whole Treaty, or only of a part of it, and what part? This question became a new source of contest between Russia and England. It opened as soon as the tide of the February crisis began to abate after their mutual declarations that they would not occupy Constantinople under certain conditions. It increased the already existing tension and threatened to bring them again into conflict.

When Andrassy invited the Great Powers to meet in a conference, he stated as its object "to establish the accord of Europe with regard to the modifications which it would be necessary to make in the treaties" regulating the political system in the East.[1] This invitation was accepted by all the Powers. Gortchakov refused to go to Vienna, where Andrassy would have presided over the Conference, and proposed another place, in the hope of presiding over it himself. Negotiations concerning another place continued throughout February and left an impression upon Bismarck, Andrassy and Disraeli that Russia wished to avoid the Conference altogether. Derby and Andrassy urged Bismarck to use his influence with Russia for its speedy meeting, Derby seeing in it the only means to prevent war. But Gortchakov answered that he would not let himself be intimidated, and that at all events the Conference could not meet before the conclusion of peace. Finally, at the beginning of March, he proposed that the Conference should be transformed into a

[1] G.P. No. 311.

congress and held at Berlin. This proposal was adopted by all the Powers, France only insisting upon the deliberations being limited to the questions directly raised by the war, excluding from it Egypt, Syria, the Far East and some others. Germany and England accepted Berlin with some reluctance. Bismarck disliked being compelled to take a more active part in the settlement of peace than he wished to; England feared lest it might lead to a more intimate co-operation between the three Northern Powers. She accepted the Congress under the condition "that all questions dealt with in the Treaty should be considered as subject to be discussed in the Congress, and that no alteration in the condition of things previously established by treaty should be acknowledged as valid until it has received the consent of the Powers".[1]

The examination of the whole Treaty by the Powers meant giving them the right to decide what conditions Russia would be allowed to impose on Turkey; it was equal to letting them participate in the conclusion of peace. This Russia had constantly refused, considering that their divergent interests rendered an agreement impossible, and that their aim was to deprive her of the fruits of her victory. For the same reason she could not consent now to the revision of the whole Treaty. The failure to secure Austria's co-operation left her to defend her claims alone, and she had to choose between war and surrender. In such circumstances Gortchakov no longer desired the meeting of the Congress; he saw that Austria and England would find themselves in the same position in it, and that a diplomatic co-operation would lead to military co-operation if Russia refused their demands.[2] He took refuge under the principle of "European interests", although he knew that he was no longer in a position to decide what they were to be. He instructed Shouvalov to answer that "if at the Congress plenipotentiaries raise questions of European interest, we could not prevent them, but in no case could we engage to accept them without knowing what they are".[3]

But if Russia could not allow the Powers to modify her conditions, England too could not accept them, such as they were. Both parties therefore kept firmly to their views. On 13 March

---

[1] G.P. No. 343. [2] R.D., Shouvalov to Gortchakov, 28 March 1878.
[3] R.D., Gortchakov to Shouvalov, 14 March 1878.

Derby repeated that the British Government "must distinctly understand, before they can enter into Congress, that every article in the Treaty between Russia and Turkey will be placed before the Congress, not necessarily for acceptance, but in order that it may be considered what articles require acceptance or concurrence by the several Powers and what not".[1] Shouvalov, realising that a complete divergence in this question might lead to a war, endeavoured to obtain a less negative answer from his Government. At his suggestion Gortchakov replied that "the entire Treaty—and we have no secret engagement—will be communicated to the Powers before the Congress: all will enter with full liberty of action, and we claim the same right".[2] On the 21st Derby informed Shouvalov that the British Government "cannot recede from the position already clearly defined by them", and asked "whether the Government of Russia are willing that the communication of the Treaty 'en entier' to the various Powers shall be treated as a placing of the Treaty before the Congress, in order that the whole Treaty, in its relation to existing Treaties, may be examined and considered by the Congress".[3] Gortchakov gave no answer to this question, but Derby insisted upon being informed in writing that no answer could be given. Thereupon Gortchakov replied: "we leave to others liberty to raise at the Congress such questions as they think fit, while reserving to ourselves the right to accept or refuse discussion."[4]

Except England, none of the Powers required the examination of the whole Treaty. Andrassy, whom Derby asked to use his influence on Russia to give way, refused to do so. "I always was of opinion", he answered, "that one could demand and ought to demand that Russia lays the whole Treaty of Peace before the Powers. This has been done, everything else is the business of the Congress. What the Congress will do, or will not do does not depend upon Russia. What Russia concedes or does not concede can in no way prejudice the decisions of the Congress."[5] He "objected strongly" to Derby's insistence upon revision of

---

[1] G.P. No. 358.
[2] R.D., Gortchakov to Shouvalov, 16 March 1878. Also G.P. No. 361.
[3] G.P. No. 367.
[4] R.D., Shouvalov to Gortchakov, 25 March 1878.
[5] B.A., Beust's communication to Derby, 24 March 1878, very conf.

the whole Treaty and endeavoured to persuade him not to reject the Congress because of a question of form. He argued that the Congress was more in their interests than in those of Russia, and that it would strengthen the position of the Powers desiring revision.[1] But the British Government did not share this opinion. "Whether it was practicable to examine selected portions of a Treaty whose character depends on the combined effect of all its parts," Salisbury replied on 4 May, "whether a congress ought, by its acquiescence to sanction the contention that a Treaty can be validly revised without the assent of the Powers who have signed it—these are not questions of form, but of substance and of principle."[2]

Germany stood aloof from this controversy, refusing only to go to the Congress without England, and insisting upon all decisions being reached unanimously. Seeing that Russia and England could not agree upon the question of the competence of the Congress, Bismarck proposed on 14 March that the Powers should meet in a preliminary Conference in order to settle that question. They would prepare the Congress both materially and formally and thus facilitate its work without prejudicing its decisions.[3] Gortchakov was opposed to this proposal, fearing lest it should bring about an unfavourable grouping of the Powers, but the Tsar accepted the idea, and the Russian Ambassador at Berlin was designed as his representative. But England saw no practical value in such a conference and refused it. She wanted a "yes" or "no" from Russia, and upon her answer depended whether she would attend the Congress or not.

Disagreement over the question of the competence of the Congress brought matters to a deadlock, from which war seemed to be the only way out. Under the influence of this growing tension, both Russia and England continued their war preparations. Russia slackened the retreat of her army from Bulgaria and mobilised some new divisions. General Obruchev was ordered to work out a plan of action. He proposed that the mouth of the Bosphorus should be seized in advance, as its possession was of vital importance for maritime communications with

[1] B.A., Andrassy to Beust, 14 April 1878, secret.
[2] B.A., Salisbury to Elliot, 4 May 1878, No. 293, conf.
[3] G.P. No. 345.

Bulgaria.[1] The Grand Duke was therefore ordered to ascertain what attitude the Sultan was likely to take in the event of war, and whether he would consent to Russia occupying the position on the Bosphorus. In the event of his refusing it, he was empowered to take it by force.[2] Nicholas paid a visit to the Sultan, but failed to extract from him more than a promise of neutrality. Layard informed Derby that the Duke tried also to win the Sultan for a "close and intimate alliance with Russia for mutual assistance and defence", but that the latter refused it and reserved liberty of action.[3]

Bismarck told the British Ambassador that Russia seemed to be resolved to accept a war with both Austria and England. In his opinion she was better prepared than Austria, but Austria and England united were able to vanquish her.[4] Gortchakov's correspondence with Shouvalov shows that he counted upon the possibility of a war with both of them. "I continue to believe in a war with England sooner or later", he wrote to Shouvalov, "and expect nothing of a Congress if it met." And again: "Our August Master is preparing for all eventualities, and I have not hidden from Baron Langenau that among these eventualities we calculate a possible war not only with England but also with Austria-Hungary."[5]

The imminent danger of a war with England induced Russia to make one more attempt and secure at least Austria's neutrality. Although at first decided to accept the struggle with both of them, Gortchakov realised after cooler thinking that Russia could not sustain a struggle on both fronts. Besides, Germany, as she had repeatedly declared, would not stand Austria being seriously hurt, which meant that fighting her would be a useless and dangerous affair. On 24 March General Ignatyev was sent to Vienna to give necessary explanations about the Treaty of San Stefano, and see under what conditions Austria would accept it and remain neutral in the event of war. But Andrassy seeing Russia in difficulty raised the price of his neutrality. Before Ignatyev arrived he assured England that he would not give up a single point of their interests.[6] Yet he promised Russia not

---

[1] S. S. Tatiščev, *op. cit.* II, pp. 474–6.   [2] *Ibid.*
[3] B.A., Layard to Derby, 28 March 1878, No. 436, most secret.
[4] B.A., Russell to Derby, 25 Feb. 1878, No. 142, secret.
[5] R.D., Gortchakov to Shouvalov, 6 March 1878 and 10 April.
[6] B.A., Beust's communication to Derby, 26 March 1878.

only to remain faithful to the Dreikaiserbund, but also to maintain neutrality in a war with England, if she accepted the following conditions: (1) That Austria should occupy Bosnia and Herzegovina as well as the territory between Serbia and Montenegro after informing the Porte of it. The occupation would take place immediately if the Congress should not meet, or later on if it met. (2) That the frontiers of Montenegro should follow the line of Korito, as far as the junction of the Rivers Piva and Tara, then to Belopolje, crossing the River Lim near Berani and then to the Lake of Skutari. Austria was to annex the territory between this lake, the sea and the River Bojana. Montenegro would be guaranteed the liberty of navigation on that river and the lake. (3) That Serbia should receive no aggrandisement in the west: as compensation she would be given Vranja and Trn in the east. That she should undertake to or let Austria construct a railway line through her territory and maintain the same tariffs as in Austria. (4) Russia's right to take Bessarabia was recognised, and Austria promised to support that view towards both Roumania and the Great Powers. (5) That the eastern frontier of Bulgaria between Kirk-Kellissi and Constantinople should take the line proposed by the Conference of 1876, leaving thus Lule-Bourgas and a part of the Black Sea to Turkey; her western frontier should be drawn from the Gulf of Orfano to Vranja: "the district remaining beyond this limit should be given administrative autonomy independent of the Bulgarian Principality, under the name of 'Macedonia'. Salonika would be part of this new province." (6) Austria desired that the occupation of Bulgaria should not last more than six months after the evacuation of the rest of Roumelia, and that the number of troops should be reduced to 20,000 men. If Russia accepted these conditions, Austria would support them at the Congress, but wished that they should be adhered to even if the Congress did not meet.[1]

In a conversation with the German Ambassador Andrassy pointed out that his demands were intended to secure the railway line through Mitrovica to Salonika and free access to the Aegean Sea for Austria. In order to be able to protect that line, she must take possession of the Sandjak of Novipazar and remove the frontier of Bulgaria to the Gulf of Orfano. The occupation of a

[1] G.P. No. 393.

portion of Albania was necessary for the protection of Albanian Catholics and for preventing Spizza and Antivari becoming Russia's naval bases. He added also that Ignatyev raised serious objections only against the proposed frontier of Montenegro and that because of the special interest which the Empress had for Prince Nicholas. Stolberg saw that Andrassy's conditions went far beyond his earlier demands, and that their tendency was to put the whole western half of the Balkans as well as the whole Adriatic coast under Austria's influence and power. He wrote to Berlin that Andrassy did not hide that he considered the present moment favourable to extract from Russia a highest price for himself.[1]

General Ignatyev had the same opinion of Andrassy's demands. He told General Schweinitz that he had offered Andrassy commercial treaties and railway tariffs with the Balkan States, and the occupation of a slice of land on both sides of the railway line. Andrassy was not satisfied with this: he wanted the whole territory of the rivers running to the Adriatic and the Gulf of Salonika. Ignatyev had proposed to him to take all these lands and make of them an autonomous state under the name of "Macedonia", and place Baron Rodić at its head; he would not object to it.[2]

In a dispatch to Langenau Andrassy argued that his demands were not inspired by any wish of conquest, but solely by the desire to make it possible for Austria to reconcile herself with the situation created by the Treaty of San Stefano. Yet he modified that Treaty in a manner which deprived him of any pretext for increasing his demands. It is beyond doubt that he intended to establish a full domination over the western part of the Balkans. This was the policy which the military circles in Austria had already urged at the Conference of 29 January 1875. They defended the same views now in their observations upon the Treaty of San Stefano, which probably served as the basis of Andrassy's demands. Starting with the assumption that Austria must annex Bosnia and Herzegovina in order to prevent their union with Serbia and Montenegro, they asked that the occupation should be extended up to Novipazar and that the frontiers of Bulgaria should be removed to Tchustendil and the River Struma.

[1] G.P. No. 377.   [2] G.P. No. 380.

In that way Austria would be able to keep Serbia and Montenegro separate, to secure for herself free access to Salonika, to
play the Greek, Albanian and Moslem element against the
Serbian, and to secure her share of spoil in the event of
Turkey breaking up altogether.[1]

Andrassy's "growing appetite of annexations" was strongly
resented in St Petersburg. Gortchakov complained bitterly of it
to the German Ambassador and asked Germany to keep Austria
neutral by all means. In that case Russia could accept war with
England, as she was sure of Italy and believed Turkey would
preserve neutrality in her own interest.[2] Bismarck advised him
to make concessions to Austria and thus oblige her to remain
neutral. Gortchakov drew his attention to the too naïve conception of peace of the Vienna Government, who were in close
connection with England, and insisted upon Austria declaring
herself openly for England or Russia.[3] Russia began to mass
her troops in Galicia and transport her army from Bulgaria to
Roumania. At the same time she made new overtures to Vienna
designed to meet Andrassy's wishes. On 17 April Novikov delivered a *pro memoria* to Andrassy stating the concessions Russia
might be willing to make. She was ready to accept the western
frontier of Bulgaria and willing to take into consideration his
demands with respect to the occupation. She made no difficulties
about Serbia, and promised every facility for the Austrian railway
to Salonika, but excluded the annexation of the Sandjak of Novipazar. She objected only to the restriction of the frontiers of
Montenegro and asked that they should stretch to Bojana.[4] It
is interesting to note that Russia insisted solely upon preserving
the acquisitions of Montenegro, while conceding almost all other
points. It is difficult to see what political reasons dictated such
a policy, unless it were the personal sympathy of the Empress
for Prince Nicholas, of which Ignatyev spoke to Andrassy.[5]

Andrassy observed to Novikov that the division of the Sandjak

---

[1] A.A., Militärische Betrachtungen über die durch den Frieden von San-
Stefano geschaffenen neuen Grenzen auf der Balkan Halb-Insel. Wien, am
24ten März 1878.

[2] A.A., Karolyi to Andrassy, 14 April 1878, No. 206, geheim.

[3] *Ibid.*

[4] A.A., Novikov's communication to Andrassy, 17 April 1878.

[5] A.A., Langenau to Andrassy, 9 April 1878, No. 17A–D, geheim; 10 April,
No. 81, Tel., and 17 May, No. 117, geheim.

between Serbia and Montenegro was considered by all parties in the Monarchy as an artificial barrier, designed to cut off her communications with the East, and that therefore it must be annexed by Austria. As to Montenegro he expected that the Tsar would abandon his protégé rather than demand from his ally the sacrifices which were contrary to her interests. He would agree to give Montenegro the port of Spizza, but not Antivari or Dulcigno, for this would make her master of Cattaro itself, and provoke permanent conflicts with Austria. He required, however, a precise answer to the proposals he had made to Ignatyev.[1]

This answer reached him on 8 May. His insistence upon the acceptance of all his points forced the Russian Government to face the question whether a war under such conditions was worth while. They did not in fact yet know what demands England was going to make. When they were communicated to Shouvalov at the beginning of May, Russia was no longer disposed to pay the price requested by Austria and repudiated all her previous concessions.

Like Russia, England too continued her war preparations. Disraeli was hardening in the conviction that war was inevitable, and having failed to win Austria over for co-operation, he was resolved now to act alone. He reverted again to his earlier project of obtaining a place in the East, which would enable him to concentrate troops and ships in the event of war. On 2 March he suggested for discussion in the Cabinet the occupation of Mytilene, St Jean d'Acre and a port on the Persian Gulf, and a committee was appointed "to consult the military and naval authorities as to the best course of action".[2] At the same time he conceived the idea of creating a League of Mediterranean Powers, with the object of securing "the trade and communications from the overshadowing interference of Russia".[3] This he considered as "a secret of secrets" and therefore conducted preliminary negotiations unofficially. But the idea found no response abroad and was soon dropped. The information from Admiral Hornby that he was prepared to force the Bosphorus and that he "could cut off the Russians from all their supplies via the Black Sea" filled him with confidence and made him believe

---

[1] A.A., Andrassy to Langenau, May (no date) 1878.
[2] Disraeli, p. 253.   [3] *Ibid.*

that he was "in a commanding position".[1] A formal resolution was passed in the Cabinet as to the acquisition of "a new naval station in the east of the Mediterranean...if necessary by force" in the event of the British maritime interests being compromised by or without the Conference.[2] On 16 March Disraeli wrote to the Queen that the Cabinet discussed "*corps d'armée*, new Gibraltars, and expeditions from India". Fresh fuel was added to the fire when after the ratification of the Treaty of San Stefano the Russians moved a detachment of their army to Buyukdere to embark for home. Though Russia was allowed by the Treaty to use Turkish ports for the evacuation of her army, this move provoked great alarm in London and Constantinople. Derby protested against it, and threatened with a written remonstrance.[3] Gortchakov revoked the order at once to avoid further complications. Meanwhile, Russia's refusal to accede to the British conditions for the Congress decided Disraeli to undertake the measures which he had long contemplated. On 27 March he proposed in the Cabinet to call out the reserves and to direct the Indian Government "to send out a considerable force, through the Suez Canal, and occupy two important posts in the Levant, which will command the Persian Gulf and all the country round Bagdad".[4] This proposal was adopted by all his colleagues, with the exception of Lord Derby, who resigned at once. Derby's chair was taken by Lord Salisbury, who had intimately collaborated with Disraeli during the last crisis.

On 4 April Salisbury issued a circular to the Great Powers stating clearly the views of the British Government on the Treaty of San Stefano and its revision. He analysed that Treaty to show that its aim was to establish Russia's complete domination in the Balkans and the Black Sea, and that it gave her a powerful instrument of coercing Turkey and suppressing "almost to the point of entire subjugation the political independence of the Government of Constantinople. These results arise not so much from the language of any single article in the treaty as from the operation of the instrument as a whole." Great Britain could not admit that the Power dominating on the Straits, the Persian

---

[1] Disraeli, p. 255. [2] *Ibid.* pp. 255-6.
[3] R.D., Shouvalov to Gortchakov, 21 March 1878; Gortchakov to Shouvalov, 19 and 20 March. [4] Disraeli, pp. 262-5.

Gulf and the shores of the Levant, and neighbouring the Suez Canal "should be so closely pressed by the political outposts of a greatly superior Power that its independent action, and even existence, is almost impossible". She must insist therefore upon the whole Treaty being submitted for revision.[1]

The arrival of Salisbury at the Foreign Office marked a turning point in British policy. Disraeli and Derby were of two opposite characters and mentalities and could work together only by constant mutual concessions. Disraeli vacillated from the idea of the preservation of Turkey to her partition, aiming always at restoring British influence and prestige in Europe. Derby spent all his energy in resisting measures which might provoke a war, but was unable to devise any constructive policy adapted to the exigencies of the situation. Contrary to Disraeli's opportunism and Derby's doctrinarianism, Salisbury combined in himself the strength of a principle with the efficiency of a practical mind. When he took up the leadership of foreign affairs, he surveyed the situation such as he found it, and set up a few principles to guide his action. He did not believe "in the possibility of setting the Turkish Government on its legs again", nor did he think it safe "to stake England's security in those seas on Turkish efficiency".[2] He rejected therefore the idea of preserving her integrity and endeavoured to find other means for the protection of British interests. Turkey should be freed from Russia's domination and rendered "tolerably independent within its reduced proportions". This could be achieved by "driving back the Slav State to the Balkans—and substituting a Greek province". But since Turkey would no longer be able to defend the seas where Britain had her interests, England had to make up for it by acquiring a new naval station in the Aegean. Russia should be left in possession of her conquests in Asia, and for this concession she could be expected to accept English demands in Europe. Beyond this limit England had no interest in opposing Russia, and she should support her in securing "good government, assured peace and freedom" for the Christian population.[3]

This was in short Salisbury's programme of policy. He was prepared to accept a war, if necessary, to realise his aims. But

[1] Salisbury, pp. 228–9.   [2] Ibid. p. 213.   [3] Ibid. pp. 213–14 and 229.

he believed that it offered a suitable basis for negotiations and a peaceful settlement. He lost no time in acquainting Bismarck with his views, hoping to obtain his support, and endeavoured to reach an understanding with Austria, believing that it would compel Russia to accept his demands.

The British Ambassador in Berlin was instructed to enter into confidential conversations with Bismarck and learn his views on this programme. "As he likes frank diplomacy", Salisbury wrote to him, "it may be useful for you to be able to tell him exactly what we want.... I still think that the division of Bulgaria in Europe and the provision of compensation for England in Asia are the two keys of this difficult lock."[1] Bismarck was found "willing to support any terms of settlement which England might think necessary for her own security—provided that they were acceptable to Russia. He would do nothing to imperil friendly relations with his eastern neighbour and his own opinion was avowedly in favour of partition."[2]

Salisbury's chief preoccupation was, however, to reach an agreement with Austria as to the modification of the Treaty. Already on 3 April he proposed to Andrassy "that some formal agreement should be come to for giving effect to the seven points enumerated in his note of 29 May".[3] The insincerity and evasion of his policy gave no hope of an easy agreement. Nevertheless, Salisbury asked his Ambassador to "take every opportunity which you decently can to press on Count Andrassy to declare his policy—not in concealed and ambiguous communications but by some act that shall pledge him to the world".[4]

The separate attitude Andrassy took in the question of Congress and the vagueness of his language with regard to the conditions of peace provoked suspicion in London as to his real intentions. Elliot complained of the impossibility of giving "any clear view of his views". He warned his Government that "Andrassy continues to concert in secret with the two other Imperial Cabinets...".[5] "I believe, however," he wrote, "that he will be found willing to assent to much in the Russian pro-

[1] *Ibid.* pp. 242, 244.
[2] *Ibid.* pp. 243–4.
[3] B.A., Elliot to Salisbury, 17 April 1878, No. 312, conf.
[4] Salisbury, pp. 245–6.
[5] B.A., Elliot to Derby, 21 March 1878, No. 213, conf.

posals, which from his language three months ago he seemed resolved not to tolerate."[1] He concluded from further conversation that Andrassy had accepted, or was at the point of accepting, Bismarck's view that Turkey was dead, and that he endeavoured to find compensation for himself in Bosnia, Herzegovina and the Sandjak: it was with that object that he asked the Delegations for a vote of credit.[2]

Austria had by that time definitely abandoned all war combinations and adopted a policy of compensation. In the Cabinet of 12 March the Finance Ministers spoke of the difficulties of effecting a loan on the British market and stressed the necessity of giving peaceful declarations in the Delegations. Andrassy still held that there was no reason for pessimism, but he pointed out that Turkey could not be maintained and that it was very well that Austria had not protested against anything that had hitherto happened. Her interests could be now protected more easily than before. If she asked for compensations she must endeavour also to preserve her other interests, and for that purpose she should take advantage of Greece. "The possibility of a solution is better than a war," he said, "for a successful war would show only that we have vanquished this time, whereas this solution would prove that Russia is not to lead in the East".[3]

The idea of compensation was now being ventilated by the Austrian press and was found acceptable, though in Hungary it was rejected. On 28 March Andrassy hinted at it to Elliot in a disguised form. He insisted upon the necessity of preventing Russia from remaining in Bulgaria longer than six months, and intimated that, as a guarantee for her evacuation, England should keep her fleet in Constantinople and Austria should occupy Bosnia, Herzegovina and northern Albania, "as a security for communications with Salonika".[4] The idea of guarantee had in fact another meaning. Andrassy undertook to occupy these provinces at once in the event of there being no Congress, if Russia accepted his conditions of neutrality. Although the occupation had to be executed in consequence of the agreement

---

[1] B.A., Elliot to Derby, 8 March, No. 187, conf.
[2] *Ibid.* 24 March, No. 243, conf.
[3] A.A., Ministerrath Protokol, 12 March 1878.
[4] B.A., Elliot to Derby, 28 March 1878, No. 258.

with Russia, he endeavoured to give it the appearance of a co-operation with England, of a common guarantee for the evacuation of Bulgaria. This duplicity was characteristic of Andrassy's conduct in the Russo-British conflict throughout the crisis. A few days later he told Elliot that he had demanded three things from Ignatyev: (1) a large restriction of the frontiers of Bulgaria, (2) her occupation by not more than 20,000 men and not longer than six months, and (3) supervision of her organisation by all the Powers. As to Bosnia and Herzegovina, he knew that Turkey was incapable of introducing reforms there, and therefore, "the only thing that she [Austria] could do would be to annex" these provinces as well as the Sandjak and northern Albania. He added that this measure would be un-popular and that "it was only...through a Congress that this could be accomplished....In fact whatever is now mentioned as desirable," wrote Elliot, "Count Andrassy at once reverts to the 'Congress' as the mode of obtaining it."[1] Andrassy had in fact by this time definitely made up his mind for occupation. But being uncertain whether the Congress would meet or not, he endeavoured to provide for both eventualities. If it met, he wanted to represent it as a necessity imposed upon him by the incapacity of Turkey to introduce reforms; if it did not meet, the occupation was to serve as a guarantee for the evacuation of Bulgaria, and undertaken in concert with England.

On 29 March Benjamin Kallay, formerly diplomatic agent in Belgrade and Andrassy's personal friend, was sent to Constanti-nople to persuade the Porte to cede Bosnia and Herzegovina to Austria. In the instructions for Count Zichy, Andrassy used his old arguments of the impossibility of an autonomous organisation in these provinces. He pointed out to the Porte that it would not be able to fulfil the promises made in the Treaty of San Stefano, and that their realisation would provoke another revolution in which Bosnia and Herzegovina would be lost to Turkey. Austria could not allow their passing into the hands of Serbia and Montenegro, for this would have en-dangered her possession of Dalmatia. She asked therefore that these provinces should be ceded to her, and promised in return

[1] B.A., Elliot to Salisbury, 1 April 1878, No. 269, most conf. and No. 272, conf.

I *

to help Turkey reduce the frontiers of Bulgaria.[1] The Porte was greatly surprised at such demands and delayed its answer under the pretext of desiring to examine the question thoroughly. At Andrassy's request, the German Ambassador was instructed to support his proposal at the Porte.[2] To overcome the Turkish resistance Austria informed them that she could no longer feed the Bosnian refugees and that if the Porte was unable to secure their repatriation and give them the reparations it had promised, she would be obliged to do it herself. Andrassy proposed that the Porte should invite Austria to occupy these provinces and keep them until the final solution of the question. He had nothing against it declaring that its sovereign rights were not prejudiced by this measure.[3] But the Porte remained unyielding. She dwelt upon the danger of Italy demanding Albania, if Bosnia were ceded to Austria; she declared that England had already promised to support her with regard to Bulgaria, and that Russia too was willing to make concessions. On 18 April the Sultan told Zichy that he had waged wars for much smaller territories and that he could not accede to the Austrian proposal.[4]

While pressing the Porte to cede the two provinces, Andrassy endeavoured also to win over the Great Powers for his project of occupation. It was only on 14 April that he communicated through Beust his opinion on the "chief objects to be attained in changing the preliminary Treaty". He asked that the frontiers of Bulgaria should be narrowed, that she should be organised under the supervision of European commission, and that the Russian occupation "must cease with the end of the Russo-Turkish War". He wished also to preserve the interests of Greece, and to secure a natural territorial connection between Constantinople, Thessaly, Macedonia and Albania. Should this be impossible, then these provinces should obtain an organisation similar to that of Bulgaria, in order to serve as a counterpoise to her. "The Ottomans as a nation", Andrassy argued, "have proved to be completely incapable of civilising the Christians." He believed "that a rational curtailing of Turkish territory would

[1] A.A., Andrassy to Zichy, 28 March 1878; B.A., Layard to Salisbury, 8 April 1878, No. 459, most conf.
[2] G.P. No. 434.
[3] A.A., Andrassy to Zichy, 15 April and 3 May 1878.
[4] A.A., Zichy to Andrassy, 18 April 1878, No. 241.

in no way be prejudicial to the stability or internal strengthening of the Turkish Empire..." There were three ways of achieving that purpose: Congress, war and adjournment of the question. Andrassy proposed that the first one should be adopted, as it left the other two ways open in case of need. He reserved discussion of the question of Bosnia and Herzegovina for another time.[1]

On 21 April Andrassy addressed a long memorandum to Salisbury on the question of Bosnia and Herzegovina, endeavouring to convince him that it was in the interests of Europe and Turkey alike that these provinces should be annexed by Austria. The arguments he used in support of his demand are well worth reproducing. He started by proving that an autonomous organisation of these provinces was impossible because of the social and religious differences of their population. The war had only aggravated these natural hindrances. Turkey was incapable of introducing reforms and giving reparations, and the old struggle would therefore be renewed. But even if she succeeded in pacifying temporarily these provinces, a revolt of the landless against the landlords would soon arise and bring to Austria as many Mohammedan refugees as it had already brought Christian ones. The result of this struggle would be their union with Serbia and Montenegro. The creation of such a Slav grouping of states would jeopardise the peace and possessions of the Austrian provinces (Dalmatia, Croatia and Slavonia), and would oblige her to annex the whole Slav complex aspiring to union, if she did not wish to be constantly threatened by it. To avoid that alternative she must annex Bosnia and Herzegovina.

From the point of view of Turkish interests such a solution would also be most advantageous. She would have to accept new obligations, though she was before the war hardly capable of fulfilling the old ones. The land would remain economically passive for a long time. The autonomies would provoke discontent among the Moslems and she could not prevent further revolts. Turkey would not be able to defend the two provinces against Serbia and Montenegro. "The next phase of complications in the Orient would be probably a co-operation of Serbia, Montenegro and Bulgaria against Turkey" provoked by the Bosnian question. The consequence of this would be the loss

[1] B.A., Andrassy to Beust, 14 April 1878.

to Turkey not only of Bosnia and Herzegovina, but also of Albania and probably of all her possessions in Europe. In such a situation she could not hold down the hostile Christian elements in the Balkans. Another rising in Bosnia would unite all the discontented elements and bring them up to the walls of Constantinople. These dangers could be avoided only by the annexation of the two provinces by a conservative non-Slav Power, which would make the union of the Panslav elements impossible. Turkey would no longer have to fear Slav aspirations, and could concentrate her power upon defending her other provinces. An autonomy would lead to the extinction of the Moslem element as it did in Serbia. It would be the task of Austria to protect them and secure their lands. This would demonstrate that, contrary to the Slav assertion, a common life of the Moslems and the Christians was possible without any of them being oppressed by the other, which would have beneficial consequences for the whole Ottoman Empire. All in all, Turkey could lose a province "the possession of which is no gain to her and the loss of which is inevitable", but a timely solution of this question would avert great dangers for her in the future.

It was also in the interest of Europe that these provinces should be definitely appeased. The preservation of Turkish rule there would only cause new conflicts: Austria alone could pacify them, protect the Albanians and prevent further disturbances. It was also of interest to Europe that no Power should obtain a predominant influence in the East. Whatever the modifications introduced in the Treaty of San Stefano, "the fact of the liberation of a great tribe by Russian intervention could not be revoked, and means at all events an increase of the Slav influence, to create an equipoise against which is in the interests of Europe". If Europe refused to allow Austria to prevent the Slavisation of the Balkans, then the maintenance of the *status quo* would be abandoned without superseding it by a formation capable of life, and whatever were the modifications of the Treaty, the results would be negative only. The erection of a "theoretical autonomy" as a counterpoise to Russia would soon collapse, whereas Bulgaria—a Russian creation—would subsist, which would only enhance her prestige. Should Austria replace Turkey in possession of Bosnia and Herzegovina, then a Slav grouping under Russia's protection would be excluded and a counterpoise to her preponderance would be created.[1]

In short, Austria did not wish to annex Bosnia and Herzegovina and had never aspired to it; on the contrary she had done everything to avoid being compelled to it. It was unpopular, fraught with many political difficulties and financially represented a burden only. But she was forced to it by the necessity of protecting herself from the consequences of the Treaty of San Stefano. Whereas for Austria it was a sacrifice only, it represented a great service to both Turkey and Europe. "For our Monarchy itself this means no increase of power," wrote Andrassy, "but an act which is at the same time apt to secure European peace from convulsion, a sacrifice that Austria-Hungary takes upon herself and the fruits of which come to Europe's good".[2]

"Nothing can be more unsatisfactory than the line which Andrassy is pursuing", wrote Salisbury to Elliot on the 24th. "If it were mere duplicity I should not mind so much. But it obviously covers intense irresolution. For if he had made up his mind to go halves with Russia in the Balkan Peninsula, I don't suppose that he would have any ground to fear Bismarck, and the harm that we could do him would be small. But he has no single definite object. He is trusting to indefatigable shiftiness to enable him to keep well at once with Hungarians, Russians, English, Turks and Italians, while he steadily obeys the orders from Berlin."[3]

Salisbury did not let himself be deceived by Andrassy's verbosity. He was informed by Colonel Wellesley of the conditions Andrassy put forward to Ignatyev for his neutrality in the event of war between Russia and England, and could therefore see through Andrassy's game.[4] He did not mind so much about Bosnia and Herzegovina, but he feared lest they were only a first step towards a complete agreement with Russia. Division of the Balkans was a possible and attractive policy. "In that case he will throw us over", wrote Salisbury, "and his course will be easy enough if he can square the Hungarians."[5]

[1] B.A., Andrassy to Beust, 21 April 1878.
[2] *Ibid.* [3] Salisbury, p. 247.
[4] B.A., Loftus to Salisbury, 15 April 1878, Inclosure No. 1, secret.
[5] Salisbury, p. 248.

On 20 April Salisbury proposed an agreement "not to accept a Bulgaria that should overstep a certain frontier line to the South", and suggested that this line should be the Balkans and that Southern Bulgaria should receive an organisation similar to that of Lebanon.[1] Andrassy refused to bind himself "with reference to the limits of Bulgaria unless it is combined with stipulations concerning other questions"...."We do not know what is the opinion of British statesmen on the subject of Russian occupation of Bulgaria and Roumania," he wired to Beust, "on the Bosnian question and on the cognate one of Montenegro and Serbia. If a common action is desired we have the right to know the English intentions in respect to all these points."[2] He wished to know whether England would go to war for Bulgaria and whether she intended to accept the Congress or delay it "till after all the separate points which have been raised by England shall have been settled from Cabinet to Cabinet".[3] Salisbury replied that he would not oppose Austrian pretensions in Bosnia and Herzegovina, but that he considered that question as one concerning Austria and Turkey. As to Serbia and Montenegro their frontiers had no importance to England. "I have been unable to draw from Count Beust's language or from the despatches which he communicated any definite conclusions as to the policy which Count Andrassy will pursue", he wrote to Elliot. "...But I am prepared to say generally that if Count Andrassy will come to terms about the southern limits of Bulgaria, Her Majesty's Government will make no difficulty respecting the points upon which he insists."[4]

In fact Andrassy deliberately avoided a separate agreement with England, though he had himself proposed it on 31 January. Was he afraid of losing Germany's support if he sided with England, or was he, which is more probable, hopeful that by refusing an understanding with both Russia and England he would more easily bring them into conflict? Russia was prepared to accept war with England if she were sure of Austria's neutrality. England would be compelled to fight, since Russia refused all her demands. It was evident that a Russo-British

[1] B.A., Salisbury to Elliot, 20 April 1878, No. 271, secret.
[2] B.A., Andrassy to Beust, 23 April 1878.   [3] Ibid.
[4] B.A., Salisbury to Elliot, 25 April 1878, Tel. No. 28.

war would force England to lean upon Austria and Germany, and that it was the best means of bringing her into an alliance with them, which was Andrassy's old dream. However, in taking such an attitude Andrassy was only following the advice Bismarck gave him as early as October 1876, namely not to interfere in the natural antagonism between England and Russia. That he constantly obeyed his advice and in fact adapted his conduct to Bismarck's wishes is clearly manifest from a telegram he addressed to Karolyi on 30 April. He asked Bismarck whether he agreed with the interests he had brought forward in his correspondence with England, and whether an arrangement with her would not be opposed by Germany but considered rather as a success. "It is of vital interest for us to be clear about this, for it would be open to objection to renounce the strength of a European co-operation before we were able to rely upon the support of Germany."[1] Bismarck answered that his proposals were "as reasonable as practical", but that he could not say more.[2] Pressure from both sides compelled him to preserve absolute neutrality, and he could not promise his support to any concrete understanding. In the Cabinet Andrassy insisted upon measures being taken which would free Austria from any dependence upon Russia and England. On the 28th he told his colleagues that Austria was not compelled to go with Russia at any price, nor to side with England for interests which were partly remote from her own.[3] He answered Salisbury that he could not "propose the line of the Balkans or any other boundary different from one which he had communicated to Ignatyev, but that he would support a more restricted frontier if proposed by England or any other Power". He objected to Southern Bulgaria being given the status of Lebanon, since this would only stimulate Bulgarian aspirations and give an opportunity for Russian propaganda. But this question could be dealt with only "in conjunction with all the other *faits accomplis*. Before anything else we must be perfectly clear about English intentions". He asked once more for an answer to his note of 14 April and about the Congress.[4]

[1] A.A., Andrassy to Karolyi, 30 April 1878, Tel.
[2] A.A., Karolyi to Andrassy, 7 May 1878, No. 24A–B, vertr.
[3] A.A., Ministerrath Protokol, 28 April 1878.
[4] B.A., Andrassy to Beust, 29 April 1878, private and conf.

On 4 May Salisbury sent a detailed answer to all Andrassy's proposals and objections from 14 April onwards, making one more effort to convince him of the necessity for common action. He explained that the Congress could not meet before a compromise was reached on the question of revision. Although England and Austria were not equally interested in all the questions raised by the Treaty, they were deeply concerned in some of them, "and in respect of which their common action would produce far more efficacious results....To both it appears of primary importance that the Slav State shall receive as small an extension of territory and influence as possible; that every condition tending to place that influence at the disposal of Russia shall be resisted, and that all practicable support shall be given to the races which are likely to act as barriers to the advance of the Slavonic power." For that reason he had insisted upon the frontier of Bulgaria being removed to the Balkans so as to prevent "the establishment of a new naval Power upon the shores of the Aegean". He had also asked Andrassy "to suggest some alternative delimitation" if he were unable to join in the line of the Balkans. England could not accept any modification of the Treaty without a new frontier of Bulgaria. She did not overlook the importance of Russian occupation but she could not "place it on the same level". She would be ready to support Austria on that point if she agreed upon the question of frontier. As to Bosnia and Herzegovina "the policy it unfolds is new and not consequent on, nor directly in harmony with the previous communications we have received from him and from the Austrian Ambassador. In the absence of any knowledge of the views entertained by the Porte and by other Powers it would be difficult for Her Majesty's Government to enter upon any appreciation of a measure which in relation to the previous system of Austria is so entirely novel, and which at the same time has so little direct bearing upon the special interests of England." But she would not offer any opposition to this project if an agreement for concordant action were reached.[1]

Meanwhile, by this time England had already opened direct negotiations with Russia for an agreement upon the modifications of the Treaty. Andrassy's procrastination and evasion of a

[1] B.A., Salisbury to Elliot, 4 May 1878, No. 293, conf.

common action and the danger of his joining Russia altogether induced Salisbury to settle his differences with Russia. In a subsequent letter to Elliot he explained what influence the attitude of Austria had upon his taking that course. "In all these negotiations our path has been marked out for us very much by Austria", he wrote. "If she would have agreed to fuller co-operation at an earlier period, no special arrangement with Russia would have been necessary. But we have been obliged to provide for the case—which is even now possible and three weeks ago seemed very probable—of Austria throwing us over altogether....If we had had anybody to help us the matter might have been different."[1]

Already at the beginning of April Salisbury took steps to remove the danger of conflict which the proximity of the Russian and the English forces at Constantinople rendered possible. He sounded Bismarck whether he would undertake to mediate between Russia and England—putting it as his own proposal— for a simultaneous withdrawal of their forces to an equal distance from Constantinople.[2] Bismarck assented to this at once, and after privately sounding Gortchakov, he offered his mediation to both countries on 9 April, with the object of reaching an arrangement for the removal of the British fleet beyond the Dardanelles and of the Russian troops to a distance "equivalent to the time the English fleet would require to take up her present position".[3] This proposal was accepted by both Governments, though on the part of Russia with some mistrust, the Tsar believing that England was unprepared and that she only wished to gain time. The negotiations were opened at once, but they were prolonged owing to the difficulty of defining the time necessary for resuming the present positions, as both Governments endeavoured to avoid being forestalled by the other. Finally on 19 April Russia accepted the formula proposed by England, but reserved the right to concert previously with the Porte about the neutral zone and to make proposals later for the date of the return of the British fleet. A complete agreement was never reached, and the two opposing forces were

[1] *Ibid.* 3 June, No. 370, most conf.
[2] Salisbury, p. 242.
[3] G.P. No. 381.

left at Constantinople. At the end of May England strengthened her position still more by concentrating 7000 Indian troops at Malta.[1]

Although these negotiations remained without result they gave time to ease the tension and improve the atmosphere generally. The firmness of England and the uncertainty as to the conduct of Austria made Russia abandon her intransigent attitude. The diplomatic game Ignatyev had started with the view of playing off both Austria and England proved to be a blunder. The confidence that Russia was strong enough to accept a war with both of them vanished as soon as its danger became imminent: Russia was neither militarily nor financially prepared to support the struggle to the end. The influence of Ignatyev and the military circles began therefore to decline. Gortchakov, who had endeavoured to carry out their policy, was no longer considered the man who could lead Russia out of this impasse. The man to whom the Tsar was inclined now to lend his ear was Shouvalov. His deep knowledge of conditions in Great Britain and his friendly relations with Bismarck designated him for the chief rôle in future events.

The desire to reach an agreement on the changes to be introduced in the Treaty of San Stefano was discreetly announced by both Governments, though at first they both preferred to conduct negotiations through Berlin. The knowledge of the British demands, which Salisbury formulated clearly and communicated to Berlin, only facilitated these negotiations. He had informed Russell of them already at the beginning of April, and on the 19th he developed at length to the German Ambassador his objections to the Treaty.[2] It is probable that Bismarck revealed them to Gortchakov and that the latter knew in advance what he had to expect from England.

Direct negotiations between Salisbury and Shouvalov were opened at the beginning of May. To avoid the delay and confusion caused by telegrams, it was agreed that Shouvalov, after obtaining the British conditions, should go to St Petersburg to explain them to his Government. On 7 May Shouvalov left London and on his way home visited Bismarck, whom he found very much surprised at the concessions England was prepared to

[1] Disraeli, p. 287.   [2] G.P. No. 401.

make, and greatly preoccupied at Russia's "having negotiated with England instead of treating with Austria". Shouvalov told him that it was England and not Austria who threatened Russia's conquest in Asia. Bismarck agreed that England "would have gone to war alone, whereas Austria would only have made war if she had allies", and promised his support for coming to an understanding with England.[1]

On 22 May Shouvalov was back in London, after paying a second visit to Bismarck. An agreement on the main questions was soon established, but the desire of the British Government to squeeze more from Russia than they originally demanded, and the obstinacy of Gortchakov against further concessions, prolonged the negotiations and at one moment brought their success into jeopardy. Shouvalov had to strain all his energy and use all his tact in a hard struggle with both St Petersburg and London. He succeeded in reaching an agreement on the principal points only and left the minor matters to be dealt with at the Congress. On 30 May a protocol was signed between Shouvalov and Salisbury, according to which Russia was to restore Bayazid and rectify the frontier of her conquests in Asia so as to leave the Trebizond road free, but retaining Batum and Kars. In Europe she consented to the frontiers of Bulgaria being removed from the Aegean and withdrawn east of the Vardar so as to exclude the non-Bulgarian population. Bulgaria was to be divided into two parts by the line of the Balkans. The northern part was to obtain a political autonomy with a Prince of its own, and the southern an administrative autonomy with a Christian Governor. The Tsar attached special importance to the Turkish troops being removed from the southern part, but consented to the Congress defining the time and manner in which they could be used for the defence of the province or restoration of order. England reserved the right to insist at the Congress that the Turkish garrisons should be retained on the frontier of the province. With regard to the organisation of the Christian provinces remaining under Turkish rule, all the Great Powers were to have a consultative voice. In return England consented, though with reluctance, to Russia's taking Bessarabia, and promised not to contest the other clauses of the Treaty of San

[1] G. Hanotaux, *op. cit.* IV, p. 340.

Stefano.[1] The long controversy as to the revision of the Treaty of San Stefano was thus ended by an agreement about the limits of modification, which enabled both Powers to accept the Congress.

The Protocol of London accomplished the first purpose of pushing the Slav power beyond the Balkans and restoring to Turkey a tolerable independence. But this was half only of Salisbury's programme. England's chief interest lay in Asia, where Russia was left in possession of practically all of her conquests, and where she was bound to use a strong corrosive influence, which Turkey was unable to withstand alone. "The mere presence of the Russians at Kars", wrote Salisbury, "will cause Persia, Mesopotamia and Syria to turn their faces northward. Then a Russian party will arise... and a chaos will follow of which, in some form or other, the Russians will take advantage to reduce the Porte to impotence, and to turn its provinces into Russian satrapies."[2] He considered that "the presence of England is the only remedy which can prevent this process of destruction from going forward". He was ready to "enter into a defensive alliance with the Porte, undertaking to join in defending her Asiatic Empire from any attacks of Russia.... But to give any strength or value to such an undertaking, some port in the Levant would be an absolute necessity."[3] After discussing several places the British Government decided that this "port" should be the island of Cyprus which was best suited for a naval base and had "the double advantage of vicinity both to Asia Minor and Syria". The need of a naval base was not the only reason for acquiring this island. The present crisis taught Salisbury that the British people "would probably abandon the task of resisting any farther Russian advance to the southward in Asia, if no other but speculative arguments can be advanced in favour of action. But it will cling to any military post occupied by England as tenaciously as it has clung to Gibraltar: and if any movements were made which would threaten it while attacking the Ottoman dominions, its actions might be counted on."[4] To make this acquisition popular at

---

[1] B.A., Salisbury to Elliot, 3 June 1878, No. 370, most conf.; G.P. No. 427.
[2] Salisbury, p. 266.   [3] *Ibid.* p. 267.
[4] Layard, Salisbury to Layard, 18 April 1878.

home he wished "that the Porte should give us specific assurances of good government to Asiatic Christians, similar to those given in the Treaty to Russia; and should thereby invest us with a special privilege of advice and remonstrance in case of any gross abuse".[1]

Throughout April and May Salisbury endeavoured to prepare Layard for this new policy. He argued at length that the Turkish "breakwater is now shattered...and the flood is pouring over it", that the centre of her power in the future lay in Asia, where she was menaced by Russia and where England alone could defend her. As soon as Shouvalov returned from St Petersburg, Salisbury instructed Layard to offer the Sultan an engagement to defend his Asiatic dominions in case of Russia retaining Batum, Kars and Ardahan. In return for this he was to cede Cyprus to Great Britain.

Layard had no great difficulty in inducing the Sultan to accept this overture. Despite England's vacillation the Turks were constantly in hope that she would wage a war on Russia and rescue their lost provinces, and had repeatedly offered their co-operation. This hope gave Layard an unrivalled influence with the Sultan, who followed his advice even in the choice of his Ministers. The long-protracted negotiations among the Powers completely exhausted the Turkish treasury. On 19 May the Sultan complained to Layard that he was no longer able to feed his army, and asked for a loan of four million pounds, promising to give "any security in his power".[2] A widespread dissatisfaction in both the army and the ruling class resulted in a plot against the Sultan which arose on 24 May. Though it was quickly suppressed, the Sultan was seized with terror and implored Layard to place a British ship at his disposal and take charge of his family if he were murdered.[3] In such a situation he could not but welcome a British overture to defend his Empire. An agreement in principle was reached already on the 27th, but the secret Convention was signed only on 4 June. It engaged England to defend the Ottoman Empire against any invasion on the part of Russia if she retained Batum, Kars and Ardahan, and Turkey,

---

[1] Salisbury, p. 269.
[2] Layard, Layard to Salisbury, 19 May 1878, most secret and personal.
[3] Layard, Layard to Salisbury, 31 May 1878.

to assign Cyprus to be occupied and administrated by England. By this Convention England obtained compensation for any territorial increase of Russia and Austria and placed herself in a better position to defend her interests in the East.

Andrassy was informed of the Anglo-Russian negotiations. Already on 28 April he told the Cabinet that Russia was trying now to come to an agreement with England in order to avoid making concessions to Austria. Although he considered that Austria was not compelled to make agreements with either of them, and that she must be prepared to defend her rights alone, the possibility of an Anglo-Russian understanding came as a painful surprise to him. His first thought was to counteract that understanding. As soon as he learned of the British proposals to Russia he disclosed to Salisbury the Russian proposals of 8 May, representing them as an attempt to separate Austria from England "by entangling them in separate negotiations". He warned Salisbury against falling into this trap, adding that "the only way to defeat it was for the two Governments to act towards each other with the most perfect openness".[1] At the same time he declared himself ready to come to an agreement with England on the basis of her note of 4 May, asking that in return for his support in the question of Bulgaria she should give her support to his demands with reference to Bosnia, Herzegovina and Montenegro.[2]

Andrassy also warned Bismarck of the danger of Austria remaining isolated in the event of Russia and England coming to an arrangement and asked him to use his influence in London for an agreement with Austria, and to give a clear promise that he would support her interest in St Petersburg or at the Congress. He told Bismarck that an Anglo-Russian understanding would leave the impression in Austria that he had sacrificed her interests to Russia, since he had mediated between Russia and England, and that this would strengthen the enemies of an Austro-German *entente*.[3]

Bismarck realised the difficulties involved in Austria remaining isolated. He was much surprised at the concessions England was

---

[1] B.A., Elliot to Salisbury, 10 May 1878, No. 374, most secret.
[2] *Ibid.*
[3] A.A., Andrassy to Karolyi, 17 May 1878, Tel. No. 49.

prepared to make to Russia, and did not hide from Shouvalov that he preferred an agreement with Austria. He expressed his anxiety in London lest "England should come to an agreement with Russia to the prejudice of Austria", and his opinion that it could hardly bring about a lasting peace.[1]

Salisbury found it strange that Andrassy who had himself conducted secret negotiations with Russia, while constantly dissuading England from them, should talk now of a trap. He doubted whether Andrassy's "inclination for a joint action" indicated really "a more honest policy.... I believe he is only trying to frighten Russia: and if Russia would abandon Montenegro he would divide with her the Balkan Peninsula by a line running from Serbia to the Gulf of Rendina."[2]

On 16 May Andrassy told the British Ambassador that he "would be willing to come to an agreement with H.M. Government as to the question relating to Bulgaria and to join in pressing them upon Russia, if England would at the same time join in pressing upon Turkey the Austrian proposition concerning Bosnia and would also join in pressing upon Russia the objections entertained by Austria to the cession of a port to Montenegro".[3] Beust made the same communication a few days later, insisting "upon the necessity of an arrangement expressed in writing". Salisbury felt that it was an Austrian trap that he had to beware of and refused to "come to any definite arrangement until we know what Shouvalov has to say...".

"I am very anxious not to break with Austria or to force her into the arms of Russia", he wrote to Elliot. "But in spite of Beust's assurances, I doubt whether any written agreement will bind Andrassy, and I fear that, the moment one is made, Russia will raise her price and buy him off. His calculation, I fear, has been to use England as a bogey to frighten Russia, and if he could not thus get his end diplomatically, then to push England into a separate war with Russia and extort terms from the latter when she is exhausted. I feel therefore that coming to close quarters with Andrassy is dangerous work, and I had rather avoid it till all hope of an amicable settlement with Russia is at an end."[4]

---

[1] B.A., Salisbury to Russell, 25 May 1878, No. 294.
[2] B.A., Salisbury to Elliot, 10 May 1878, No. 319, secret.
[3] B.A., Elliot to Salisbury, 16 May 1878, No. 398, secret.
[4] Salisbury, p. 258.

It was only on 27 May, after an agreement with Russia was practically reached, and in order "to dissipate these fears", that he authorised his Ambassador to offer Andrassy an agreement binding the two Governments to urge at the Congress the organisation of Bulgaria in the manner already agreed upon with Russia. In that event "England will support any proposition with respect to Bosnia which Austria shall make at Congress".[1] Andrassy accepted this proposal but insisted upon the words Herzegovina and the Sandjak being added to Bosnia. Salisbury refused to include the Sandjak as it did not belong to Bosnia, but accepted "Herzegovina" with the reserve that England should not engage "to contest definitely boundaries assigned to Serbia and Montenegro.... We cannot undertake to go to war about them or to break up the Congress upon them."[2] As Andrassy refused this reserve, the document was signed with reference to Bosnia only. On 6 June the secret agreement on the basis of Salisbury's proposal was signed in Vienna by Elliot and Andrassy. England and Austria engaged themselves to urge at the Congress that the autonomous tributary state should not extend south of the line of the summits of the Balkans and west of the River Morava. The rest of Bulgaria was to be cut off from the Aegean and subjected to provisions securing to the Sultan adequate political and military supremacy to guard against invasion or insurrection. The occupation of the northern part was not to last more than six months and with 20,000 men only. In the Articles VI, VII and XI of the Treaty of San Stefano the word "Russian" was to be superseded by the word "European". England promised to support any proposition with respect to Bosnia, which Austria should make at the Congress.[3] Andrassy, though dissatisfied with Salisbury's refusal to insert Herzegovina and the Sandjak, told Elliot that he considered the agreement "as between gentlemen", and hoped that a further understanding would be reached at the Congress.[4]

With Russia no special agreement was reached. As soon as Russia entered into direct negotiations with England she changed her attitude towards Austria. In a note of 8 May she put forward

[1] B.A., Salisbury to Elliot, 27 May 1878, No. 349, most secret.
[2] Ibid. 2 June, No. 362.   [3] Ibid. 27 May 1878.
[4] Elliot to Salisbury, 6 June 1878, Tel. No. 454.

new proposals, which though intended to remove Andrassy's objections, in fact repudiated all previous concessions. To meet the objection against a great Slav state, Russia proposed that Bulgaria should be divided into two separate states on the line decided by the Conference of Constantinople and that their exterior limits should remain the same as indicated in the Treaty of San Stefano, rectified by an international commission on the bases of the majority of population. Both states would remain vassal and enjoy complete internal autonomy. Austria would be free to conclude an arrangement with the western part of Bulgaria and Serbia, without, however, prejudicing their autonomy, in order to secure her railway line to Salonika and its junction through the Serbian territory. She would also be free to occupy and annex Bosnia and Herzegovina "according to the terms and in the limits concluded between the two Governments". If she accepted these proposals she would have to engage herself by an act in writing to remain solid with Russia with regard to the other clauses of the Treaty of San Stefano and to maintain neutrality in the event of renewal of war, whatever extension it took.[1]

Andrassy considered these proposals inacceptable. The division of the Sandjak would close the road to the East for Austria; the division of Bulgaria was, in his opinion, a concession in appearance only, since both parts had an expressly Slav character, thus creating a Slav confederation instead of a great Slav state.[2] Bismarck shared the opinion that the Russian proposal closed Austria hermetically from the East. He held the division of Bulgaria to be of some importance only if the western part were to come more under the influence of Austria.[3] Although the Budapest Convention did not concede the Sandjak to Austria, he considered her claims to be justified, since Russia had also violated that Convention, and Russia should make concessions to Austria in order to keep her from going with England. Bülow's commentary was more significant. In his opinion the whole question centred now round Montenegro, as the tendency of Russia was to create a great Slav state stretching from Antivari to Varna. It is therefore conceivable that Bismarck should have

---

[1] A.A., Novikov's communication to Andrassy, 8 May 1878. Also G.P. No. 404.　　　[2] G.P. No. 405.　　　[3] G.P. No. 406.

taken advantage of Shouvalov's visit to acquaint him with his views and stress the importance he placed on an agreement with Austria.[1]

Meanwhile the Russian Government seemed unwilling to make further concessions to Austria. The prospect of an agreement with England made them stiffen. On the contrary they endeavoured to obtain England's support in the question of Serbia and Montenegro in order to be able to exert pressure on Austria.[2] Yet on his return from St Petersburg Shouvalov communicated to Bismarck the proposals he was about to make to England and told him that Russia had nothing against the occupation of Bosnia and that she renounced the division of the Sandjak. The question of Antivari was to be settled at the Congress.[3] Andrassy was not quite satisfied with the Russian proposals. He objected specially to the division of Bulgaria, believing that the two parts would soon unite and thus counteract the whole plan. But he was ready to leave that and other minor questions for the Congress. Bismarck urged him not to insist upon all details being regulated before the Congress, as the danger was of its not meeting at all. Both Russia and England were ready to sacrifice Austrian interests to an agreement between themselves. He promised his full support at the Congress but only to the limit of "no breach with Russia".[4]

The attempt to win Turkey over to cede Bosnia and Herzegovina proved to be equally unsuccessful. Having failed to persuade her that it was in her own interest to do so, Andrassy tried to frighten her out by the Russian demands of 8 May. On the 15th he communicated them to the Porte and renewed his proposal that she should invite Austria to occupy the two provinces, and await the decision of the Congress without asking any previous declaration from Austria.[5] A few days later he extended his demands to the Sandjak under the plea that it would enable Austria to defend Turkey from Serbia, Montenegro and Bulgaria.[6] At the same time he asked England and Germany to support his demands with the Porte, and invited

[1] G.P. No. 410.
[2] B.A., Loftus to Salisbury, 14 May 1878, No. 435, secret.
[3] G.P. No. 410.   [4] G.P. Nos. 413, 415.
[5] A.A., Andrassy to Zichy, 14 May 1878, No. 76.
[6] *Ibid.* 18 May, No. 77.

Bismarck to use his influence in London to that effect. Salisbury consented to give the Porte friendly advice since, as he told the German Ambassador, the question was not one of annexation, but of an occupation only.[1] In fact it was Andrassy's overture for co-operation in Bulgaria that induced him to change his attitude. But although Layard did his "utmost to persuade the Sultan to accede to the demands of Austria-Hungary", the Turks remained inflexible. On the 24th they consented to Austria occupying temporarily some strategic points in Bosnia and Herzegovina if she would conclude an alliance with them for mutual defence against Serbia and Montenegro. Austria was to occupy the main places on the frontiers of Serbia and Montenegro in order to prevent an invasion on their part, but would not interfere in the internal administration of these provinces, and would evacuate them as soon as order and peace were restored.[2]

Andrassy was very much disappointed with such a result and began to think of a forcible occupation. This measure was indeed strongly advised by Bismarck, who feared that not only Turkey, but also Italy and France would oppose occupation at the Congress. The Treaty of San Stefano gave no pretext for proposing an occupation, and the question was whether the Congress would admit it at all. Were Austria already in possession of these provinces, she could plead an accomplished fact.[3] But Andrassy could not make up his mind upon adopting this measure. He was without financial means for a speedy occupation and feared also the resistance of Turkey and the bad effect it would have in Hungary. The Hungarians were strongly opposed to annexing these provinces as a compensation for Russia's aggrandisement, which Tisza called the policy of "Trinkgeld". He wrote to Andrassy on 22 May that he regarded it as an evil event in case of Austria being compelled by circumstances to adopt that course. He did not know whether Andrassy intended an occupation or annexation, but considered that even an occupation was admissible only as a part of a general action against Russia, for preventing the realisation of the Treaty of San Stefano. This must be put forward as the purpose of Austria's

[1] G.P. No. 417.
[2] A.A., Zichy to Andrassy, 24 May 1878, No. 304; G.P. No. 436.
[3] G.P. Nos. 415, 437–8.

action, showing thus that she did not aim at a secret acquisition of territory, at a partition of Turkey or a compensation for Russia's spoil.[1]

Andrassy refused the Porte's proposal and suggested that she should adopt his project of the 15th or omit from her own the clauses relating to alliance and the Sultan's sovereign rights. After reaching an agreement with England and securing the support of Germany, Russia and France for occupation, he advised the Porte not to put any obstacles to his demands at the Congress. But the Turks refused to bind themselves to anything and left the question to be decided by the Great Powers.

[1] A.A., Tisza to Andrassy, 22 May 1878.

CHAPTER XI

*

THE CONGRESS OF BERLIN

THE London Agreement laid down the limits of the revision of the Treaty of San Stefano, and Russia was able now to consent to its being discussed as a whole at the Congress, without fearing inacceptable demands being put upon her. She could not, however, hide from herself the truth that this agreement was possible only by her making the concessions which at the time of conclusion of that Treaty she was resolved not to make. The negotiations of the last five months convinced her that not only England and Austria, but all the Great Powers were opposed to her dominating in the Balkans, and that a peaceful settlement could be reached only by her abandoning these pretensions. This unity of Europe against Russia was emphasised at the Congress still more. To use the words which Wertheimer puts in Andrassy's mouth, Russia was put "in the dock" before Europe.[1]

The Congress of Berlin was opened on 13 June. Elected as president, Bismarck proposed at once that the questions should be discussed according to their importance, and that therefore that of Bulgaria should be dealt with first. Knowing that the main questions were already substantially settled in direct negotiations between the interested Powers, he wished that their agreement should be formally recorded before proceeding to other points. The danger of war would thus be averted, and a basis laid down for the solution of outstanding questions.

Russia and England agreed in London as to the boundaries and division of Bulgaria, but the question of the organisation of the southern part was left to be settled at the Congress. The Tsar attached special importance to Turkish troops being removed from it, seeing in it the guarantee for security of the province, but consented to the Congress finding the mode and cases in

[1] Andrassy, III, p. 102.

which the Sultan would be permitted to enter with his troops to prevent an insurrection or invasion. Salisbury accepted in principle the evacuation of the province, but reserved the right to insist at the Congress upon the Sultan being allowed to retain his troops on the frontier. To this point Russia reserved full liberty of discussion.[1] Both parties desired now to make use of their reserves to the utmost. Russia's aim was to secure the Christians from Turkish abuses; England desired to make the Sultan complete master of the southern province. Both parties had to count upon a strong warlike current at home, which for months resisted every concession to the opponent. The position of England was further aggravated by the disclosure of her agreement with Russia, which was published by *The Globe* on 14 June. The Jingoes saw in it the betrayal of the policy which Disraeli had led them to believe he pursued. Disraeli, for whom the chief object of the Congress was "consolidating and restoring the authority and stability of Turkey",[2] was not much inclined to observe his agreement with Russia, and insisted strongly upon his demands being accepted. On the 17th he proposed two resolutions: (1) "That the chain of the Balkans should be the new frontier of Turkey. (2) That in the country south of the Balkans, the Sultan should exercise a real political and military power." He was to be allowed to fortify the frontiers and maintain his troops there, and to occupy the province if its security were menaced.[3] Since Russia opposed both these demands, Bismarck proposed that the question should be settled in direct negotiations between the interested Powers. At the request of Austria, her representative was also included in the negotiations.

Although consenting to Bulgaria being divided by the chain of the Balkans, Russia endeavoured now to obtain its division by a vertical line, creating an eastern and a western province. It is interesting that Andrassy should have also tried to win over Disraeli for another line, trying to persuade him that the line of the Balkans was inferior to his own. "In truth common persons understand what the line of the Balkans means", reported Disraeli to the Queen, "but the complications of Count Andrassy, all arising out of little interests and obscure influences of his own, would only convey an impression that we were surrendering

---

[1] G.P. No. 426.   [2] Disraeli, p. 335.   [3] *Ibid.* p. 322.

something intelligible and substantial."[1] He refused to accept any other line, and Shouvalov abandoned his proposal.

But in the question of retreat of the Turkish troops from Southern Bulgaria, which at Disraeli's request was to be called Eastern Roumelia, England and Russia remained equally unyielding. Some attempts were made to reach a compromise, but Disraeli refused to recede from his demands, and declared them an ultimatum. He spread the rumour among the delegates that he would break up the Congress if Russia did not accept all his points. On the 21st he even ordered a special train to be ready to take the British Delegation back to London. Alarmed by this news Bismarck tried to mediate, proposing "some plans for a compromise". At the last moment the Russians yielded, and Disraeli wrote to the Queen: "before I went to bed I had the satisfaction of knowing that St Petersburg had surrendered."[2]

The Russians accepted British demands in principle, but endeavoured to mitigate them by insisting upon the Congress defining the cases and the mode of occupation of the province, and a European commission fixing up the points which Turkey was to garrison on the frontiers. Disraeli resolutely refused these proposals. Bismarck, desiring to show his friendship to the French, offered them the task of reconciling these divergences, and Waddington, France's first delegate, gladly accepted this overture.[3] Though taking "a rôle non-inactive but reserved", he hastened to learn the views of England and Austria as soon as he arrived in Berlin. He considered British demands identical with France's interests. "We remained thus faithful...to our old traditions of good will towards Turkey", he reported to Paris, "and to the interests which command us to assure, if possible, the guarantees of duration for what remained of that great body mutilated by the Treaty of San Stefano."[4] But Russia's desire to protect the Christians was in his opinion also in accordance with France's traditions, and he endeavoured therefore to provide for it too. He found, however, his task unrealisable. Russia succeeded only in obtaining that Turkey should not use irregular troops on the frontier, and that she

[1] Disraeli, p. 317.   [2] *Ibid.* pp. 323–6.
[3] D.F. No. 320.   [4] *Ibid.*

should notify the Powers of her decision to occupy the province if its security were menaced.

In this conflict over Bulgaria England was strongly supported by Austria. She had promised it before the Congress in return for England's support in Bosnia, and now endeavoured to deserve her favours for the important rôle England was to play in the acquisition of Bosnia and Herzegovina. "Throughout the discussion Austria entirely supported England", wrote Disraeli to the Queen. "...Much mortification among Russians at our understanding with Austria."[1] And again: "I have gained him [Andrassy] quite, and he supports me in everything."[2] The Russians had counted upon England's opposition, but the attitude of Austria came as a painful surprise to them. The Tsar told the Prince of Hesse that Andrassy was pushing to war, and that if he were placed between war and humiliation his choice was made.[3] The possibility of war was taken into consideration again and preparations for it were hurriedly made. General Fadeef was sent by the War Office on a secret mission to Serbia to learn the disposition of the Austrian troops on the frontiers of Serbia and Bosnia and the possibility of resisting the occupation of Bosnia and Herzegovina.[4] Shouvalov gave expression to these feelings in a different way. "If as a special privilege I were given permission to let one of our colleagues hang, I would choose Haymerle (Austria's third delegate); no one has tormented me so much as that one; when one believed one was ready he would always come again to change a comma."[5] The Russians were discontented still more with Bismarck, who while steadily refusing to interfere with Austria in their favour, energetically supported all her proposals.

After Bulgaria the Congress discussed the question of Bosnia and Herzegovina. That they were to be occupied by Austria was a foregone conclusion. In various ways all the Powers, except Italy, had given their consent to it. Even Italy did not mean to oppose it, but only to make a formal protest. The Turks alone persisted in resisting it, and did not give way even after Andrassy's threat to break up the Congress.[6] On the 28th, when

[1] Disraeli, p. 323. [2] *Ibid.* p. 328.
[3] Schweinitz, II, p. 32. [4] *Zapisi Jevrema Grujića*, III, pp. 338-9.
[5] Schweinitz, II, p. 35. [6] Andrassy, III, p. 126.

this question was to be presented to the Congress, the Sultan ordered his delegates to refuse the occupation. Bismarck offered Andrassy to adjourn the session, but the latter was convinced that the Turks could not prevent a resolution of the Powers, which for him was the most important. When the session opened he expounded again his old arguments of the impossibility of the execution of reforms foreseen in the Treaty of San Stefano for Bosnia and Herzegovina, of the incapacity of the Turks to preserve these provinces and the danger of their uniting with Serbia and Montenegro. Without demanding them for Austria, he declared that she could only accept such a solution as would guarantee their permanent appeasement.[1] Lord Salisbury tried to convince the Congress that a permanent appeasement was a European interest and that it could be preserved only by Austria. He proposed therefore that she should be entrusted with the occupation and administration of Bosnia and Herzegovina. Bismarck supported it with ardour, and the other Powers associated themselves with it. The Turks alone protested against it, declaring that they were able to introduce reforms and preserve order in the provinces. But they were soon silenced by Bismarck and Disraeli. The protocol was left open for them to sign it subsequently.[2]

Despite all insistence and threats the Turks refused to accept the decision of the Congress. On 4 July they declared that they had complete confidence in the Powers and that they would come to a direct agreement with Austria.[3] But this agreement could not be reached, as the Turks insisted upon Austria declaring in writing that the occupation was provisional and that the sovereign rights of the Sultan were not thereby injured. They stuck to it up to the last day of the Congress, when Andrassy finally consented to sign this declaration.[4]

In accepting Salisbury's proposal for occupation Andrassy declared that the Sandjak of Novipazar would remain under Turkish rule, but that Austria would keep her garrisons there in order to secure military and commercial communications through it. Russia objected to this new demand, desiring to secure previously Austria's consent for Antivari, which the Tsar

[1] *Ibid.* pp. 128–30. [2] D.F. No. 322; Andrassy, III, p. 132.
[3] Andrassy, III, p. 132. [4] G. Hanotaux, *op. cit.* IV, p. 369.

wished to give to Montenegro. The matter was regulated when the question of Montenegro came up for discussion. Moreover, an agreement was reached on 13 July between Russia and Austria by which Russia engaged not to raise any objection if Austria should be compelled to occupy the Sandjak definitely "like the rest of Bosnia and Herzegovina". In return for this Austria promised her diplomatic support for removing all the difficulties which might arise from the execution of the Treaty of Berlin.[1]

Next came the question of Asia. By the London Protocol Russia promised to restore Bayazid and the valley of Alashkert to Turkey, and England engaged not to contest the acquisition of Batum and Ardahan, reserving for herself the right to protect Turkey from the dangers which these acquisitions might bring about in the future. This protection she meant to effect by the occupation of Cyprus, and Salisbury had arranged that the Convention with Turkey should be placed before Parliament on the same day when the Congress took up the question of Asia. Meanwhile *The Globe* revelation had provoked great dissatisfaction in the Conservative ranks and the publication of the Cyprus Convention, which was intended to appease them, might be interpreted now as selling Batum and Kars for Cyprus. "We should be out before you could get home", wrote Northcote, urging that its publication should be postponed.[2] Alarmed by such a situation, Disraeli abandoned his engagements towards Russia and endeavoured to push her farther north and deprive her of Batum, or at least turn it into a free port. He insisted upon the Russians making concessions, warning them that they might be otherwise faced by a more warlike Government in England. The question was discussed directly between him and Gortchakov and a misunderstanding in the maps made them believe they were agreed. But when this agreement was announced to the Congress, they found out that they meant two different things. Bismarck offered his mediation and the matter was settled by compromise, Russia consenting to Batum being converted into a free port, "essentially commercial".[3]

The desire to announce the Cyprus Convention only after "earnest, but unavailing, attempts to persuade Russia not to

[1] Andrassy, III, p. 134.   [2] Salisbury, p. 288.
[3] Disraeli, pp. 336-8.

take Kars", had to be abandoned as the secret of it began to leak out. To avert another disclosure Salisbury communicated its substance to Waddington on 7 July,[1] which was fortunate, for on the next day the *Daily Telegraph* published its text, thus compelling the Government to lay it before the Parliament on the same afternoon. Salisbury had some difficulties in inducing the Porte to issue a *firman* about the occupation, and succeeded in overcoming its resistance only by a threat of abandoning its cause at the Congress. On 1 July an annex to the Convention was signed by which England engaged to restore Cyprus in case of Russia abandoning her conquests in Asia.[2]

With the settlement of these questions the main causes of conflict among the most interested Powers were removed. Russia was forced to renounce the pretension of dominating the Balkans, but the changes produced by the war could not be completely annulled, and Austria and England therefore sought territorial compensations for themselves in order to strengthen their position in the East in so far as Turkey was weakened. The proportion of power of the Great Powers had to be preserved in the East despite the transformations which were taking place there. To this principle all other interests were subordinated: the destiny of the Christians as well as that of Turkey.

Italy and France were left without compensations, but France obtained promise of support for her claims in Africa, and Italy was also encouraged to seek her future extension in that direction. On 7 July Salisbury informed Waddington that since France and Austria had refused England's invitation to act upon the Treaty of 15 April 1856, England was driven to seek alone for the means of protecting her interests in Asia, that she had refused to take Egypt, which had been offered her, and had resolved provisionally to occupy Cyprus.[3] Alarmed at first by this news, the French found in it a pretext to put forward their claims for compensation. Waddington explained to Salisbury that while England was essentially an Asiatic, France was essentially a Mediterranean Power, and that she should be given a free hand there for her development. Salisbury advised him to take Tunis. "Do what

---

[1] D.F. No. 325.
[2] G. Norandounghian, *Recueil d'actes internationaux de l'Empire Ottoman*, III, pp. 522–4.　　　　[3] D.F. No. 325.

you like there," he said, "it is not our affair." He recognised France's rights in Syria and disclaimed every intention of pre-judicing her interests there; he promised also co-operation in Egypt and partition of the sphere of influence.[1] Bismarck assured Waddington too that he assented completely to this proposal.[2] After the Congress the French Government elicited from England a formal confirmation of the promises made in Berlin.

Italy had followed with anxiety Austria's aspirations upon Bosnia and Herzegovina and had endeavoured to counteract them or obtain some compensations. In 1876 the irredentist movement in Trentino had become more active, and by the autumn a sharp press campaign against Austria ensued. The Vienna Government was seriously alarmed by it, and Andrassy hastened to sound Bismarck as to his attitude in the event of an attack by Italy.[3] When Russia went to war it was evident that Austria would get hold of the two provinces. Crispi, the Italian Foreign Minister, visited Bismarck at Gastein in August 1877 and offered him an alliance against Austria and France, and an understanding for settlement of the questions arising out of war. This Bismarck refused, but advised him to take Albania or some other part of Turkey on the Adriatic.[4] In Vienna and London Crispi found, however, no encouragement for com-pensations. In 1878 he was superseded by Count Corti, who did not think Italy's interests were threatened by Austria's advance in the Balkans. Corti went to the Congress with instructions not to oppose a provisional occupation, but to prevent an annexation, or, should this prove impossible, to seek for compensation.[5] But he dared not even broach the question of compensation, and was glad that Austria asked only for occupation, being thus able to resist all pressure from home. Yet it seems that England, Germany and even France were not opposed to her obtaining some compensation, though not in Europe. Waddington says that in offering him Tunis, Salisbury suggested that Italy might take Tripoli. Waddington agreed with this, and a few months later he endeavoured himself to encourage Italy in that direction in order to remove her resistance in Tunis.[6]

[1] D.F. Nos. 330–2.   [2] D.F. No. 330.
[3] A.A., Bericht des Baron Münch...8 Oct. 1876, cited before.
[4] The Memoirs of Francesco Crispi, ii, pp. 30–5.
[5] R. W. Seton-Watson, op. cit. p. 478.   [6] D.F. Nos. 330, 342.

To this side indeed the attention of Italy turned after the Congress.

That all the Powers should obtain some territorial compensation was the basic idea of Bismarck's programme of partition of Turkey. Though this programme was not realised entirely, it was in this spirit that the questions were settled at the Congress and the future relations of the Powers regulated. The Treaty of Berlin was in fact a compromise between Bismarck's plan of partition and Disraeli's plan of maintenance of Turkey—a compromise which was imposed by the results of war.

Russia's associates, Serbia, Montenegro and Roumania, were not admitted to the Congress, but they were allowed to state their claims to the Assembly. As Russia had refused to recognise them formally as her allies and to let them participate in the conclusion of peace with Turkey, so also the Powers considered the Eastern Question as a matter of their own, and meant to settle it among themselves, irrespective of the wishes and interests of the Balkan peoples. Russia had no reason to desire their presence at the Congress. Two out of her three associates were utterly dissatisfied with her conduct and the gains allotted to them in San Stefano. If they went to the Congress, it was not to help Russia preserve that Treaty, but to find support with other Powers to accomplish the aims Russia had contested against them.

Two days after the fall of Plevna Serbia had again declared war on Turkey. She was advised by the Grand Duke already in September to be prepared, as she might be soon asked to enter into action, but her demands for financial assistance received evasive answers only.[1] On 22 November Nicholas invited Serbia to begin operations within ten days, and her delay was much resented at headquarters. In answering Milan's congratulation for the conquest of Plevna, the Tsar said that he "could not conceal his regret that the Serbian army had not come earlier after the example of the Roumanians, who had together with the Russians shed their blood at Plevna".[2] Nevertheless, Serbia's action was not without importance for Russia. After besieging Nish Serbia directed her operations towards Pirot, occupied it on 28 December, and continued advancing towards Sofia, falling upon the back of the Turkish defence. When Sofia

[1] *Zapisi Jevrema Grujića*, III, pp. 301–5.   [2] *Ibid.* p. 309.

fell her army stood four hours distant from it, and her action contributed considerably to forcing the Turks to evacuate that city. She turned then to the south and occupied the whole territory between Pirot, Vranja and Prishtina.

When the negotiations for peace opened, Serbia tried to present her claims to the Grand Duke, but he refused even to listen to her delegate and directed him to inform St Petersburg of it. Milosav Protić was sent to Russia to point out the danger of future rivalry between Serbia and Bulgaria and the necessity of Slav co-operation, but he failed to change the decisions of the Tsar. He was told bluntly by Giers that "the interests of Russia came first, then came those of Bulgaria, and only after them came Serbia's; but that there were occasions on which Bulgarian interests stood on equal footing with the Russian".[1] The Treaty of San Stefano deprived Serbia of almost all her conquests in the East, leaving her Nish only and a small strip of territory on the south-west up to Mitrovica and Novipazar. Serbia reconciled herself with losing Bosnia and Herzegovina, which Russia had already ceded to Austria, but she could not consent to shedding her blood for a great Bulgaria. Russia's conduct provoked great discontent with both public opinion and the Government. The Government refused to evacuate the territory assigned to Bulgaria by the Treaty, alleging that the Turks had not evacuated that assigned to Serbia. There was a resolve to resist the Russians by force if necessary; the Commander-in-Chief was ordered not to reduce his army too much and to be ready for every eventuality.[2]

The resistance of England and Austria against the Treaty of San Stefano raised the hope that its revision would bring about an improvement in the position of Serbia. Rumours were current that Russia was prepared to cede the whole western half of the Balkan peninsula to Austria in order to win her over to her side, and that Austria would bind Serbia by a military convention and a customs union. It seemed evident that the destiny of Serbia was entirely dependent upon Austria whether the latter joined Russia or England. Prince Milan and Ristić were not slow in realising this altered situation and adapting their conduct to it.

[1] J. Ristić, *Diplomatska istorija Srbije*, II, p. 143.
[2] S. Jovanović, *Vlada Milana Obrenovića*, I, pp. 417-18.

Already by the end of February Ristić approached Wrede and expressed his desire for an improvement of relations with Austria and his conviction that her attitude at the Conference might contribute very much to it.[1] This sudden reversal of the policy of Serbia was gladly received and immediately exploited by the Government of Vienna. It corresponded exactly to Andrassy's principal aim, that of bringing the Balkan peoples under the political and economic control of the Monarchy and establishing her supremacy there. He informed Ristić through Wrede of his readiness to support Serbia under certain conditions. These conditions foresaw neither a military convention nor customs union, the two points which were particularly feared in Belgrade.[2] On his way to Berlin Ristić visited Andrassy and delivered him a letter from Prince Milan, in which the latter spoke of the common interests of the two countries, of his desire to maintain intimate relations with the Dual Monarchy and his hope that she would help him to obtain increase of territory.[3] Andrassy consented to defend Serbia's claim for Pirot and Vranja at the Congress on the condition that she should renounce every extension in the Sandjak and that she should take some commercial and railway engagements. Negotiations were continued at Berlin, Andrassy insisting upon the agreement being signed before the question of Serbian boundaries was discussed by the Congress. If Serbia refused this, Ristić feared that even the frontiers of San Stefano would come into question. He signed the convention on 8 July, binding Serbia to build a railway line through her territory connecting Vienna with Constantinople and Salonika, to conclude a commercial treaty with Austria, and to allow a temporary use of her soil for the regulation of the Iron Gates.[4] Andrassy had endeavoured to induce Serbia to leave the exploitation of her railways to the same company which exploited the Turkish railways, and to conclude with Austria a customs union if she should wish it. But Ristić succeeded in avoiding engagements which would have placed Serbia entirely under Austria's domination. The customs union was to be concluded only by consent of both sides, it could not be

[1] *Ibid.* p. 452.
[2] *Ibid.* p. 453; J. Ristić, *op. cit.* II, p. 162.
[3] J. Ristić, *op. cit.* II, pp. 162–5.
[4] *Zapisi Jevrema Grujića*, III, pp. 376–7; J. Ristić, *op. cit.* II, p. 184.

imposed by Austria; with regard to the railways, only the territory newly acquired was subject to the obligations taken by Turkey.[1]

Serbia was advised by Russia herself to come to an arrangement with Austria. Shouvalov warned Ristić not to do anything without Austria's approval. Yet he himself opposed Serbia's claim to Pirot, which Austria was disposed to give her. Ristić made great effort to remove his resistance, pointing out that it only enabled Austria to extract more concessions from Serbia. He spoke to Shouvalov of Slav solidarity and the damage to its cause from a rivalry between Serbia and Bulgaria; of the importance of Serbia in Russia's future plans against Austria, "with whom they will soon have to settle accounts".[2] Shouvalov yielded at the last moment, and chiefly at the insistence of Andrassy, who, after having obtained the concessions from Serbia, fought energetically for her cause. By the Treaty of Berlin Serbia was assigned the whole territory from Kopaonik to Vragna and Pirot, or fifty square kilometres more than by the Treaty of San Stefano.

While leaving Serbia to the mercy of Austria, Russia stood by the side of Montenegro with all her power. Apart from the Tsar's sympathy for the tiny Principality, his conduct was inspired also by the desire to reduce the territory to be occupied by Austria as much as possible. But he was no more able here than in Bulgaria to preserve the frontiers of San Stefano in face of the opposition of Austria, which was backed up by the other Powers. Prince Nicholas realised at once that Russia could no longer secure his gains, and hastened to come nearer to Austria. He had all along maintained good relations with her, and had been attentive to her advice and interests. His conduct had been fully appreciated and rewarded by the Vienna Government. On 15 February he sent his cousin, Božo Petrović, to Vienna with an autograph letter for Francis Joseph, in which he thanked him for his benevolent attitude during the war, without which the greater part of his successes "would not have been possible", and prayed him for his support in the future.[3] But the Austrians did not mean to recede from their claims, and the

---

[1] *Zapisi Jevrema Grujića*, III, pp. 376–7.
[2] *Ibid.* pp. 340–1. [3] Djordjević, *op. cit.* pp. 426–7.

San Stefano frontier of Montenegro was reduced to a half at the Congress. Out of three ports given her by Russia, she was left one only, Antivari, and there she was forbidden to keep ships of war or to receive foreign ones. Even the territory left to her was to be accepted as Austria's grace. Nicholas bowed to the inevitable and endeavoured to make the best of it. His conduct during the occupation of Bosnia and Herzegovina earned him the special gratitude of Francis Joseph, and the subvention he had received before the war was renewed.[1]

The position of Roumania was most peculiar. She had allowed Russia to use her territory and had helped her crush the Turks at Plevna, and as a reward she was asked now to cede Bessarabia. Both Gortchakov and Ignatyev made it plain to the Bucarest Ministers that this decision was irrevocable and that it could not be the subject of negotiation.[2] The Roumanians were at first determined to resist this demand, and the Chamber voted the inviolability of their territory.[3] They hoped that England and Austria would offer resistance to Russia, and that in co-operation with them they might save Bessarabia. Feelers were sent to Vienna to sound the intentions of Austria and offer assistance in case of war.[4] A protest against the Treaty of San Stefano was sent to all the Powers. But the situation was not favourable to their action, as the Powers were themselves looking for compensation. At the Congress they were allowed to state their claims, but this remained unavailing. They found Bismarck opposed to their demands, and with him all the principal Powers. Italy and France, though sympathising with Roumania, were not inclined to stand against the other Powers. The fate of Bessarabia was sealed, and Roumania succeeded only in obtaining a stretch of land in Dobrudja beyond the line assigned to her at San Stefano.

The irresolution and hesitation of Greece had brought her to an undesirable and impotent position after the war. The hegemony of the Slavs, which she most dreaded, seemed to be accomplished by Russia's victory, without Greece being able either to prevent it or to secure her share of spoil. The hope that she would be rewarded for her neutrality was shattered after the conclusion

[1] Ibid. pp. 433–7. [2] R. W. Seton-Watson, op. cit. p. 488.
[3] P. Lindenberg, op. cit. p. 455. [4] Andrassy, III, p. 103.

of the armistice, and she hastened now to get hold of the territory she claimed, by invading Thessaly with her army. But this move came too late to have any prospect of success. It was strongly disapproved by Great Britain and the other Powers, who compelled her to retreat. As a counterweight to the Slavs, Greece was a suitable weapon in the hands of England and Austria, and they seemed disposed to favour her claims. England counted upon her support in the event of war with Russia and endeavoured to smooth over her differences with Turkey. Salisbury tried to persuade Bismarck of the necessity of giving Greece Thessaly and Epirus.[1] Having failed in this, he advised the Porte to cede her a part of these provinces up to the Rivers Kalamas and Peneus in order to secure herself from future agitation.[2] Greece failed to be admitted to the Congress, though her demand was favoured by England, France and Italy, but she was allowed to be present at the sessions which discussed the questions of the bordering provinces. Waddington proposed that Turkey and Greece should come to a direct agreement as to the rectification of the frontier on the line Kalamas–Peneus and the Powers adopted this proposal, reserving for themselves the right of mediation in the event of their failing to reach an agreement.[3] But the Turks avoided ceding their territory, and it was only at the pressure of the Powers that in 1881 a settlement was effected by which Greece obtained an extension in Thessaly, though much smaller than that proposed at the Congress.

Serbia, Roumania and Montenegro were declared independent and took an obligation to maintain religious equality and freedom of worship. For other provinces of European Turkey an organisation similar to the Cretan Organic Statute of 1868 was provided, to be worked out by special Turkish commissions. Armenia was to obtain reforms adapted to the needs of the population, and their execution was to be supervised by the Great Powers.

The Congress of Berlin altered the Treaty of San Stefano in a manner which substituted Austrian for Russian supremacy in the Balkans. The big Bulgaria was narrowed and divided into a vassal principality and a semi-autonomous province, leaving

---

[1] Salisbury, p. 243.
[2] Layard, Salisbury to Layard, 30 May 1878.
[3] D.F. No. 324.

Turkey a large direct path to her western provinces and a strong frontier on the north. As a basis for future operations, which it was intended to become, the new Bulgaria was practically useless. While Russia was thus prevented from establishing herself in the Balkans, Austria was allowed to occupy Bosnia, Herzegovina and the Sandjak, thus frustrating the idea of a great Slav state and opening the doors to her further extension towards Salonika. Even the frontiers of Serbia and Montenegro were reduced or enlarged according to Austria's interests. The predominant position she obtained in the Balkans soon brought under her influence all the Balkan peoples, and she exploited their rivalry to maintain them under her domination. Her aim, to drive Russia out of the Balkans and take a position there from which she could control events and turn them to her own advantage, seemed to be realised. Russia, who had shed her blood for the liberation of the Christians, was deprived of all influence with them.

But although the Treaty of Berlin represented a diplomatic defeat for Russia, her sacrifices were not in vain. The situation created by that Treaty marked a considerable advance on the way of weakening Turkey and emancipating the Christians. The whole northern half of the Balkan peninsula was wrested from Turkey. A new Christian state was created on the Black Sea, and Serbia and Montenegro were enlarged. Though separated by the Sandjak, they constituted together with Bulgaria a chain of Christian states stretching from the Black Sea to the Adriatic. The purpose for which Russia fought was thus materially achieved. The changes effected in 1878 owing to Russia's sacrifices were the foundation for the successes achieved in 1912.

While Austria was dominating the Balkans, the decade following the Congress of Berlin marked a great ascendency of Germany's influence in Europe. Bismarck had failed to realise his plan of partition of Turkey, the purpose of which was to isolate France, to direct all the Powers to mutual rivalry, which would prevent anti-German coalitions and give them the same interest in preserving the *status quo* as Germany had herself. But it was in its spirit that the Berlin settlement was effected, for the principle of compensation underlay all major solutions of the Congress. The conditions created thereby did not secure

Germany that dominating position Bismarck aspired to, but they gave her a preponderant influence in European affairs. The Imperial league which had been hitherto the only political formation in Europe and which, though discordant, was strong enough to preserve peace, was destroyed. Put on trial during the crisis, it proved incapable of bridging the gulf which separated Russia and Austria in the East. It was replaced by a dual alliance between Germany and Austria, which was long prepared by both Bismarck and Andrassy. This alliance became the pivot around which revolved the whole system of European Powers. It was soon enlarged by the addition of Italy, and its ramifications spread on one side to Serbia and Roumania, and on the other to England, who was connected with it through the Mediterranean Agreements. Russia and France stood isolated and divided, and far from joining hands against Germany were both looking for her support. Russia found herself compelled to return to the alliance of the three Emperors and accept there a subordinate position, in order to escape isolation and check Austria's supremacy in the Balkans. France was encouraged to extend her possessions in Africa, where she came into conflict with Italy and England. If Bismarck's dream was not completely realised, he could still be quite satisfied with his achievements.

Viewed in retrospect of the next decade, the Congress of Berlin seemed to be a manifest success of Bismarckian policy. The situation created by it strengthened the position of Germany and gave her an unrivalled influence in Europe. Yet his game proved to be wrong in the long run. Based on the system of playing off one Power against another, it could not be played with safety to the end. Sooner or later those Powers and states would realise the identity of their interests against Germany and would unite to defend them. Despite all Austria's intrigues, the Balkan states created an alliance in 1912, which stood under Russia's protection, and which succeeded in breaking up the Ottoman Empire in Europe. Russia and France concluded an alliance and secured England's support for it. By promoting Austria's interests against the Russian, Germany had tied up her fate with that of Austria—the Power whose national heterogeneity had doomed her to dissolution.

The real gainer by the Treaty of Berlin was England. Although without a determined policy, she had instinctively followed the road which proved to be most advantageous for her. By refusing the plan of partition and by preventing its being imposed upon her by a dissolution of Turkey, England had frustrated the scheme which was intended to strengthen the Imperial Alliance and secure Germany's domination in Europe. The dissolution of that Alliance meant the weakening of Germany and the strengthening of England, who was to become her chief rival.

INDEX

✳